Aristotle and the Rediscovery of Citizenship

Aristotle and the Rediscovery of Citizenship confronts a question that is central to Aristotle's political philosophy as well as to contemporary political theory: What is a citizen? Answers prove to be elusive, in part because late-twentieth-century critiques of the Enlightenment called into doubt fundamental tenets that once guided us. Engaging the two major works of Aristotle's political philosophy, his *Nicomachean Ethics* and his *Politics*, Professor Susan D. Collins poses questions that current discussions of liberal citizenship do not adequately address. Drawing a path from contemporary disputes to Aristotle, she examines in detail his complex presentations of moral virtue, civic education, and law; his view of the aims and limits of the political community; and his treatment of the connection between citizenship and the human good. Collins thereby shows how Aristotle continues to be an indispensable source of enlightenment, as he has been for political and religious traditions of the past.

Susan D. Collins is assistant professor of political science at the University of Houston. Her research focuses on political thought in classical antiquity. She has contributed to the *American Journal of Political Science* and the *Review of Politics*, and she is coeditor of *Action and Contemplation: Studies in the Moral and Political Thought of Aristotle* and cotranslator of *Empire and the Ends of Politics: Plato's "Menexenus" and Pericles' Funeral Oration*.

Aristotle and the Rediscovery of Citizenship

SUSAN D. COLLINS

University of Houston

CAMBRIDGE
UNIVERSITY PRESS

CAMBRIDGE UNIVERSITY PRESS
Cambridge, New York, Melbourne, Madrid, Cape Town, Singapore, São Paulo, Delhi

Cambridge University Press
32 Avenue of the Americas, New York, NY 10013-2473, USA

www.cambridge.org
Information on this title: www.cambridge.org/9780521110211

First published 2006
This digitally printed version 2009

A catalog record for this publication is available from the British Library

Library of Congress Cataloging in Publication data

Collins, Susan D., 1960–
Aristotle and the rediscovery of citizenship /
Susan D. Collins.
p.   cm.
Includes bibliographical references and index.
ISBN 0-521-86046-6 (hardback)
1. Aristotle – Political and social views.   2. Citizenship – Philosophy.   I. Title.
JC71.A7C65   2006
323.601 – dc22   2005026788

ISBN 978-0-521-86046-8 hardback
ISBN 978-0-521-11021-1 paperback

In memory of my parents
Elizabeth and Thomas Collins

Contents

Acknowledgments   *page* ix

   Introduction: The Rediscovery of Citizenship   1

1 Liberal Citizenship and Aristotle's Ethics   6
   Liberalism and Its Critics   7
   The Limits of Liberal Citizenship   19
   Aristotle on Law, Education, and Moral Virtue   41

2 Citizen Virtue and the Longing for the Noble   47
   Courage as Noble Sacrifice and Self-Concern   52
   Noble Deeds and the Ascent of Virtue   58
   Magnanimity and Virtue as the Highest Good   61

3 Justice as a Virtue   67
   Justice as the Lawful   69
   Justice as Fairness   71
   Reciprocity and the Regime   74
   Justice and the Dual Ends of Moral Virtue   76
   Law and Right Reason   80

4 Prudence, the Good Citizen, and the Good Life   91
   The Problem of Prudence   91
   Education, Law, and Compulsion   98
   The Political Community as Natural End   102
   Recasting the Question of the Good Life   108

5 Citizenship and the Limits of Law   119
   The Identity of the Citizen   119
   Citizenship, Revolution, and the Regime   122

    The Good Citizen and the Good Man   124
    Citizenship and the Rule of Law   132

6   Political Wit and Enlightenment   147
    Nobility and Irony   148
    Politics and Wit   154
    Education, Liberty, and Leisure   160

    Conclusion: Aristotle and the Rediscovery of Citizenship   166

Bibliography   179
Index   189

Acknowledgments

In the course of my education, I have had the support of teachers, colleagues, friends, and family. I dedicate the book to the memory of my parents, Elizabeth and Thomas Collins, whose love and care for their children seemed infinite and who were models of decency and humanity. I am especially grateful to two teachers, Leon Craig and Christopher Bruell; their example and thought continue to inspire me, and I will always remain in their debt. My gratitude also to the faculty at Boston College, Robert Faulkner, Susan Shell, and the late Ernest Fortin, who enriched my studies. Four friends in particular, Monty Brown, Lorna Dawson, Robert Bartlett, and Devin Stauffer, have made my life and thought better in every way, and I am very grateful to Lorna and Bob for their tireless comments on the manuscript in its various phases. In writing the book, I have also benefited from the advice of several colleagues and friends. Paul Rahe and Harvey Mansfield assisted at critical points in the publication process and provided extensive comments on the manuscript. Stephen Salkever, Arlene Saxonhouse, and Mary Nichols were incisive readers whose suggestions greatly improved the work. Others have given their support along the way, including David Bolotin, Matthew Davis, Charles Griswold, John Scott, Lorraine Pangle, Thomas Pangle, Ty Tessitore, Sandy Thatcher, and Catherine Zuckert, and I have had the good fortune of wonderful colleagues at the University of Houston, in particular, Ted Estess, Cynthia Freeland, Ross Lence, Donald Lutz, Rick Matland, Susan Scarrow, and Robert

Zaretsky, whose fellowship always managed to lift my spirits. My grad-
uate assistants, Sarah Neal and Carol Brown, cheerfully and expertly
took on every task, however tedious, and made my work so much eas-
ier. My warm thanks to the editors at Cambridge, Lewis Bateman and
Beatrice Rehl, who supported the manuscript from the beginning; to
Louise Calabro, who guided it through the production process; and
to Helen Greenberg, whose careful copyediting helped to polish it.

Finally, I want to express my deep gratitude to my husband, Joseph,
and daughter, Isabella. I cannot imagine my life without them; their
existence alone makes it worth living.

Parts of Chapters 2, 3, and 4 appeared in an earlier form in "Moral
Virtue and the Limits of the Political Community in Aristotle's *Nicomachean Ethics*" in the *American Journal of Political Science* 48 (January
2004). I am grateful to the John M. Olin Foundation for supporting
a critical year's leave to work on the manuscript and to the Earhart
Foundation for their generous summer support, which helped me to
complete the publication process.

Aristotle and the Rediscovery of Citizenship

Introduction

The Rediscovery of Citizenship

During an interview on the first anniversary of September 11th, author David Halberstam was suddenly moved to remark, "I used to say I was a New Yorker. Now I like to think of myself as a citizen of the city."[1] As a response to the attacks on America's most cosmopolitan city, Halberstam's comment spoke powerfully to the newfound sense of citizenship that then gripped the nation and has since struggled for definition. For what, indeed, does it mean to be a "citizen"?

To be sure, the events of September 11th and their aftermath have impelled all serious observers to speak anew of the sacrifices and duties of citizenship or of a deeper commitment to community. Beyond this, however, language often fails. With Rousseau, perhaps, some had sought to efface the very word citizen from our vocabulary, or, with Kant, to search out a higher notion of world citizenship, or, with Hobbes, to rest content as subjects rather than citizens as long as life and liberty were otherwise preserved. But if, in the face of present challenges, such notions seem inadequate – if, in particular, we are awake to aspects of citizenship that our own principles and assumptions obscure or resist – where might we turn for understanding? This study turns to Aristotle's *Nicomachean Ethics* and *Politics*, the two works in the history of political philosophy that together contain the most comprehensive and systematic investigation of the question "What is a citizen?"

---

[1] CNN, "Newsnight with Aaron Brown," 9 September 2002, Interview with David Halberstam.

1

The Aristotelian tradition became almost moribund with the success of modern liberalism and of attacks such as those of Hobbes on the many "absurdities" of the "old Morall Philosophers," Aristotle chief among them. Yet today Aristotle's thought enjoys a remarkable renaissance. Against the orthodox liberal concept of the state as an association of rights-bearing free agents who contract with one another for the sake of peace and the pursuit of happiness, scholars are again taking seriously the idea articulated most fully by Aristotle that human beings are "political animals." By giving new currency to the old view that individuals are naturally situated within a political community that requires specific virtues, molds character, and shapes its citizens' vision of the good, the revival of Aristotelianism has challenged even such staunch defenders of liberalism as John Rawls to examine again the sphere of the citizen. This reexamination of citizenship belongs also to the recent work of scholars as diverse as Alasdair MacIntyre, Richard Rorty, Amy Gutmann and Dennis Thompson, Michael Sandel, Peter Berkowitz, Stephen Macedo, William Galston, and Martha Nussbaum. Yet, for all their diversity, the efforts of these scholars are typically unified by certain liberal presuppositions or ends and, in particular, by the concern to marry liberal principles of equality and individual freedom with a more or less Aristotelian view of community.

Although my book begins from current efforts, it does not seek to duplicate them. In undertaking a study of Aristotle's account of citizenship, I contend that this account is a source of insight for us precisely because it does *not* begin from liberal presuppositions. Aristotle's presentation of citizenship's foundation in law and moral virtue is the classic statement of the preliberal view of political authority and civic education, according to which the community is prior to the individual and the highest purpose of the law is the education to virtue. Moreover, his investigation of citizenship and its connection with virtuous action and the good life addresses the question that is in principle left open by liberal thought: the question of the highest human good. Aristotle's treatment of these matters clarifies the limitations of the current rediscovery of citizenship, with its distinctive liberal assumptions, as well as attachments and concerns that persist within our experience and yet are scarcely acknowledged, let alone explained, by liberal theory. By illuminating dimensions of citizenship that we either overlook or obscure, Aristotle invites our rediscovery of citizenship in its own right.

He thereby helps us to comprehend not only the perspective of cultures or communities that do not share liberal principles, but also the full significance of the question "What is a citizen?" as an enduring human concern.

In following Aristotle's investigation of this question through both the *Nicomachean Ethics* and the *Politics*, my study reflects his view of the deep connection between ethics and politics and brings into their proper relation two works that are too often treated apart. Besides its introduction and conclusion, the book has six chapters. Chapter 1 draws a path to Aristotle's thought, beginning from the general critique of the Enlightenment and the specific criticisms of Rawls's influential account of liberalism that opened the door not only to post-Enlightenment views but also to the return to Aristotle. I trace in this context Rawls's reformulation of his original account – his "political liberalism" – as well as other current efforts to describe a citizenship that is robust enough to support political order yet compatible with individual freedom and equality. In the disputes provoked by these efforts, two problems have emerged that provide a bridge to Aristotle's thought, even as they underline its distinctiveness: first, the priority of justice, or "the right," over the good, which remains a crucial but controversial claim of Rawlsian liberalism; and second, the nature of civic education, which raises difficult questions for scholars who wish to establish the moral and political supports of liberal politics while preserving a sphere within which individuals can freely pursue the good as they see fit.

The disputes over these problems indicate the limitations of the current rediscovery of citizenship and the initial reasons for turning to Aristotle's thought. To explore fully the relation between the right and the good, and the nature of civic education, one must begin from Aristotle's treatment of law and the education to moral virtue in his *Nicomachean Ethics*. This treatment opens the way to his direct investigation of the meaning and limits of citizenship in the *Politics*.

The next five chapters proceed thematically, examining in turn the connection of citizenship with moral virtue, education, and the good, and its relation to the political community and law. In Chapters 2 and 3, I show that the *Nicomachean Ethics* offers an account of civic education that is superior to those currently available, first, because it acknowledges the authoritative role of the political community and the law with regard to education, and, second, because it clarifies how this education bears on the question of the good. In particular, by bringing out the moral and political dimensions of the good, Aristotle is able to explore a concern central to human experience that liberal thought necessarily obscures: the relation between the good life and the nobility and justice that constitute morally virtuous action. Aristotle shows that as the educator to virtue, the political community necessarily elevates this life as best and seeks to reconcile two ends as proper to right action: the common good and the perfection in virtue as an end in itself. In his account of the most complete virtue, justice, he establishes that the deepest problem of civic education is the irrepressible tension between these two ends. Against the claims of the political community and the law, this difficulty reopens the question of how one determines the proper end of action and indicates that the law, for all its authority, cannot be the final arbiter concerning the good. In contrast to others, I do not believe that Aristotle has or desires a single solution to the problem of right action. Nevertheless, his careful treatment of this problem comprehends the perfection that is the highest pedagogic end of the law and illuminates its significance for our good as citizens and human beings.

My argument then moves to two chapters that focus on Aristotle's *Politics*. In Chapters 4 and 5, I examine the demands and necessities of citizenship in connection with the question of the good and then outline more fully Aristotle's treatment of citizenship in the context of the political community's legal prerequisites and natural end. I argue that while Aristotle gives full due to the political community's authority regarding moral virtue and the good, his analysis of the dispute over distributive justice establishes the boundaries of this authority in every regime or political order. His precision about these matters further illuminates the law's limitations with respect to its pedagogic aims and reveals the necessity of a move to a natural or transpolitical, as opposed to a legal or political, perspective on human action and political life.

In his analysis, Aristotle sheds light on the difficulty that may be most troubling for us as liberal citizens: the potential tension between the demands of civic devotion and the independence of individual reason. Accordingly, in Chapter 6, I argue that Aristotle sketches a middle ground between thoughtless or dogmatic commitment to convention and skeptical alienation from it. The possibility of this middle ground

emerges in his account of education in the *Politics* and in his eluci-
dation of an apparently minor moral virtue in the *Nicomachean Ethics*,
wittiness. Against a view popular today that the tensions, conflicts, and
evils inherent in political life are proof of its tragic and ultimately
incomprehensible nature, I suggest that there is in Aristotle's political
philosophy a comic vision in the highest sense: a vision, in short, that
appreciates both the nobility and the limits of human striving and that
in no way despairs of wisdom about human affairs. Such a perspective, Aristotle indicates, supports a form of prudence by which citizens
understand and defend the benefits of a decent political community
while remaining clear-eyed about its failings or limitations.

My conclusion returns to the current rediscovery of citizenship to
explore directly the guidance offered by Aristotle. That Aristotle is
not a liberal democrat bears repeating. To mention a few obvious
issues: He lists democracy as a deviant regime, his own best order is
aristocratic, and his treatments of slavery and of the political status
of women and foreigners are hardly models of inclusiveness. But as
antidemocratic as Aristotle's thought may be in some respects, it does
not suffer from many of our own blind spots and frequently speaks to
our most serious concerns. Indeed, for all the clear goods of a liberal
order, recent events have underscored that citizenship does not simply confer benefits but requires sacrifices, and involves not only rights
but also duties – in short, citizenship frequently asks not what your
country can do for you, but what you can do for your country. For us,
then, Aristotle's treatment of the relation between individual and community, the connection between justice and the good, and the nature
of civic education elucidates aspects of citizenship that we acknowledge without always exploring and for which liberal theory offers little insight. Moreover, because Aristotle's investigation of citizenship
addresses the question of the human good with a completeness that
liberal thought necessarily eschews, it offers Halberstam's "citizen of
the city" a path to understanding the relation between being a citizen
and living well as a human being. By thus challenging us to rediscover
these dimensions of citizenship and to reflect anew on the question
of the good, Aristotle's political philosophy can be for us, as it was for
thinkers across the Christian, Jewish, and Islamic traditions of the past,
an indispensable source of enlightenment.

1

Liberal Citizenship and Aristotle's Ethics

The current debate about liberal citizenship is marked by a pervasive doubt about such fundamental liberal principles as the primacy of the individual, the neutrality of the contractual state, and the priority and universality of rights. To be sure, there have been past disputes about the political and legal terms of citizenship. In the American case, for example, disputes have ranged from the arguments concerning naturalization at the Constitutional Convention to the battle over voting rights to more recent discussions of immigration. But these past disagreements also reflected a more fundamental consensus that "the first mark of American citizenship," and of liberal citizenship in general, is the "political equality of rights," and that defining citizenship largely entailed working out the full meaning of these terms.[1] Since the current debate follows from critiques of liberal thought itself, however, we now confront fundamental questions concerning the very ideals and principles that have traditionally undergirded discussions of citizenship.

In providing an overview of these critiques and the ways in which scholars have subsequently sought to reconceive liberal citizenship, I seek not to recapitulate this ongoing debate but to describe the general context within which it has arisen and to draw out problems that provide a bridge to Aristotle's thought. I begin from two developments.

[1] Judith Shklar, *American Citizenship: The Quest for Inclusion* (Cambridge, MA: Harvard University Press, 1991), p. 1.

First, in the last decades of the twentieth century, a growing perception that liberal thought, and the Enlightenment project in general, failed to make good on its promise to ground morality in a rational and nonteleological framework raised serious doubts about liberalism's capacity to defend its own moral and political principles. These doubts opened the way to a return to the Aristotelian tradition that the Enlightenment had rejected, as well as to post-Enlightenment views.[2] Second, criticisms of Kantian moral philosophy and of John Rawls's influential Kantian politics in *A Theory of Justice* raised questions about the relation between the individual and the political community that have significantly shaped the present efforts to reconceive citizenship.

LIBERALISM AND ITS CRITICS

The remarkable renaissance of Aristotle's thought in the late twentieth century was made possible in part because of doubts arising within the tradition of liberal thought. In returning to classical philosophy, neo-Aristotelianism represents a break with what Stephen Salkever has called "the intransigently antiteleological character" of liberalism's "founding texts."[3] But as a sketch of some of the developments leading

---

[2] The school of thought having its inspiration in Aristotle is wide and diverse, and while I hope to capture some of this breadth and diversity in the notes, my discussion in the text is limited by my immediate purposes. I therefore confine my references to the works of several well-known thinkers involved in the revival of Aristotle's thought in the 1980s and 1990s. More detailed critical surveys of the rise of Aristotelianism, and the related return to an ethics of virtue, include Gregory Trianosky, "What Is Virtue Ethics All About?," *American Philosophical Quarterly* 27 (October 1990): 335–44; Peter Simpson, "Contemporary Virtue Ethics and Aristotle," *Review of Metaphysics* 45 (March 1992): 503–24; and John C. Wallach, "Contemporary Aristotelianism," *Political Theory* 20 (November 1992): 613–41. Volume XIII of *Midwest Studies in Philosophy* (Notre Dame, IN: University of Notre Dame Press, 1988) contains representative articles.

[3] Salkever, "'Lopp'd and Bound': How Liberal Theory Obscures the Goods of Liberal Practices," in *Liberalism and the Good*, eds. R. Bruce Douglass, Gerald R. Mara, and Henry S. Richardson (New York: Routledge, 1990), p. 167. See also Alasdair MacIntyre, "The Privatization of the Good: An Inaugural Lecture," *Review of Politics* 52 (Summer 1990): 348 and *After Virtue: A Study in Moral Theory* (Notre Dame, IN: University of Notre Dame Press, 1981), p. 54; Michael Sandel, *Liberalism and the Limits of Justice*, 2nd ed. (Cambridge: Cambridge University Press, 1998), p. 175. For fuller discussions of liberalism and the question of teleology, see Salkever's *Finding the Mean: Theory and Practice in Aristotelian Political Philosophy* (Princeton, NJ: Princeton University Press, 1990), pp. 21–36; William Galston, *Justice and the Human Good* (Chicago: University of Chicago Press, 1980), ch. 2 and *Liberal Purposes: Goods, Virtues, and Diversity in the Liberal State* (Cambridge: Cambridge University Press, 1991), chs. 4–7.

up to it indicates, this break resulted less from a reevaluation of ancient teleology than from critiques that called into question liberalism's own moral and political principles. For, alongside Aristotle's natural philosophy, early liberals such as Hobbes and Locke jettisoned also the classical view that the end of government is the human good, understood as virtue and the perfection of human nature. Armed with a new mechanistic and materialistic science of nature, they sought to comprehend the brute facts of our original or prepolitical condition – the "state of nature" – and especially what they saw to be the inevitable conflict or war among human beings in the pursuit of their individual goods, within a political compact whose central purposes were the protection of its members from harm, regulation of their various interests, and preservation of their natural freedom. Despite abandoning an overarching idea of the human good, then, early liberalism sought to establish natural and rational principles for ordering civic life. Although in the state of nature the pursuit of our individual good has no moral import of its own, it becomes a matter of moral and political import when we enter into association with one another, as we are compelled to do if we desire peace and prosperity. In the face of the war and oppression that the unbounded pursuit of our desires would produce, it is both necessary and right to establish an association in which peace and freedom are preserved – in which our natural freedoms, our rights to life and property, for example, are enjoyed in the fullest way without harm to others. From this point of view, the main tasks of government become the regulation of competition and protection of individual freedom, and the central problem of politics, the abuse of power.

Liberalism's story, however, is only just beginning. Under the influence of later Enlightenment thinkers on both sides of the English Channel – with Rousseau and Montesquieu and Hume and Burke as obvious exemplars – and with the rise of Romanticism, German Idealism, and Marxism in the eighteenth and nineteenth centuries, the view of nature and human nature grounding the denial of a highest human good succumbed first to an emerging and then to a full-blown sense of the basic historicity of human existence. Under this new dispensation, human nature came to be seen as a product of and not a constant within the continual flux of time and events. More generally, the idea of nature itself appeared as a salutary myth, a conceptual fabrication for the purposes of justifying the liberal ideal of the state. This new sense of our historicity obviously did not allay but deepened doubt concerning the existence of a highest human good – in a world of flux, the good or happiness too is radically contingent – yet, more importantly, it eventually also engulfed the principles informing liberal politics itself. It thus darkened liberalism's horizon with a new thought. For although Kant and Hegel sought to show that our status as historical beings need not undercut the possibility of a rational moral or political order, if indeed reason can stand above the historical flux, contemporary scholars began to grapple also with the more radical views of Nietzsche, Heidegger, and their intellectual heirs. To recall Alasdair MacIntyre's influential formulation in *After Virtue*, the view drawn out by Nietzsche (and his "emotivist and existentialist successors") is that "all rational vindications of morality manifestly fail and that *therefore* belief in the tenets of morality needs to be explained in terms of a set of rationalizations which conceal the fundamentally non-rational phenomena of the will."[4]

In rejecting the tradition of which Aristotle was the core, the Enlightenment claimed to be able to ground a new, if leaner, morality in true science and rationality. But liberalism's deepening skepticism, following the break with the ancient tradition, finally called into question its own principles of justice and morality. This development has been greeted by some as a crisis and by others as a liberation. According to MacIntyre, for example, the failure of the Enlightenment to secure a rational foundation for moral consensus and political life means that the liberal tradition cannot defend against challenges to the public authority and a disintegration of individual life into self-absorption and private gratification – if everything is permitted, then anything goes.[5] Arguing that "the defensibility of the Nietzschean position turns

---

4 MacIntyre, *After Virtue*, p. 117 (emphasis in text).
5 The effort to reform moral and political life gave rise to the communitarian movement with which many contemporary Aristotelians are identified. But the terms "neo-Aristotelian", "communitarian," and "liberal" are somewhat amorphous in their application to any one position. Even those who would identify themselves as liberal might yet argue in favor of what Michael Walzer has called a "communitarian correction" ("The Communitarian Critique of Liberalism," *Political Theory* 18 [February 1990]:

in the end on the answer to the question: was it right in the first place to reject Aristotle?", MacIntyre has sought to replace liberal theory with "something like Aristotle's ethics."[6] Others have pursued less radical strategies, seeking, for example, to find resources within the Enlightenment tradition for its defense, to modify liberalism in an Aristotelian direction, or to rediscover the republican elements of liberal thought. Efforts of this kind are represented by the work of Peter Berkowitz, Stephen Macedo, William Galston, Martha Nussbaum, and Michael Sandel.[7] Still others, who assert and even celebrate the demise of Enlightenment metaphysics, strive, like Habermas, to formulate a "postmetaphysical" but still liberal framework for ethics and politics or, like Richard Rorty, to search out new possibilities of "individual

---

15), and communitarians typically have commitments to certain liberal goals, since, as Galston observes, "most Anglo-Americans are, in one way or another, liberals; all are deeply influenced by the experience of life in liberal societies" (*Liberal Purposes*, p. 79). As Charles Griswold has noted, "Among those who in some sense wish to return to the Greeks, there is remarkable consensus that the political offspring of the Enlightenment are, at least in good part, worth preserving. (I refer to liberal institutions and political arrangements)" (*Adam Smith and the Virtues of Enlightenment* [Cambridge: Cambridge University Press, 1999], p. 4). For overviews of communitarianism, see Amitai Etzioni, ed., *Rights and the Common Good: The Communitarian Perspective* (New York: St. Martin's Press, 1995), and C. F. Delaney, ed., *The Liberalism–Communitarianism Debate* (Lanham, MD: Rowman & Littlefield, 1994).

[6] MacIntyre, *After Virtue*, p. 117 (emphasis in text).

[7] See, for example, Peter Berkowitz, *Virtue and the Making of Modern Liberalism* (Princeton, NJ: Princeton University Press, 1999); Stephen Macedo, *Liberal Virtues: Citizenship, Virtue, and Community in Liberal Constitutionalism* (Oxford: Oxford University Press, 1996) and *Diversity and Distrust: Civic Education in a Multicultural Democracy* (Cambridge, MA: Harvard University Press, 2000); Galston, *Justice and the Human Good*, *Liberal Purposes: Goods, Virtues, and Diversity in the Liberal State* (Cambridge: Cambridge University Press, 1991), and *Liberal Pluralism: The Implication of Value Pluralism for Political Theory and Practice* (Cambridge: Cambridge University Press, 2002); Martha Nussbaum, "Non-Relative Virtues: An Aristotelian Approach," in *Midwest Studies in Philosophy, Volume XIII: Ethical Theory, Character and Virtue*, ed. Peter A. French, Theodore E. Uehling, Jr., and Howard K. Wettstein (Notre Dame, IN: University of Notre Dame Press, 1988); pp. 32–53, "Human Functioning and Social Justice: In Defense of Aristotelian Essentialism," *Political Theory* 20 (May 1992): 202–46, and "Aristotelian Social Democracy" in *Aristotle and Modern Politics: The Persistence of Political Philosophy*, ed. Aristide Tessitore (Notre Dame, IN: University of Notre Dame Press, 2002); Sandel, *Liberalism and the Limits of Justice* and *Democracy's Discontent: America in Search of a Public Philosophy* (Cambridge, MA: Harvard University Press, 1996). Malcolm Schofield offers a helpful overview of several uses to which Aristotle's political thought has been variously put in *Saving the City: Philosopher-Kings and Other Classical Paradigms* (New York: Routledge, 1999), pp. 100–1.

and private spiritual liberation."[8] These challenges to Enlightenment thought and the attempts to reconceive ethics and politics form the general context within which the debate about liberal citizenship is pursued.

At the same time, specific criticisms of Kantian moral philosophy and of Rawls's well-known account of liberalism in *A Theory of Justice* have significantly shaped this debate. The influence of the Kantian view in the liberal tradition can be traced in part to Kant's effort to vindicate morality in the face of liberalism's own skepticism and, at the same time, to elevate the liberal claim concerning the fundamental freedom of human beings.[9] In short, according to Kant, the most compelling evidence of human freedom, and the true locus of morality and law, are to be found in our capacity through reason to formulate and act in accord with a universal law, which we legislate for ourselves and which is, by virtue of its universality, free from any contingency and subjective interest.[10] Whereas our desire for our own good leads to "heteronomy," or many particular and subjective maxims of action, reason enables us to transcend this particularity by asking the question "Can this maxim become a universal law?" By placing the locus of moral action in our very freedom from the desires and passions, and in the sense of duty that accompanies the self-legislated moral law, Kant is thus able to dispense with notions of nature and the good while both elevating individual freedom as an end and establishing strict standards for moral action.

In *A Theory of Justice*, Rawls conjoins the idea of law and duty at the center of Kant's moral thought with the liberal contract theory of political association carried to "a higher level of abstraction."[11] To recall

---

[8] Jürgen Habermas, *Between Facts and Norms: Contributions to a Discourse Theory of Law and Democracy*, trans. William Rehg (Cambridge, MA: MIT Press, 1998); Richard Rorty, "The Priority of Democracy to Philosophy" in *The Virginia Statute for Religious Freedom: Its Evolution and Consequences in American History*, eds. Merrill D. Peterson and Robert C. Vaughan (Cambridge: Cambridge University Press, 1988), pp. 272–3.

[9] See Sandel's discussion of "deontology with a Humean face" in *Liberalism and the Limits of Justice*, pp. 14, 21.

[10] I follow here especially Kant's *Groundwork of the Metaphysic of Morals*, trans. H. J. Paton (New York: Harper & Row, 1964).

[11] Unless otherwise noted, all references to *A Theory of Justice* are to the first edition. John Rawls, *A Theory of Justice* (Cambridge, MA: Harvard University Press, 1971), pp. 3, 11. Chapter 1 is Rawls's summary of his position, especially as it stands to his main opponent, utilitarianism. See pp. 251–7 for a specific discussion of the Kantian

Rawls's argument in brief: When we imagine the founding moment of the political contract, the "original position," we must abstract from all particular ends or preferences of the individuals who are parties to this contract and conceive of a "self prior to its ends." We are then to imagine these parties collectively establishing, under a veil of ignorance concerning their own circumstances and ends, the universal rules to govern their future association. By this account, there is no need to evaluate the specific ends actually desired by individuals; the key is to ensure that the process established for negotiating their differences is fair. In this way, Rawls's "procedural liberalism," his emphasis on "justice as fairness," understands itself to be accommodating a multiplicity of subjective ends – and so preserving the freedom of individuals to pursue them – while offering a rational and nonutilitarian account of the rules governing our political association.[12]

In following Kant, Rawls is able to derive the rules of political justice as well as to supply a moral ground for liberal institutions and processes.[13] "Though it rejects the possibility of an objective moral order," Michael Sandel notes in *Liberalism and the Limits of Justice*, "this liberalism does not hold that just anything goes. It affirms justice, not nihilism."[14] Our reverence for the law as moral is connected with its detachment from any particular and merely subjective end, and our obedience to justice is to a universal rule that does not specifically advantage any individual or set of individuals. Liberalism thus entails, in Rawls's well-known phrase, "the priority of the right over the good," a priority justified in part because "the desire to express our nature as

---

derivation – the "high point of the contractarian tradition in Kant and Rousseau" – of the principle of "justice as fairness." See also *Political Liberalism* (New York: Columbia University Press, 1993), p. xv.

[12] Sandel's observation is helpful: "'Deontological liberalism' is above all a theory about justice, and in particular about the primacy of justice among moral and political ideals. Its core thesis can be stated as follows: society, being composed of a plurality of persons, each with his own aims, interests, and conceptions of the good, is best arranged when it is governed by principles that do not themselves presuppose any particular conception of the good; what justifies these regulative principles above all is not that they maximize the social welfare or otherwise promote the good, but rather that they conform to the concept of right, a moral category given prior to the good and independent of it" (*Liberalism and the Limits of Justice*, p. 1).

[13] See also Rawls's summary of the aims of *A Theory of Justice* in his *Political Liberalism*, p. xv.

[14] Sandel, *Liberalism and the Limits of Justice*, p. 176.

a free and equal rational being can be fulfilled only by acting on the principles of right and justice as having first priority."[15]

Yet, for all their persuasive power and liberal underpinnings, Kantian moral philosophy and the liberalism it inspired became so much the object of criticism that Rawls ultimately modified elements of his theory of justice.[16] In general, critics argued, reverence for the moral law and justice cannot be sustained in the face of the morally diminished or arbitrary character of the ends the law superintends. The defense of the law as moral, that is, collapses if we cannot supply reasonable arguments in behalf of the goods that are protected. Moreover, in insisting on a separation between the right and the good, Rawlsian liberalism both covers over the connection between liberal justice and a uniquely liberal vision of the good, and relies on a picture of the self that misrepresents the relation between the individual and the political community.[17]

According to the first of these criticisms, the elevation of the moral law and justice, which is grounded in their supposed universality and neutrality, is undercut by the fact that their task is to superintend an arena that has no moral elevation of its own.[18] That our highest and

[15] Rawls, *A Theory of Justice*, p. 574. Rawls does not alter this statement in his revised edition; see p. 504.

[16] It is difficult to overstate the influence of Kantianism on the view of liberalism that prevailed in 1970s and 1980s, an influence for which Rawls especially is to be credited: "Within academic philosophy, the last decade or so has seen the ascendance of the rights-based ethic over the utilitarian one, due in large part to the powerful influence of John Rawls's *A Theory of Justice*" (Sandel, *Liberalism and Its Critics*, p. 4). See also Galston, *Justice and the Human Good*, p. 9: "Robert Nozick has remarked that the eminence of John Rawls's theory is such that 'political philosophers now must either work within [it] or explain why not'."

[17] For detailed critiques of Kant and Rawls, see all of Sandel's *Liberalism and the Limits of Justice* and Galston's *Justice and the Human Good*, as well as chs. 6 and 7 of his *Liberal Purposes*. Also, there is an entire neo-Aristotelian school of virtue ethics that has its inspiration in G. E. M. Anscombe's influential repudiation of any "law-based" ethics in her seminal article "Modern Moral Philosophy," *Philosophy* 33 (January 1958): 1–19. I do not rely on Anscombe's argument here, which is on the order of MacIntyre's global critique of liberalism. See Trianosky, "What Is Virtue Ethics All About?" and Simpson, "Contemporary Virtue Ethics and Aristotle," for fuller discussions of the school of virtue ethics having its source in Anscombe. For recent works, see Philippa Foot, *Natural Goodness* (Oxford: Clarendon Press, 2001); Rosalind Hursthouse, *On Virtue Ethics* (Oxford: Oxford University Press, 1999); and Roger Crisp and Michael Slote, eds., *Virtue Ethics* (Oxford: Oxford University Press, 1997).

[18] In allowing for different ends or "life plans," Rawls makes room for the operation of reason in "carrying through a rational plan" with a view to attaining those ends and

truly free – truly human – action is the formation of and obedience to the self-legislated law underlines the fact that all our other actions and choices are unfree or slavish, tied as they are said to be to inclination or preference.[19] Our most serious action proves in this way to be for the sake of our less serious pursuits, our freest deeds for the fulfillment of our slavish desires. But if there is no more to the sphere of individual ends than a kind of self-serving acquisitiveness having its source in inclination or desire, how worthy is this sphere of protection? The difficulty, Sandel suggests, is that "the morally diminished status of the good must inevitably call into question the status of justice as well."[20] Our reverence for the law, so necessary to our sense of duty and law-abidingness, is inevitably connected with its purposes. In protecting pursuits and ends lower than itself, then, the law invariably declines in dignity.

Indeed, according to Sandel, "once it is conceded that our conceptions of the good are morally arbitrary, it becomes difficult to see why the highest of all (social) virtues should be the one that enables us to pursue these arbitrary conceptions 'as fully as circumstances permit'."[21] At a minimum, in commanding the protection of practices and pursuits that have no moral dignity of their own, and that some individuals may abhor, the law requires citizens to exercise the highest of

---

even, to a certain extent, in assessing them. But, as he further argues, "we eventually reach a point though where we just have to decide which plan we most prefer without further guidance from principle . . . we may narrow the scope of purely preferential choice, but we cannot eliminate it altogether." Thus, his objection to utilitarianism is less its view that choice is rooted in desire or inclination and more that it "does not take seriously enough the distinction between persons" (*A Theory of Justice*, pp. 548–54, 27). For this reason, among others, Sandel criticizes Rawls's view of moral agency, which he describes as only "apparently voluntaristic" in its being grounded in "something already there (in this case the shape and intensity of [his] pre-existing desires)" and as finally limited only by the "unchosen" principles of justice (*Liberalism and the Limits of Justice*, p. 167).

[19] Consider MacIntyre's remark: "Kant of course denies that morality is 'based on human nature', but what he means by 'human nature' is merely the physiological non-rational side of man" (*After Virtue*, p. 52).

[20] Sandel, *Liberalism and the Limits of Justice*, pp. 167–8. For his full criticism, see pp. 154–68. Galston takes up Rawls's later effort to offer a more robust account of moral agency and concludes that "Rawls's conception of moral personality will appeal only to those who have accepted a particular understanding of liberal political community" (*Liberal Purposes*, p. 131).

[21] Sandel, *Liberalism and the Limits of Justice*, p. 168.

all the social virtues while also averting their eyes or holding their nose.[22] Yet this very requirement suggests that for all their claims to universality and neutrality, the law and justice are not truly separable from the ends of the nonmoral or subjective sphere they superintend – that judgments concerning these ends must be barred from the public sphere lest they undercut citizens' reverence for the law and justice. But if so, the law is neither a true expression of autonomy nor simply neutral as to our private pursuits. Rather, in abstracting from the preferences or ends of individuals, it either compels assent by silencing objections or it ultimately transforms these objections.

In fact, critics also observe, the very claim that the law and justice are universal and neutral obscures the connection between the principles of the liberal order and the vision of the human good that informs it. For undergirding liberal justice, and reflected in the ends it promotes, are distinctively liberal judgments about the good: In presupposing that rights are prior to duties, for example, liberal justice assumes that the individual is of higher dignity or sanctity than the community; in preferring open markets to sumptuary laws, it judges free exchange and prosperity to be superior to cultural and religious habits that may impede them; in insisting that there can be no taxation without representation, it identifies individual labor and the enjoyment of its fruits, as compared to need or membership in a certain community, as the true ground of property.

To speak in the most general terms, the other side of liberalism's professed skepticism about the existence of a human good, and its corresponding concern about power, is its reverence for individual freedom. As open-ended an aim as this freedom may seem to be, no political order, even the most well-intentioned liberal order, can secure itself and perpetuate its specific form without influencing the character and moral vision of its members. To the contrary, according to William Galston, liberalism "is rather committed to a distinctive conception of the human good, a conception that undergirds

---

[22] Drawing a Christian inference, Charles Taylor suggests that this form of liberalism requires that we must "hate the sin, love the sinner." See Taylor, "Living with Difference" in *Debating Democracy's Discontent: Essays on American Politics, Law and Public Philosophy*, eds. Anita L. Allen and Milton C. Regan, Jr. (Oxford: Oxford University Press, 1998), p. 215.

the liberal conception of social justice."[23] In the first place, the protection of individual freedom carries clear constitutional prescriptions, such as popular sovereignty, elective office, divided government, an independent judiciary, and individual rights, to name a few. The support of such an order, moreover, entails a whole set of virtues exclusive of other possibilities: tolerance and sturdy self-reliance instead of righteousness and obedience, for instance; the work ethic and not the renunciation of worldly goods. Indeed, as Rawls himself acknowledges even in his early work and most fully in *Political Liberalism*, the institutions and practices of a liberal order require of citizens specific excellences or virtues.[24] Behind the apparent universality and neutrality of liberalism, then, a certain educative influence operates.[25]

The fact of liberalism's educative power also reveals a fundamental error in the Kantian–Rawlsian view of the self, and therefore of the relation between the individual and the political community.[26] In asking us to conceive of the individual as a "self prior to its ends,"

---

[23] Galston, *Liberal Purposes*, p. 18. See chs. 4–7 for Galston's exploration of the claims in favor of liberal neutrality, particularly those of Rawls. For Rawls's response to Galston's objections, see *Political Liberalism*, pp. 195–200.

[24] One of the questions in debate is how broadly and deeply liberalism's educative influence extends, that is, whether there is a limited or "thin" theory of the good, as Rawls argues, by which public life and public virtues are defined and shaped but which does not constitute a "way of life" specific to liberalism. For other examples, see Lyle A. Downing and Robert B. Thigpen, "Virtue and the Common Good in Liberal Theory," *The Journal of Politics* 55 (November 1993): 1046–59, and Michael Walzer, "The Communitarian Critique of Liberalism," *Political Theory* 18 (February 1990): 6–23.

[25] Galston, *Liberal Purposes*, p. 18. Suggestions as to how liberals might defend specifically liberal virtues, and examples of such virtues, are offered by Salkever in *Finding the Mean*, ch. 6 (his "Lopp'd and Bound" has such a project as its central task), as well as by Galston in *Liberal Purposes*, pp. 213–37. One could consider also Nussbaum's "thick, vague theory of the good," the most recent version of which she lays out in "Aristotelian Social Democracy" in *Aristotle and Modern Politics*. For another effort to make a quasi-Aristotelian defense of liberal virtues, see Berkowitz's *Virtue and the Making of Modern Liberalism*. By comparison, see Sharon Krause's treatment of the moral resources in a liberal concept of honor in *Liberalism with Honor* (Cambridge, MA: Harvard University Press, 2002).

[26] This argument clearly applies to the reigning Kantianism of the 1970s, but there have been more recent treatments of Kant's thought about virtue and education that would appear to provide a more subtle view. See Martha Nussbaum's summary of this literature in "Virtue Ethics: A Misleading Category?" *The Journal of Ethics* 3 (1999): 163–201.

and so as prior to association with others, this view presupposes that through the operation of reason, individuals can be radically free from the communities – family, friends, and nation – that are the primary source of their moral experience and judgment.[27] Individuals are thus said to be, to use Rawls's words, "self-originating sources of valid claims."[28] Yet as Habermas has pointed out and Rawls has acknowledged, the self of the original position requires moral powers that can be acquired only within society and through association with others.[29] These powers are not conceivable, that is, prior to these associations. In this respect and more generally, the picture of the "unencumbered self" in *A Theory of Justice* obscures the ways in which the communities within which we are raised give impetus and substance to individual moral agency and confer upon us obligations of a morally relevant kind.[30]

It is not surprising, then, that critics of Kantian ethics and Rawlsian liberalism are often considered, their own protests notwithstanding, communitarians.[31] For even scholars who disown the label, including MacIntyre and Sandel, nonetheless insist that an individual is significantly shaped by the community within which he or she is raised. Indeed, Rorty has approvingly suggested, Sandel goes so far as to reject the "ahistorical self" of Enlightenment metaphysics in favor of a "theory of the self that incorporates Hegel's and Heidegger's sense of the historicity of the self."[32] Yet, it is not necessary to understand

---

[27] Susan Mollar Okin provides a classic feminist critique of Rawls in ch. 5 of her *Justice, Gender, and the Family* (New York: Basic Books, 1989).

[28] Rawls, "Kantian Constructivism in Moral Theory," *Journal of Philosophy* 77 (August 1980): 543. Cf. *Political Liberalism*, p. 32, where Rawls speaks not of "self-*originating* sources of valid claims," but of "self-*authenticating* sources of valid claims."

[29] See the exchange between Rawls and Habermas in *The Journal of Philosophy* 92 (March 1995): 109–80.

[30] See especially Sandel's discussion in *Liberalism and the Limits of Justice*, pp. 178–83. Consider also Alasdair MacIntyre's general criticism of the "privatization of the good" in liberalism in "The Privatization of the Good," as well as Martha Nussbaum's shift toward a more Kantian–Rawlsian view from her early position in *The Fragility of Goodness: Luck and Ethics in Greek Tragedy and Philosophy*, rev. ed. (Cambridge: Cambridge University Press, 2001) to her later work, a shift that she discusses in the Preface to the revised edition of the former work, pp. xviii–xxiv.

[31] See, e.g., Alasdair MacIntyre, "The Spectre of Communitarianism," *Radical Philosophy* 70 (March–April 1995): 34, and Michael J. Sandel, "Political Liberalism," *Harvard Law Review* 107(7) (May 1994): 1766–7.

[32] Rorty, "The Priority of Democracy to Philosophy," p. 260.

our situation in such radical terms to see that the challenge to the Enlightenment, and to the Kantian and early Rawlsian views of ethics and politics, raises deep questions about the relation between the individual and the political community. If, for example, the individual is properly understood as situated within a political community, then does this community have primacy and authority over individual pursuits and aims? If no political order is neutral with respect to the moral education and good of its members, what is the nature and scope of its educative influence? If, as members of a particular political community, individuals acquire duties not derivative of rights, what is the status of these duties, especially with respect to rights and the pursuit of happiness? If, in sum, the political community cannot be understood simply in terms of a contract among unencumbered or free agents, and is undergirded and defined by certain practices and virtues, then what are the "distinctive marks" of liberal citizenship?

As scholars struggle with these questions, moreover, they find themselves in a radically unsettled world. For not only have doubts about liberal principles arisen from within, but the attacks of September 11, 2001, informed us with stunning ferocity of the challenges, practical and theoretical, presented by those who deny the truth of these principles and who take their bearings from divine law. In what is frequently called the "post-9/11 world," it is clear that a full account of the foundations and aims of citizenship cannot proceed in an isolated world of liberal assumptions. Both our own doubts and the challenges from without require us to get to the root of the matter and, by returning to a fundamental reconsideration of the relation between the individual and community, to ask again the question "What is a citizen?" In a way that is not true of liberal thought, this question is central in Aristotle's political philosophy; nevertheless, there are problems belonging to the current debates about citizenship that offer a bridge to his thought even as they clarify its distinctiveness. By outlining Rawls's reformulation of his theory of justice, the treatment of moral disagreement by deliberative democrats Dennis Thompson and Amy Gutmann, and the recent work of Sandel, Berkowitz, Macedo, and Galston, I draw out two problems in particular: the relation between justice, or the right, and the good, and the nature of civic education.

THE LIMITS OF LIBERAL CITIZENSHIP

In response to criticism that the argument of *A Theory of Justice* is grounded in a Kantian conception of the person as autonomous and therefore relies upon a comprehensive doctrine or theory of the good even as it claims not to do so, Rawls refashions his account to present a liberalism that is "political, not metaphysical."[33] Replacing some of the Kantian elements of his original argument, he begins from the problem presented by a modern democratic society: "A modern democratic society is characterized not simply by a pluralism of comprehensive religious, philosophical, and moral doctrines but by a pluralism of incompatible yet reasonable comprehensive doctrines."[34] Given the "fact of reasonable pluralism," Rawls's political liberalism confines its authority and operation to questions of "social cooperation" and seeks an "overlapping consensus" among comprehensive doctrines that can endorse, each from its own point of view, a political conception of justice.[35]

Accordingly, the political sphere is the sphere within which the individual as citizen takes on a "public identity" and members of the same political community come together to deliberate concerning "the fair terms of social cooperation between citizens regarded as free and equal."[36] This form of deliberation requires an "idea of public reason" in accord with which "comprehensive doctrines of truth or right [are] replaced by an idea of the politically reasonable addressed

[33] See Rawls's own account of this reformulation in his Introduction to *Political Liberalism*.

[34] Ibid., p. xvi. See also Rawls's discussion of the meaning of "reasonableness" in *Justice as Fairness: A Restatement* (Cambridge, MA: Harvard University Press, 2001), p. 191.

[35] Rawls, *Political Liberalism*, pp. xvi, 10, and all of Lecture IV. Rawls rejects Habermas's effort to derive these principles from a "norm of rational dialogue" or idealized speech situation (see pp. 191–2).

[36] Rawls, *Political Liberalism*, p. 47. See also his Introduction, pp. xiii–xxx, in which he describes his overall project. Rawls continues to draw inspiration from Kant, though now from Kant's distinction between public and private reason in "What Is Enlightenment?" (see p. 213). But consider also "The Idea of Public Reason Revisited" in *The Law of Peoples, With "The Idea of Public Reason Revisited"* (Cambridge, MA: Harvard University Press, 1999), pp. 175–80, as well as Stephen Salkever's critique of Rawls in "The Deliberative Model of Democracy and Aristotle's Ethics of Natural Questions" in *Aristotle and Modern Politics: The Persistence of Political Philosophy*, ed. Aristide Tessitore (Notre Dame, IN: University of Notre Dame Press, 2002), pp. 342–74.

to citizens as citizens."[37] Public reason seeks not to dictate the ends or goods of the free and equal citizens to whom it refers but to set the standards and procedures by which to adjudicate disputes arising from the diverse pursuits of the good. Reflecting a version of the social contract, public reason requires citizens "to propose principles and standards as fair terms of cooperation and to abide by these willingly, given the assurance that others will likewise do so."[38] While the pursuit of the good on the part of an individual may belong to a comprehensive view, then, the content of public reason is given by "the principles and values of the family of liberal political conceptions of justice" that meet three conditions: (1) they "apply to basic political and social institutions," (2) they are "presented independently from comprehensive doctrines," and (3) they "can be worked out from fundamental ideas seen as implicit in the public political culture of a constitutional regime."[39]

Rawls argues that the idea of justice thus understood is "freestanding," requiring at most that citizens endorse the "essentials of a democratic regime" or "constitutional democracy."[40] As the modern alternative to the ancient regime in which citizens are bound together in a common vision of the good, political liberalism has its roots in the "clash between Salvationist, creedal, and expansionist religions" – a clash born of the Reformation and its aftermath.[41] As a solution to this problem, moreover, it is neither an answer to the question of the human good nor a branch of moral philosophy; the "moral psychology of the person" consistent with political liberalism is but a "scheme of concepts and principles for expressing a certain conception of the person and an ideal of citizenship."[42] In this regard, political philosophy

---

[37] Rawls, "The Idea of Public Reason Revisited," pp. 132, 136–8.

[38] Rawls, *Political Liberalism*, pp. 48–9. For a full account of the idea of public reason, see Rawls's "The Idea of Public Reason Revisited." See also *Justice as Fairness*, in which he makes explicit the problem that citizens must act "at the expense of their own interest" (p. 191).

[39] Rawls, "The Idea of Public Reason Revisited," p. 143; *Political Liberalism*, p. 254.

[40] Rawls, *Political Liberalism*, pp. xvi, xxx, 10–11. Rawls argues that a comprehensive doctrine cannot reject the essentials of a democratic regime as a minimal requirement of reasonableness, but Galston counters that "this criterion packs far too much into the idea of the 'reasonable'." See Galston, "Two Concepts of Liberalism," *Ethics* 105 (April 1995): 518.

[41] Rawls, *Political Liberalism*, p. xxv.

[42] Ibid., pp. 87–8.

is "autonomous." While it cannot say anything it wishes since it is limited by human psychology and history, it nonetheless constructs its schemes in response to the problem of modern society with which it is presented: "We strive for the best we can attain within the scope the world allows."[43]

According to Rorty, Rawls's reformulation of his theory of justice represents a welcome turn on his part to pragmatism, and it would seem that the effort to eschew metaphysics or comprehensive doctrines of any kind opens the door to a pragmatic politics that not only takes its bearings from the practices and problems of the age, but brackets all foundational disputes in search of a present consensus. Rorty perhaps endorses the fullest version of this view in arguing that Rawls's pragmatic (and Hegelian) turn reflects the conclusion at which we have arrived in history: the conclusion that "democracy takes precedence over philosophy."[44] Indeed, he argues, "disenchantment" with or detachment from foundational principles, religious and philosophic, is "the price we pay for individual and private spiritual liberation, the kind of liberation that Emerson thought characteristically American."[45] Beginning from a deeply communitarian premise – the historical self of the post-Enlightenment era is constituted by the community – Rorty arrives at a liberal outcome: individual liberation. The effort to reenchant the world by returning to foundational principles, he contends, would entail the highest of costs: "the freedom of individuals to work out their own salvation."[46]

Whether or not Rorty faithfully captures Rawls's own position, his insistence on the priority of democracy to philosophy helps to illuminate the impetus for and the consequences of Rawls's move away from Kant and his sharpened emphasis on the problem to which political liberalism is the solution. The ideas of justice as fairness and of public reason represent the tools with which those who hold conflicting

---

43 Ibid., p. 88. See also Lecture III, as well as Rawls's discussion of the four roles of political philosophy in *Justice as Fairness*, pp. 1–5, and Galston's criticism in *Liberal Pluralism*, pp. 42–6.
44 Rorty, "The Priority of Democracy to Philosophy," p. 269. See also Chandran Kukathas and Phillip Pettit, *Rawls: "A Theory of Justice" and Its Critics* (Stanford, CA: Stanford University Press, 1990), p. 144.
45 Rorty, "The Priority of Democracy to Philosophy," p. 272. Rorty claims to be following Dewey, but cf. Sandel, *Debating Democracy's Discontent*, pp. 322–3.
46 Rorty, "The Priority of Democracy to Philosophy," p. 272.

religious or moral doctrines formulate the terms of peace and secure the freedom of each to live as he or she sees fit within the same political association. For the sake of this peace and freedom, individuals in their "public identity" appeal only to reasons that are acceptable or "reasonable" to their fellow citizens. As Rawls notes in his final restatement of justice as fairness:

Together, the values of justice and of public reason express the liberal ideal that since political power is the coercive power of citizens as a corporate body – a power in which each has an equal share – this power is to be exercised, at least when constitutional essentials and questions of basic justice are at stake, only in ways that *all* citizens may reasonably be expected to endorse.[47]

The appeal to fairness – to the priority of the right and democracy – seeks common ground within diversity and thus rules out, for political purposes, recourse to the opinions, beliefs, and principles that constitute this very diversity. Or, to be more precise, the ideas of the good that are allowed into the political realm have to be political ideas, which means that they must "belong to a reasonable political conception of justice."[48]

Rawls thus appears to secure the priority of the right on new grounds – the "fact of reasonable pluralism" as opposed to the nature of a free self – and to rest the moral elevation of justice and the law on their protection not of the sphere of merely subjective preferences, but of the diversity of comprehensive doctrines of the good. Yet even scholars who are sympathetic to Rawls's liberalism doubt that his new position wholly achieves its aims. In particular, critics are unconvinced that it adequately captures the character of moral disagreement within a democratic order, the relation between liberal justice and the human good, and the nature of civic education. Some of the central disputes concerning these matters provide an opening to Aristotle's view of the law, education, and moral virtue in his *Nicomachean Ethics*. Although liberal thought has traditionally rejected this view, we must now recover it if we are to achieve clarity about the question of citizenship. I trace a path to this recovery with the aid of Gutmann and Thompson's discussion of the problem of moral disagreement, Sandel's criticism of

---

[47] Rawls, *Justice as Fairness*, p. 190 (my emphasis).
[48] Rawls, *Political Liberalism*, p. 176.

Rawls's political liberalism, and recent discussions of liberal virtue and civic education by Berkowitz, Macedo, and Galston.

In their defense of a form of democracy that is fundamentally deliberative, Gutmann and Thompson argue that Rawls's "constitutionalism" – his focus on the principles of justice that order a democratic society – leaves untouched the area of "middle democracy" in which moral disagreements arise in everyday political life and require our deliberation.[49] Indeed, they argue, both the constitutional democracy of Rawls and the "procedural democracy" of Robert Dahl place obstacles in the way of a robust deliberative politics: the latter by telling citizens "to agree on some neutral rules of play and keep their moral disagreements to themselves" and the former by leaving moral deliberation and the defense of rights "to an institution that is supposed to be above politics – the Supreme Court."[50] The difficulty with these views is that moral disagreement does not cease at the constitutional or procedural doorstep; as Rawls himself recognizes, "issues such as abortion, preferential hiring, and health care are central to the question of justice in democratic societies."[51] Following Rawls, Gutmann and Thompson largely agree that individuals in their capacity as citizens must conform to the requirements of public reason, specified in the principles of reciprocity, publicity, and accountability.[52] Nevertheless, they also contend, the conflicts over issues such as abortion or affirmative action are grounded not simply in interpretive disputes concerning the constitutional meaning of liberty and equality, but

[49] As Bohman and Rehg observe, "The term 'deliberative democracy' seems to have been first coined by Joseph Bessette, who argued against elitist (or 'aristocratic') interpretations of the Constitution. Bessette's challenge joined the chorus of voices calling for a participatory view of democratic politics." See James Bohman and William Rehg, eds., *Deliberative Democracy: Essays on Reason and Politics* (Cambridge, MA: MIT Press, 1997), p. xii. Deliberative or "participatory" democracy found powerful inspiration in the thought of Hannah Arendt; see especially *The Human Condition* (Chicago: University of Chicago Press, 1998).

[50] Amy Gutmann and Dennis Thompson, *Democracy and Disagreement* (Cambridge, MA: Harvard University Press, 1996), p. 347.

[51] Ibid., pp. 35–8.

[52] They lay out these three principles in chs. 2 to 4 of *Democracy and Disagreement*. Particularly with respect to the principle of reciprocity – "the foundation of reciprocity is the capacity to seek fair terms of social cooperation for their own sake" – they acknowledge a debt to Rawls (as well as to T. M. Scanlon) but add that "we give greater emphasis than they do to actual political deliberation and draw different implications with respect to the content of the principles of justice" (pp. 52–3, n. 1).

also in fundamental disagreements concerning the good for individuals and society. While acknowledging Rawls's "deliberative turn" in his later work, Gutmann and Thompson contend that his view of deliberation is too narrow to capture the scope and nature of moral disagreement in democratic politics, and that, in particular, the principles of deliberation ought to allow public discussion of claims grounded in comprehensive views. By barring such claims, they argue, both procedural and constitutional democracy attempt to enforce a kind of truce among citizens at the expense of real consensus and political progress. In short, the question at the heart of the matter is whether claims deriving from doctrines of the good can, and indeed must, be brought into deliberation concerning the just or the right in public affairs. As Gutmann and Thompson conclude, "Moral argument will almost certainly intrude into politics no matter what our theories say or what our practices imply. The important question is what kind of moral argument our democracy should foster – what its content should be, and under what conditions it should be conducted."[53]

Notwithstanding the much-debated question of whether Gutmann and Thompson offer an account of deliberative democracy that succeeds in truly accommodating moral disagreement,[54] their extensive analysis of actual moral argument amply illustrates that battles over abortion and capital punishment, as well as a whole host of issues regarding education, health and welfare, employment practices, and so forth, bring to the deliberative forum ideas of justice firmly rooted in views of the good life and good society. These views frequently conflict: the sanctity of a fetus as created and conceived in God's grace as opposed to the control of a woman over her own body; equal opportunity for the sexes as compared to the roles endorsed by nature or by God; the righteousness of vengeance versus the charity of forgiveness.[55] Within the realm of middle democracy, it seems impossible to

---

[53] Ibid. See also Gutmann and Thompson "Why Deliberative Democracy Is Different," *Social Philosophy and Policy* 17 (Winter 2000), p. 161: "In modern pluralist societies, political disagreement often reflects moral disagreement.... Any satisfactory theory of democracy must provide a way of dealing with this moral disagreement."

[54] See, for example, the essays compiled in *Deliberative Politics: Essays on Democracy and Disagreement*, ed. Stephen Macedo (New York: Oxford University Press, 1999).

[55] Thompson and Gutmann's treatment of *Mozert v Hawkins* is particularly illuminating concerning the clash of such fundamental ideas, and their interpretation of the case

avoid moral conflict among comprehensive views that are overtly or covertly brought into the debate. Yet, in the absence of real deliberation, Gutmann and Thompson suggest, we never confront the true grounds of our disagreement and thus fail to exploit the opportunities to arrive at real consensus, if only about why we must agree to disagree.

Clarity about questions of the good, moreover, sheds light on liberalism's own claims and assumptions. Even if we limit the idea of justice to Rawls's strict view that justice is social cooperation among citizens understood as free and equal, the principles of freedom and equality are themselves connected with certain views of what is truly good: a life lived free from coercion and as a truly autonomous being, for instance, or a society that cares for its least advantaged members. And Rawls, too, ultimately rejects Rorty's radical historicist version of his position by defending political liberalism in terms of the goods it achieves, such as those inherent in the exercise of the moral powers required of citizens of a well-ordered democratic society and in the "public recognition" of one's status as a free and equal citizen.[56] To assert with Rawls that these goods are not anchored in a comprehensive doctrine – that they are strictly "political goods" – does not undercut the more basic fact that justice carries with it an idea of the good, if an ostensibly political one.

Indeed, it is by pressing hard on Rawls's "political conception of the person" – his separation of our public and personal identities – that Sandel begins to find fault with his effort in *Political Liberalism* to "[rescue] the priority of the right from controversies about the nature of the self" by attaching it to the fact of reasonable pluralism.[57] "The fundamental question," Sandel insists in response to Rawls's reformulation of his position, "is whether the right is prior to the good": whether, for example, "rights can be identified and justified in a way that does not presuppose any particular conception of the good life," and whether "the case for rights [rests] on the moral importance of

is the subject of some debate. See, for example, Galston, *Liberal Pluralism*, pp. 114–22, and Stanley Fish's comments in *Deliberative Politics: Essays on "Democracy and Disagreement,"* pp. 88–102

[56] Rawls, *Political Liberalism*, p. 203.

[57] Sandel, *Liberalism and the Limits of Justice*, p. 195.

the purposes or ends rights promote."[58] For Rawls, as for Rorty, the justification for adopting the political standpoint or a public identity is precisely the fact that no one comprehensive doctrine is accepted by all. The reasonable citizen thus understands that his or her own religious and moral ideals cannot be awarded constitutional status in a democratic society marked by a pluralism of comprehensive views. Yet the treatment of moral disagreement by Gutmann and Thompson, and the dispute between Rawls and Sandel, raise the question of whether liberalism can subordinate moral and religious ideals to the requirements of liberal justice without confronting the question of their truth or, more precisely, without addressing their claims, as well as liberalism's own claims, with regard to the human good.

As Sandel notes, the liberal conception of justice is not a mere *modus vivendi* if its appeal to justice necessarily imports ideas of the good into the architecture of the political order. Sandel's argument against Rawls on this point is both descriptive and prescriptive. The moral and religious principles that informed the Lincoln–Douglas debates and the arguments of the early abolitionists would have been disallowed by the requirements of public reason, and these same requirements prevent us from offering a moral argument, as opposed to a limited constitutional one, in defense of gay rights.[59] Yet, the fight against slavery

[58] Sandel importantly distinguishes the problem that he raises from the critique by communitarians. In his view, justice is linked with good because "the principles of justice depend for their justification on the moral worth or intrinsic good of the ends they serve," whereas in the communitarian view, "the case for recognizing a right depends on showing that such a right is implicit in the shared understandings that inform the tradition or community in question" (*Liberalism and the Limits of Justice,* pp. x–xi). As Ronald Beiner, commenting on Sandel's *Democracy's Discontent,* observes, "The real issue in the debate with Rawls and his followers, as Sandel rightly says, is whether a liberal theory of justice can be vindicated while avoiding appeal to one among a set of rival and controversial conceptions of the good" (*Debating Democracy's Discontent*), p. 3. See also MacIntyre's latest revision of his position in *Dependent Rational Animals: Why Human Beings Need the Virtues* (Chicago: Open Court, 1999): "No account of the goods, rules and virtues that are definitive of our moral life can be adequate that does not explain – or at least point us towards an explanation – how that form of life is possible for beings who are biologically constituted as we are, by providing us with an account of our development towards and into that form of life" (p. x).

[59] Sandel, *Liberalism and the Limits of Justice,* pp. 198–202, 207–10. See also Galston, *Liberal Pluralism:* "It is true that after political institutions have functioned for some time, their legitimacy may come to be taken for granted, and their constitutive values may come to be seen as freestanding. But this is an illusion, quickly dispelled in

illustrates liberalism's necessary recourse, especially in times of crisis, to comprehensive ideas of the good, and the arguments on behalf of justice for other oppressed groups will lack the same transformative power if the strictures of public reason prohibit such comprehensive claims. In the end, Sandel observes, it is not at all clear that the mutual respect and accommodation that public reason demands for diverse views of the good are achieved in the absence of real engagement with these views. As compared with the liberal position, according to which "we respect our fellow citizen's moral and religious convictions by ignoring them (for political purposes)," the "deliberative" position entails that "we respect our fellow citizen's moral and religious convictions by engaging, or attending to, them – sometimes by challenging and contesting them, sometimes by listening and learning from them – especially when those convictions bear on important political questions."[60] A liberalism that does not provide a political space for such engagement, Sandel insists, is in danger of losing its political robustness and moral self-confidence.

Against the liberalism espoused by Rawls, Sandel offers a "rival public philosophy" – a "republican" theory that centers on the idea that "liberty depends on sharing in self-government."[61] The Rawlsian view of "procedural democracy," he argues in his *Democracy's Discontent*, is a rather late arrival on the American stage. This strand of liberalism has its roots in the thought that informed the Founding, but it vied with a civic republican strand that emphasized virtue, duty, and civic education. Sandel is not alone in his emphasis on civic virtue and its supports. Amid concerns about moral decline and political fragmentation, the communitarian critique of the late twentieth century led to what Berkowitz has called a "chastened understanding" on the part of many scholars of liberalism, "who have increasingly come to appreciate the capacity of a liberal framework to respect the role of moral virtue, civic association, and even religious faith in the preservation of a political society based on free and democratic institutions."[62] For this

---

times of internal or external crisis. Slavery drove President Lincoln to philosophical arguments for human equality, and the Civil War drove him to theological reflections on divine judgment" (p. 41).

[60] Sandel, *Liberalism and the Limits of Justice*, p. 217.
[61] Sandel, *Democracy's Discontent*, p. 5.
[62] Berkowitz, *Virtue and the Making of Modern Liberalism*, p. 23.

reason, scholars have been ever more willing to speak of the "liberal virtues," emphasize the educative role of religious, civic, and familial associations, and underscore the duties rather than the rights of citizenship.

To be sure, Rawls himself acknowledges the necessity of virtue in the practice of liberal politics, especially "the virtues of fair social cooperation," civility, tolerance, reasonableness, and the sense of fairness. [63] But scholars who pursue the question of virtue more comprehensively and systematically offer more extensive lists of the virtues. Sandel, for instance, mines American history to present a rich array, including marital fidelity, religious piety, economic industry, frugality, individual self-control, manly courage, and practical judgment.[64] Amy Gutmann argues that in requiring citizens capable of taking a "civic standpoint" and of deliberating together concerning their common welfare, deliberative democracy requires a "democratic education": "the virtues that deliberation encompasses include veracity, nonviolence, practical judgment, civic integrity and magnanimity."[65] In general, different views as to the character of liberal political practices and goods produce different lists of liberal virtues, ranging from filial piety and patriotic love of country to individual autonomy and critical distance from convention and law. Whether rooted in civic republicanism, deliberative democracy, or even the requirements of social cooperation, more robust notions of liberal citizenship naturally call for more robust accounts of virtue and civic education than procedural or constitutional liberals have been willing to offer.

Yet there is a danger for liberalism in venturing too far down the road of virtue. The question that confronts those who, chastened by

---

[63] Rawls, *Political Liberalism*, pp. 194, 301–2.

[64] Thomas Pangle's "The Retrieval of Civic Virtue: A Critical Appreciation of Sandel's *Democracy's Discontent*" (in *Debating Democracy's Discontent*) offers a detailed account of the many virtues, and sources of inspiration for them, in Sandel's argument; see especially pp. 21–6. Pangle's critique is also helpful in drawing out the question of whether Sandel himself confronts the full implications of his effort to retrieve civic virtue.

[65] Amy Gutmann, *Democratic Education*, p. xiii. Or, as Bohman and Rehg argue, deliberative democracy occupies the terrain between liberal theorists, such as Hobbes and Locke, who emphasize self-interest and civil strife, and civic republicans, such as Harrington and Rousseau, who focus on the common interest and harmony. *Deliberative Democracy*, p. x.

the communitarian critique, seek to articulate the moral core and ped-agogic requirements of liberal citizenship is whether, in specifying the liberal virtues and mandating civic education, a liberal order consti-tutes what it professes to eschew: a comprehensive good and moral order – in the ancient sense, a regime. At the heart of the rediscovery of liberal citizenship lies a fundamental challenge to liberalism itself. Indeed, it is in confronting this challenge that Rawls, having thrown off the comprehensive claims of Kantianism, continues to insist on the priority of the right and the political conception of the person. For if liberalism is to preserve its liberal character, it must protect as sacrosanct a realm within which individuals freely pursue the good, understood now not as their mere subjective preferences but as the values and comprehensive doctrines that give their lives deepest mean-ing. The ostensible aim of a liberal civic education is therefore to edu-cate liberal citizens without transforming their comprehensive views or imposing a "way of life." To paraphrase a distinction from Aristo-tle, liberalism must strive to create good citizens but not good human beings.[66]

Rawls's defense of a political liberalism that would sustain this distinction, however, has reignited rather than resolved the ques-tion of how "transformative" liberalism is or needs to be. This ques-tion informs the "long-standing dialogue" and disagreement between Stephen Macedo and William Galston concerning the "moral and prac-tical requirements of a liberal public order."[67] Macedo's account of "civic liberalism" – a liberalism that attends to its moral and political supports through civic education – presents a robust conception of liberal citizenship and its pedagogic underpinnings. He argues that liberals must become more self-conscious not only of liberalism's sup-ports but also of its transformative ambitions. "The success of our civic project," he observes, "relies upon a transformative project that includes the remaking of moral and religious communities."[68] In this matter, Macedo is critical of liberal scholars, such as Iris Young and

---

[66] See Charles Larmore, *Patterns of Moral Complexity* (Cambridge: Cambridge University Press, 1987): "We do better to recognize that liberalism is not a philosophy of man, but a philosophy of politics" (p. 129).

[67] Galston, "Review of Stephen Macedo's *Diversity and Distrust: Civic Education in a Multicultural Democracy*," *Ethics* 112 (January 2002): 386–91.

[68] Macedo, *Diversity and Distrust*, p. x.

Richard Flathman, who praise diversity or "difference" and yet rely upon "an account of citizen virtue without articulating it, defending it, and describing how it can and should be promoted."[69] Defenders of liberalism, he argues, suffer a kind of "false consciousness" in failing to acknowledge the manner and extent to which liberal politics transforms individuals' deepest moral and political beliefs.[70]

The clearest resistance to this transformation is also the source of the intolerance and strife that distinguished the religious wars of the sixteenth and seventeenth centuries and that, according to Rawls, gave rise to liberalism's political project: orthodox (creedal and Salvationist) religion. In seeking to construct a political order in which the "true believers" – with their comprehensive doctrines and deference to divine law – can live together in peace, Macedo argues, the liberal project necessarily did more than establish a neutral institutional framework within which conflicting doctrines can coexist. This project transformed these doctrines. Although Macedo stops short of recommending what he calls "civic totalism," the education to a comprehensive liberal view of the good such as that offered by John Dewey, he is nevertheless suspicious of a simple distinction between public and private that obscures the ways that this very distinction and liberal public principles shape individual lives: "widespread acceptance of the rule of law and the distinction between public and private represent ways of constructing the world as a whole."[71] On the one hand, it is essential to liberalism's mission to establish the separation between private and public, and between church and state; on the other, the success of such a separation requires that the wall between the two be breached in fundamental ways. Looking to Locke's *Letter on Toleration*, Macedo concludes, "Lockean politics cannot, any more than our own, leave private moral beliefs altogether to one side; it cannot leave the soul alone to care only for the body. It counts on a convergence of public and private."[72]

According to Macedo, the nature and necessity of this convergence are manifest in American historical experience, and particularly in the

---

[69] Ibid., p. 26.
[70] See Macedo's *Liberal Virtues*, pp. 45, 51 and his *Democracy and Distrust*, pp. 217, 227.
[71] Macedo, *Diversity and Distrust*, p. 15; see also *Liberal Virtues*, pp. 16–21.
[72] Macedo, *Diversity and Distrust*, p. 34.

transformation of American Catholicism. The abatement of the "gen-uine tension that existed between American republicanism and the nineteenth century Catholic hierarchy," he argues, is attributable in no small part to post–Vatican II changes within the Catholic Church that "may be regarded as concessions to liberal democracy."[73] To be sure, these changes were often justified in doctrinal terms – in terms, for example, of Catholic social justice – but they represent a funda-mental shift in the moral perspective of the Catholic Church in the direction of distinctively liberal values. Although this shift reduces "the range of significant normative diversity," Macedo observes, it is to be lauded, not mourned: "What we want are healthy forms of diversity, and from a political standpoint that means forms of diversity support-ive of basic principles of justice and a liberal democratic civic life."[74]

Even as such liberalization is to be embraced, then, it must be seen for what it is. In addition to dampening the doctrinal or dogmatic zeal that has historically been a cause of sectarian strife, the conver-gence of public and private in the education of liberal citizens has essentially undercut traditional religious principles that give priority to divine authority and its representatives over secular authority and the individual, to the salvation of the soul over the preservation of the body, and to the one true faith over the many false ones. The conver-gence of public and private has thus secured the separation of church and state and the disestablishment or privatization of religion. Indeed, according to Macedo, a wholly self-aware liberalism understands the necessity of a shared civic morality that is able "to turn people's deep-est convictions – including their religious beliefs – in directions that are congruent with the ways of a liberal republic."[75] A shared civic morality cannot help but shape private life; as he observes in an ear-lier work, "Liberal political norms have a private life: they help shape and structure the private lives of liberal citizens. To a greater extent than liberals usually allow, freedom is a way of life."[76]

---

[73] Ibid., p. 88. See generally pp. 59–87 and p. 130: "While the animus against Irish Catholics was indeed based partly on race prejudice, there were more substantial and honorable grounds for worrying that the teachings of the Roman Catholic Church before Vatican II were inconsistent with liberalism."

[74] Ibid., p. 134.

[75] Ibid., p. 43.

[76] Macedo, *Liberal Virtues*, p. 265.

But given his view of the extent of liberalism's reach, how does Macedo separate his own civic liberalism from the civic totalism of a John Dewey? In response to this difficulty, Macedo has recourse to the Rawlsian notion of public reason. With Rawls, he insists that the diversity of comprehensive "worldviews" – religious and philosophic – requires that public deliberation and judgment appeal only to reasons that are accessible and acceptable to all "reasonable" citizens, that is, to "reasons and arguments that we can share in spite of our differences."[77] In this regard, liberal justice itself is not grounded in a single religious or philosophic comprehensive view: "Political liberal principles are justified only in being justified independently of religious and other comprehensive claims."[78] When it comes to political matters, no comprehensive doctrine can have priority. Political authority, as a common concern, requires common consensus and therefore a public, as opposed to private, reason that can represent such a consensus.

In taking issue with Macedo, however, Galston points out that Rawls's liberalism is "political in two senses": "not only are public reasons political rather than comprehensive but they are also addressed to the basic structure of society rather than to social life as a whole."[79] For Galston, it is Macedo's insistence on the convergence of public and private in the latter sense that is the deeply illiberal element of his civic liberalism. In this important regard, "Macedo is a totalist while Rawls is not." Regarding the scope or effect of liberal principles, rather than the basis of their public justification, then, it would seem that Macedo destroys and Rawls preserves the "traditional liberal distinction between public and private."[80]

As Galston acknowledges, his own early work also underscores the connection between liberal political principles and a particular vision of the human good, and he rejects the view that the liberal state is wholly neutral.[81] Galston is at one with Macedo, therefore, in insisting

---

[77] Macedo, *Diversity and Distrust*, p. 172; see pp. 167–87 for his discussion of Rawls and public justification.

[78] Ibid., p. 179.

[79] Galston, "Review of Macedo's *Diversity and Distrust*," p. 388.

[80] Ibid.

[81] See Galston, *Liberal Purposes*, p. 3: "Like every other political community, it [the liberal state] embraces a view of the human good that favors certain ways of life and tilts against others."

on the connection between liberalism's public principles and ideas of the good, and he agrees with those who suggest that liberal practices and purposes necessitate distinctively liberal virtues, such as tolerance or openness to diverse views, willingness to settle disagreements openly and through persuasion, and a certain "magnanimity" or reciprocity.[82] In his most recent work, *Liberal Pluralism*, he observes that theorists like Macedo have rightly drawn attention to the educative effects of liberalism: "Liberal democratic citizens are made, not born, and we cannot blithely rely on the invisible hand of civil society to carry out civic paideia."[83] Yet, Galston also insists, the liberal state, as compared to the ancient regime, does not impose a comprehensive way of life or doctrine of the good. To the contrary, its great achievement has been to create a constitutional framework of institutions and practices that accommodate and even protect the diverse pursuit of the good. His central disagreement with Macedo pertains to what he calls Macedo's "civic presumption," a presumption that "gives inadequate weight to a core human value that helps justify liberalism." This core human value is "expressive liberty" or "the ability to live one's life in a manner that freely expresses one's deepest convictions about the sources of value and meaning."[84]

Arising from this liberty, Galston also argues, is "value-pluralism," the existence of which further justifies the liberal state's presumption in favor of individual liberty. On this subject, Galston takes his bearings from Isaiah Berlin's view that "our moral universe is characterized by plural and conflicting values that cannot be harmonized in a single comprehensive way of life."[85] Galston's liberal pluralism is a comprehensive, as compared to freestanding, theory precisely because it purports to be consistent with the "basic structure of the moral world we actually inhabit" – a world in which there is a range of "rationally defensible" comprehensive views or in which "no single uniquely rational ordering or combination of such values [is]... binding on all individuals." Now, by rationally defensible, Galston means most simply that these views "fall above the Hampshire–Hart line of minimum

---

[82] Ibid., pp. 226–7; see also Galston, "Review of Gutmann and Thompson's *Democracy and Disagreement*," *Ethics* 108 (April 1998): 607–10.

[83] Galston, *Liberal Pluralism*, p. 15.

[84] Galston, "Review of Macedo," p. 390.

[85] Galston, *Liberal Pluralism*, pp. 27–8.

decency."[86] In his more expansive moments, however, he suggests also that a view of the good is rationally defensible because it represents an ordering of goods that is objectively good for the individual or that constitutes a truly rich and worthwhile way of life for human beings.[87] Indeed, Galston defines "diversity" itself as "*legitimate* differences among individuals and groups over such matters as the nature of the good life, sources of moral authority, reason versus faith, and the like."[88]

Yet how are we to know what the actual structure of the moral universe is? The empirical evidence proves ambiguous at best. In the first place, the homogeneity or heterogeneity of the moral world we inhabit is fundamentally shaped by the "regime" that constitutes it. Galston notes, for example, that there are political communities that are more rather than less homogeneous, and he is himself against forms of liberalism that, by giving pride of place to the principles of autonomy or individuality, exert a "homogenizing pressure" on ways of life that do not accept such a principle.[89] As Galston also acknowledges, moreover, the mere fact of diversity is insufficient to establish its naturalness or desirability. Judging whether the heterogeneity of the moral world under a properly constituted liberal democracy, or under any other condition, reflects the "actual structure of the normative universe" requires establishing that these conditions are also natural to and naturally good for human beings. It is this important question that ultimately undergirds the disagreement between Macedo and Galston concerning the constitution of a liberal order and the character of liberal citizenship.

For most deeply at issue between Macedo and Galston is the question of the best conditions for both the political community and its individual members. This question becomes all the more complex in light of their agreement that it cannot be settled by direct recourse to the principle of state neutrality – to the principle that Ronald Dworkin

---

[86] Ibid., p. 57. Galston's case concerning the heterogeneity of the good is in fact even more complicated, since he draws upon three orders of diversity as evidence: the clash among values within the same value system, the differences of goods relative to individuals, and the diversity of worthwhile lives (p. 34).

[87] Ibid., pp. 30–2, 37, 57.

[88] Ibid., p. 21, my emphasis.

[89] Ibid., pp. 20–4.

could once insist upon in saying that political decisions should strive to remain "independent of any particular conception of the good life, or of what gives value to life."[90] To be sure, Macedo is less convinced than Galston that a liberal state, as a civic educator, can remain at all independent of a particular conception of the good, and he considers it a matter of "self-consciousness," not to say honesty, on the part of liberals to acknowledge this fact. But more importantly, short of recommending civic totalism, Macedo is also more convinced than Galston that a distinctively liberal conception of what gives value to life is also good for those who hold it. Macedo is more willing, therefore, to wield the instruments of political authority and civic education in support of this conception.

In rejecting Macedo's civic presumption in favor of liberal pluralism, however, Galston establishes that the "underlying assumption" of the pluralist argument is a presumption against coercion:

This argument draws its force from the underlying assumption that coercion always stands exposed to a potential demand for justification. Individuals and groups whose desires and values are thwarted by existing arrangements have an incentive to question those arrangements, and they are entitled to a reply. No one asks why it is legitimate for our movements to be influenced by gravity; they just are. But coercion is not a fact of nature, nor is it self-justifying. Just the reverse: There is a presumption against it, grounded in the pervasive human desire to go our own way in accordance with our own desires and beliefs.[91]

Galston proceeds to argue that coercion cannot be justified by the claim that a certain understanding of the human good is defective. Rather, since the natural presumption favors individual liberty, "sufficient" reasons must be offered if liberty is to be restricted. Indeed, if there are such reasons, then the failure to restrict liberty – "to intervene in wrongful or self-destructive behavior" – may itself be judged "morally culpable."[92]

But Galston's argument is more complicated than he admits, and its complications illuminate the need to confront the question of the human good more fully than he does. For gravity and the pervasive

---

[90] Ronald Dworkin, *A Matter of Principle* (Cambridge, MA: Harvard University Press, 1985), p. 191.
[91] Galston, *Liberal Pluralism*, p. 58.
[92] Ibid.

human desire to go our own way are natural facts of different orders, and in the context of a political community, the mere existence of the latter does not justify its free rein simply. If sufficient reasons for the limitation of liberty must be offered, so too must sufficient reasons for its enjoyment: The wish to "go my own way," in other words, also "stands exposed to a potential demand for justification," and I may be judged "morally culpable" if I cannot offer a reason for doing so. Just as the mere fact of liberalism's pervasive or coercive educative influence would not on its own justify that influence, neither does the existence or nature of human desire by itself offer a sufficient reason for its free rein. What, then, would justify either coercion or liberty? What is the standard of "sufficient reason"? What constitute legitimate differences over such matters as the nature of the good life, sources of moral authority, or reason versus faith? It is with respect to these difficulties that the question of the human good necessarily reemerges. For, if, as Galston insists, the "superiority of democratic practices" – the defense of liberal democracy as better than the alternatives – rests on its allowing a diversity of *rationally defensible* worthwhile and good lives, we cannot establish that there is in fact such a diversity simply by appealing to the standard of "minimum decency."[93] We are compelled, that is, to address the question of what makes a human life worthwhile and good.

Concerning this question, it is important first to be clear about what precisely is at stake. For when scholars such as Rawls, Sandel, Macedo, and Galston now speak of the good, they are no longer referring to the subjective preferences of the individual, as Rawls, following Kant, originally meant. Rather they are referring to that "comprehensive doctrine" of values or beliefs – grounded in individual conscience, religious belief, or philosophical outlook – that gives life its deepest meaning and constitutes an individual's view of what it means to be a good human being and to live a good life. Citizenship and the virtues that belong to it, from the liberal point of view, do not or ought not to constitute the good in this sense. Even if these virtues and the obligations of citizenship have a certain moral claim over us – in demanding our devotion to and participation in a liberal order – they do not define an order or a comprehensive good in accord with which we

---

[93] Ibid., pp. 46, 52–3.

must direct our individual lives. In eschewing a claim to be such an order, moreover, liberalism is deeply suspicious of any authority, especially religious authority, whose political or public end is the imposition of a single comprehensive view on individuals.

Yet the current disputes about the relation between the right and the good, and the nature of civic education, have shown that liberalism itself cannot be absolved from addressing questions about its authoritative claims with respect to the good, the character and extent of its moral education, and the relation between the good liberal citizen and the good human being. These questions call for investigation at several levels. Most simply, however much we may strive to circumscribe the virtues within an instrumental or political frame – and to insist that the ideas of the good be political ideas – the inculcation of these virtues inevitably raises the question of the good simply. Even as he recommends a political or instrumental conception of virtue, for instance, Berkowitz concedes that "insofar as the link between the lesser virtues, which are exercised as a means to various ends, and the higher virtues or the virtues of human excellence, which are exercised for their own sake, is severed, virtue threatens to become a mercenary undertaking."[94] Indeed, it is not even clear, prior to examination, whether any virtue can be presented as merely instrumental or whether it makes a claim, implicit or explicit, to belong to individual excellence: Courage may be required for the preservation of the political community but, especially in light of its risks, it is inevitably honored as a noble quality worthy of possession in its own right; toleration may be necessary for the peaceful coexistence of religious sects, but it belongs also to the person whom Galston approvingly calls a "self-aware pluralist," that is, to the wisest or most self-aware human being.[95] However much liberalism wishes to abide by the separation of public and private, it invariably makes claims concerning the human good that it must acknowledge and defend.

Indeed, it is impossible to establish with the requisite certainty Galston's premise in justifying liberalism as the best political order – the existence of a diversity of rationally defensible comprehensive

---

94 Berkowitz, *Virtue and the Making of Modern Liberalism*, p. 152. See also Galston's remark concerning "the instrumental view of virtue" in *Justice and the Human Good*, p. 54.
95 Galston, *Liberal Pluralism*, pp. 53, 62

views – in the absence of an examination of these views. In an early treatment of this question, Galston observes, "It seems ridiculous to be asked to choose among Jesus, Da Vinci, Caesar, and Socrates; without doing so, we can respect each for having fully developed an important kind of human possibility."[96] But can we? Three of these possibilities – Jesus, Caesar, and Socrates – represent ways of life that reject one another's fundamental claims. These lives themselves, that is, ask us to choose among them, and how are we to decide the matter without examining the specific claims of each? In fact, a liberal political order invariably makes such choices for us. For it cannot accommodate every possibility, a Caesar, for example, and perhaps not even the highest or most fully developed ones. Yet, in admitting some possibilities and excluding others, is a liberal order to decide among ways of life and then to deny its own citizens the right, not to say the very hope, of investigating the matter?

As the disputes that inform the current rediscovery of citizenship suggest, however, we cannot justify liberal political principles merely by asserting the fact of reasonable pluralism; nor can we achieve clarity about liberalism's own comprehensive claims by falling back on the public–private distinction. An investigation of citizenship that begins from liberal presuppositions is a partial investigation. Even Galston's self-aware defense of liberalism rests in the final analysis on a liberal presumption against coercion and in favor of going one's own way, but this is a presumption not shared by doctrines that start from the fundamental authority of the law. As such, Galston's argument does not confront these doctrines on their own grounds. He does not, in fact, wholly account for his own claims concerning the right of a political order to preserve itself and its constitution when threatened with destruction – a right that exists, apparently, even when its exercise may involve the killing of innocents.[97] Are there no limits or bounds to such a right? Is every political community and its constitution simply sacrosanct in this regard? As Galston himself points out, "the traditional task of political philosophy – defining and defending the difference

---

[96] Galston, *Justice and the Human Good*, p. 68.
[97] Galston goes very far: "if the Israelis were faced with imminent defeat and probably genocide at the hands of Arab military forces, they would be justified in using atomic weapons against Damascus and Baghdad if there were no other way of averting catastrophe" (*Liberal Pluralism*, pp. 76–7).

between better and worse forms of political organization – remains relevant today."[98] If we are to undertake such a task, we must investigate also dimensions of politics that liberal thought neglects or obscures. To avoid what Galston calls "a kind of democratic dogmatism," the current debate about citizenship must enlarge the horizon within which it examines the question "What is a citizen?"

In this regard, however, scholars of liberalism are typically limited by their concern, on the one hand, to establish supports for liberal principles and, on the other, to preserve room for individual freedom and diverse pursuits of the good. In seeking to accommodate these dual aims, some, such as Martha Nussbaum, have formulated a view of "cosmopolitan citizenship" that makes room for plural and local attachments but locates our most fundamental allegiance in the liberal (and universal) principle of equal human dignity.[99] Others, such as Rorty, have emphasized the primacy of local and national communities in forming civic identity while nonetheless assigning the highest priority to individual liberation.[100] Others, such as Gutmann, have sought to define a distinctively "democratic identity" that supports a deliberative democracy and yet leaves room for other identities or allegiances.[101] And still others, such as Galston, have laid out a range of possibilities "short of full citizenship" that accommodate groups who obey the basic laws of the land but do not make full claims on the community or participate fully in its institutions and practices. These formulations certainly do not exhaust the field, but they exemplify the common effort within the current rediscovery of citizenship to support and justify liberal political principles while sustaining the traditional liberal distinction between public and private.[102] The

---

[98] Ibid., p. 45.

[99] Martha Nussbaum, *For Love of Country: Debating the Limits of Patriotism* (Boston: Beacon Press, 1996).

[100] Richard Rorty, *Philosophy and Social Hope* (London: Penguin Books, 1999). See especially the essays "Globalization, the Politics of Identity, and Social Hope" and "The Unpatriotic Academy."

[101] Amy Gutmann, *Identity in Democracy* (Princeton, NJ: Princeton University Press, 2003).

[102] The literature on citizenship ranges widely; for example, compare Walter Berns, *Making Patriots* (Chicago: Chicago University Press, 2001); Diane Ravitch and Joseph P. Viteritti, eds., *Making Good Citizens: Education and Civil Society* (New Haven, CT: Yale University Press, 2001); Thomas Janoski, *Citizenship and Civil Society* (Cambridge: Cambridge University Press, 1998); Will Kymlicka, *Politics in the Vernacular:*

consequence of this effort, however, is that the questions raised by the disputes between Rawls and Sandel, and between Macedo and Galston, are never addressed comprehensively. To understand the nature of citizenship with the requisite fullness, we require greater clarity than is now available about the relation between the right and the good, and about the connection between the education of a citizen and the "comprehensive good" that makes human life truly worthwhile and good.

But how is one to address these questions? In this matter, the distinctiveness of Aristotle's political philosophy – the fact that it does *not* begin from liberal premises or assumptions – proves crucial. For Aristotle undertakes his investigation first by acknowledging the political community's authoritative and architectonic power as educator. His acknowledgment of this power, moreover, is intended as a statement of fact: Whether it does so well or badly, every political community educates its citizens (*NE* 1103b3–6). He also shows that the highest pedagogic aim of civic education is not simply good citizens but morally serious human beings and that, from this point of view, the human good is properly understood as the possession and activity of moral virtue – in current terms, the comprehensive doctrine of values or beliefs that gives life its deepest meaning.

Because Aristotle suggests that the human good in this sense is fundamentally tied to the political community, his political thought is frequently classified as "perfectionist."[103] Yet, this classification obscures the fact that the point from which Aristotle begins is not the point at which he ends. Although he begins by acknowledging that the political community is the first and most authoritative educator with

---

Nationalism, Multiculturalism, and Citizenship (Oxford: Oxford University Press, 2001); David Miller, *Citizenship and National Identity* (Oxford: Blackwell, 2000); Ruth Lister, *Citizenship: Feminist Perspectives* (New York: New York University Press, 2003); and Dana Villa, *Socratic Citizenship* (Princeton, NJ: Princeton University Press, 2001). Most recently, Jill Frank has sought to articulate and defend the idea of a "democracy of distinction," in which she brings out the "democratic possibilities" of Aristotle's thought and argues that the "work" of citizens individually and together is "to unify the polity in a way that preserves its essential plurality." See Jill Frank, *A Democracy of Distinction: Aristotle and the Work of Politics* (Chicago: University of Chicago Press, 2005), pp. 8, 52.

[103] See, for example, Rawls, *Political Liberalism*, p. 195; Sandel, *Democracy's Discontent*, pp. 7–8; and Berkowitz, *Virtue and the Making of Modern Liberalism*, pp. 7–14.

regard to the good, his investigation in the *Nicomachean Ethics* seeks also to establish this community's true authority in this regard. By starting from the broadest view of the political community, however, Aristotle is able to explore its scope and the nature of its pedagogic aims, and to address fully the two fundamental questions that the current debate raises but does not adequately confront: the relation between the right and the good, and the connection between the education of a citizen and that of a good human being simply. To address these questions, Aristotle indicates, we first must investigate the life that the political community, as educator, presents as best: the life of moral virtue.

ARISTOTLE ON LAW, EDUCATION, AND MORAL VIRTUE

A summary statement of Aristotle's view of the significance of moral virtue is that moral virtue is a matter of intense concern for both the political community and the individual because the happiness of each is at stake. Aristotle's opening presentation of the relation between action and happiness in the *Nicomachean Ethics* can be most obviously contrasted with the argument of Kant. For inasmuch as Kant and Aristotle would agree that moral or virtuous action involves an orientation "toward another," and is connected with duty and law, their accounts of ethics find a point of agreement. Yet, by separating moral action from the longing of a human being to achieve the good – by understanding it in terms of duty alone – Kant does more than divorce it from happiness as its end. By Aristotle's account, such a separation also severs the morally serious human being's pursuit of happiness from its moral and political content, that is, from "noble and just" action (*NE* 1094b9–10, 14–19, 1099a22–31; *Pol.* 1253a14–21, 35–9).[104]

According to Aristotle, good action is understood first in connection with the end that is "nobler and more divine" to secure and preserve than that of any individual – the good of the community or nation (*NE* 1094b9–10). In suggesting that such noble and just action is the highest end in the realm of action (*praxis*), however, Aristotle does not take his bearings from the requirements of politics or the

---

[104] Citations of the *Nicomachean Ethics* and *Politics* are to the Oxford Classical Text editions; they will be indicated by the Bekker numbers in parentheses. Translations are my own.

common good simply. Rather, this action is understood, by the political community itself, as good also for the one who performs it: as good
in itself and as grounded in good character. The inculcation of good
character requires the education supplied by the law (*nomos*), which,
as the most authoritative voice of command in the political community, invariably shapes human action. Since no action proceeds in the
absence of desire, and since choice (*prohairesis*), the "starting point"
(*archē*) of action, is either intelligence operating through longing
(*orektikos nous*) or longing operating through thought (*orexis
dianoētikē*) (*NE* 1139a31, 1139b4–5), we choose and act well or badly
in accordance with the disposition of our desires.[105] Neither perfectly
rational nor wholly irrational, the desires are amenable to and require
habituation, which proceeds through command and a certain force
and, in the best case, aims at making desire obedient to "right reason" (*orthos logos*) (*NE* 1103b31–4).[106] Through habituation, then, we
acquire the moral virtues, and the law is the most authoritative voice
of command and so the arbiter of right reason in the education to
virtue. The investigation of the good is "a kind of political investigation" because the highest or most authoritative good, moral virtue,
is the same for both the political community and the individual (*NE*
1094b10–11).

   In addition to its contrast with the approach of Kant, Aristotle's initial presentation of virtue and the good stands in significant contrast
with that of his current students. Most present-day Aristotelians begin
by establishing either the political principles in accord with which they

---

[105] The usual translation of *prohairesis* is "choice," but the English word perhaps does
not fully capture the sense of the Greek, which connotes "deliberate choice": a
decision preceded by prior deliberation, such that one's choosing it has purpose
and resolution. On the other hand, the choice that issues from the characteristic
(*hexis*) formed by habit is not necessarily preceded by deliberation: As Aristotle
suggests in the discussion of courage, we more readily see the character of a person
who must act or react quickly, for in seeing something coming, a person is able to
choose on the basis of calculation and reason (1117a17–22; see also 1105a27–b5).

[106] As Aristotle's etymological note in Book II suggests, the Greek terms for moral virtue,
ēthikē aretē, point to this link between habit (*ethos*) and the virtue (*aretē*) that is the seat
of good action (*NE* 1103a17–18). This is true also of the Latin root (*mos*, pl. *morēs*)
of our English word "moral." On the etymological derivation of *ēthikē aretē*, see John
Burnet (with commentary), *The "Ethics" of Aristotle* (London: Methuen & Co.
[reprinted ed. Salem, NH: Ayer Co. Publishers, 1988],), p. 74 and G. Ramsauer, ed.
(with commentary), *Aristotle, Nicomachean Ethics*, vol. 2 of *Greek and Roman Philosophy*
(New York: Garland, 1987), pp. 77–8.

define the virtues of a good citizen or the overarching principle of the good from which they derive the virtues of human "flourishing."[107] Aristotle, by contrast, does not derive the virtues from overarching principles. In this kind of matter, he points out, it is impossible to start from what is "known unqualifiedly" (*NE* 1095a30–b7).[108] Rather, we must start from what is "known to us," which are the opinions of the community – what it praises as noble and just, and blames as shameful and unjust (*NE* 1129b11–19, 1134a26–31, 1180a14–24; *Pol.* 1253a14–21, 35–9). In questions of ethics, of course, we do not seek out just any old opinion; we do not survey, for example, the local prison population. We turn to those we trust as decent and serious role models. On these grounds, the most competent student of matters pertaining to "the noble and the just, and politics generally," is someone who already has the proper habits since, in possessing these habits, this person is already in possession of the right principles (*archas*, "starting points") (*NE* 1095b3–6). In the education to virtue, therefore, the community looks to those exemplars of the law who hold the correct opinions. To be most precise, the good in the realm of action is given first in the principles held by the morally serious (*spoudaios*) and prudent (*phronimos*) human being: the person who, having been "nobly raised," identifies the good life with noble and just action, and so with moral

---

[107] See, for example, MacIntyre, *After Virtue*, pp. 219–20; Galston, *Justice and the Human Good*, pp. 56–8 and *Liberal Purposes*, ch. 8; Nussbaum, "Non-Relative Virtues," pp. 32–6 and "Aristotle on Human Functioning and Social Justice," pp. 214–33; Salkever, *Finding the Mean*, p. 264, and "'Lopp'd and Bound'," p. 192.

[108] Richard Kraut, in *Aristotle and the Human Good* (Princeton, NJ: Princeton University Press, 1989), offers a somewhat different view, calling the argument concerning human function (*ergon*) in ch. 7 of Book I "the most important single argument in [Aristotle's] treatment of happiness" (p. 237). For Kraut's full defense of this view, as well as the use he makes of the function argument, see especially ch. 6. In the course of establishing the significance of the function argument, however, Kraut makes an important qualification concerning the moral virtues. After noting that "not a word is said in the function argument about the particular virtues that occupy so much of Aristotle's attention in later portions of the *NE*," he observes a little later, "I agree that the function argument does not by itself show that temperance (for example), as Aristotle conceives of it, is a virtue. But we would be impatient students of the *NE* if we expected it to present the whole of its argument at once. Instead of regarding the function argument as a complete but defective argument on behalf of the ethical virtues, we should treat it as the foundation for a defense that Aristotle continues to develop throughout the rest of his work. Obviously, the function argument cannot by itself show why temperance and other particular virtues are important; to do that, one must first have a proper understanding of these virtues" (pp. 322–3).

virtue (*NE* 1094b14–19, 1098a14–18, 1099a22–31, 1103a31–b25, 1105b2–9, 1105b28–1106a2, 1106a6–9, 1106b24–7, 1106b36–1107a2, 1113a25–33).

In contrast to his students today, then, Aristotle begins by defining the human good in terms of moral virtue, and not the reverse.[109] More particularly, he offers a provisional definition of the good as an activity of the soul in accord with reason, and action in conformity with this, and he adopts the morally serious perspective in identifying moral virtue as the rational perfection of that part of the soul – the desiring and longing part – from which action issues (*NE* 1098a13–18). Proceeding on this supposition, Aristotle offers also a provisional definition of moral virtue: Concerning the passions and actions, moral virtue is a "mean" (*meson*) with respect to two vices, which are the excess and deficiency in relation to what is necessary (*deon*), and a mean that accords with the rational principle (*logos*) defined by the prudent human being (*NE* 1106b36–1107a6). Aristotle's definition remains provisional since he postpones the investigation of the rational principle or right reason that underlies moral virtue until his account of intellectual virtue in Book VI (*NE* 1103b31–4). In taking up the discussion of the morally serious life, Aristotle simply accepts the law's claim to be the voice of right reason, and, indeed, he powerfully reiterates this claim in his discussion of justice (*NE* 1138a5–11).

According to Aristotle, then, the law strives not only to guard the common good, but also to make citizens "noble and good," *kalos k'agathos*, the two terms often used in Greek to describe the exemplar of virtue. In this regard, the virtue inculcated by the authoritative

---

[109] Peter Simpson's criticism of contemporary Aristotelianism sums up the difficulty: "Flourishing is the prior notion and the virtues are to be understood in terms of it. But Aristotle's understanding of the relation between flourishing and the virtues is the opposite of this. Aristotle does not argue to the virtues from some prior notion of flourishing, nor does he even attempt to do this. The virtues fall into the definition of *eudaimonia* but *eudaimonia* does not fall into the definition of the virtues.... So the notion of virtue must be prior to the notion of *eudaimonia* and must be understood before *eudaimonia* can be understood" ("Contemporary Virtue Ethics and Aristotle," p. 507). See also John Cooper's criticism of those who would designate Aristotle's ethics as "teleological": "although [Aristotle] does hold that virtuous action is a means to *eudaimonia*, or human good, *eudaimonia* is itself not specified independently of virtuous action; on the contrary, *eudaimonia* is conceived as identical with a lifetime of morally serious action" (John M. Cooper, *Reason and Human Good in Aristotle* [Cambridge, MA: Harvard University Press, 1975], p. 88).

education of the political community is presented as both instrumentally and intrinsically good. Or to put this in terms that Aristotle uses, the education provided by the law necessarily authorizes two ends for virtuous action that it also seeks to reconcile: the common good, on the one hand, and moral virtue or moral perfection in its own right, on the other.

Having accepted at face value the political community's claim to be the architect of the human good, Aristotle undertakes an investigation of the complex end at which the law aims in his discussion of the eleven moral virtues in the *Nicomachean Ethics*. These virtues belong to the morally serious life, at the peaks of which are two complete virtues, magnanimity and justice. By illuminating the peaks of the moral life, Aristotle both clarifies the highest possibilities of the education supplied by the law and reveals, on the basis of the law's own standards, the limits of its education.

Aristotle's examination of the particular moral virtues is the focus of the next two chapters. Chapter 2 follows his treatment of the noble as the end or *telos* of virtue, beginning with the first virtue, courage, through the first complete virtue, magnanimity. I show that it is virtue's connection with the noble that elevates it as an end and good in its own right. At its height in magnanimity, however, this elevation of virtue proves to entail an abstraction from justice or the common good, the other end to which the law demands the devotion of morally serious human beings.[110] Chapter 3 thus examines Aristotle's account of

---

[110] As for the logic of the discussion, I take my bearings from Aristotle's several explicit textual indications (*NE* 1117b23–4, 1119b22–3, 1122a18–24, 1125b1–8) and the description of the virtues. Aristotle's dialectical or pedagogical strategy in the *Ethics* has been addressed most recently by Richard Bodéüs, *The Political Dimensions of Aristotle's "Ethics,"* trans. Jan Edward Garrett (Albany: State University of New York Press, 1993); Aristide Tessitore, *Reading Aristotle's "Ethics": Virtue, Rhetoric, and Political Philosophy* (Albany: State University of New York Press, 1996); Thomas Smith, *Revaluing Ethics: Aristotle's Dialectical Pedagogy* (Albany: State University of New York Press, 2001); and Jacob Howland, "Aristotle's Great-Souled Man," *Review of Politics* 64 (Winter 2002): 27–56. While these scholars agree that Aristotle seeks to educate his readers concerning the best life, they diverge on important questions, some of which my discussion will address. See also Salkever, *Finding the Mean*, ch. 4; R. A. Gauthier and J. Y. Jolif, *L'Éthique à Nicomaque*, 2nd ed. (Louvain, FR: Publications Universitaires de Louvain, 1970), p. 155; H. H. Joachim, *Aristotle: The "Nicomachean Ethics"* (Oxford: Clarendon Press, 1951), pp. 111, 144; Alexander Grant, *The "Ethics" of Aristotle*, 2 vols. (New York: Arno Press, 1973), II.55–6; J. A. Stewart, *Notes on the "Nicomachean Ethics" of Aristotle's*, 2 vols. (Oxford: Clarendon Press, 1892),

justice as the more complete virtue that promises to reconcile devotion to the common good with the dedication to moral virtue simply. Yet this discussion of the virtue central to citizenship fails ultimately to resolve the tension between virtue's orientation toward the common good and its independence as an end in its own right.

By elucidating the grounds of this failure, Aristotle's treatment of justice reveals the fundamental limits of the political community as educator, clarifies the deepest problem of civic education, and raises the difficult question of the standard to which the law and the good human being must look in choosing between the two ends of a morally serious life. Of course, this difficulty, and its significance for the human good, disappear from view if we simply begin from a denial of a highest good and from the conclusions of modern realism that human action is motivated by desire and guided by calculation and self-interest. By contrast, Aristotle indicates that it is only in grappling with the problem presented by moral virtue, and with the need for wisdom in the face of it, that we see the question of the good emerge in its full dimensions.

Chapters 4 and 5 continue the exploration of this question in the context of the demands and inherent limits of the law and the political community. In particular, Aristotle's investigation of the definition of citizenship, the nature of the regime, and the dispute over distributive justice at the heart of every regime clarifies both our necessary obedience to law as citizens and the grounds of our freedom from it. This important dimension of Aristotle's treatment of citizenship becomes the theme of Chapter 6.

I.213; W. F. R. Hardie, *Aristotle's Ethical Theory* (London: Oxford University Press, 1968), pp. 116–20; Harry V. Jaffa, *Thomism and Aristotelianism: A Study of the Commentary by Thomas Aquinas on the "Nicomachean Ethics"* (Chicago: University of Chicago Press, 1953), ch. 4; David Ross, *Aristotle*, 6th ed. (London: Routledge Press, 1995), pp. 209–11.

2

Citizen Virtue and the Longing for the Noble

Understanding the complexity of moral virtue and the perspective that informs it requires attention to the substance and order of Aristotle's discussion of the particular virtues in the *Nicomachean Ethics*. It is necessary, before turning to this discussion, to address a couple of objections to this claim, objections represented by the strong statement of Sir David Ross and largely responsible for a general neglect of the virtues:

This part of the *Ethics* presents a lively and often amusing account of the qualities admired or disliked by cultivated Greeks of Aristotle's time...no attempt is made at an exhaustive logical division of either feelings or actions. The order is haphazard; two of the cardinal virtues are treated first and in considerable detail (the other two being reserved for treatment in Books V and VI); the other virtues are taken up just as they occur to Aristotle's mind, one no doubt suggesting another as he proceeds.[1]

Such a view would supply a good reason for the neglect of the particular virtues, and while students of Aristotle rarely subscribe to the whole of Ross's view, many assume the validity of some part of it.[2] The full case

---

[1] David Ross, *Aristotle*, 6th ed. (London: Routledge Press, 1995), pp. 209 and 211.

[2] Having observed that "the order in which Aristotle discusses the moral virtues in Books III and IV seems to depend on some kind of psychological theory," H. H. Joachim then asserts that "this portion of the *Nicomachean Ethics* contains Aristotle's analysis of the 'best life' as it was lived in his time – as it was manifested in the speculative and political (social and moral) ideals and achievements of the Greeks" (*Aristotle: The "Nicomachean Ethics"* [Oxford: Clarendon Press, 1951], pp. 111, 144). Alexander Grant, rejecting

against this position requires the substantive examination of the virtues (cf. *NE* 1107b14–16, 20–1, 1108a1–2), yet it is possible to address the main propositions in a prefatory way by speaking first to the question of the organization and order of the list and then to the connection of the virtues to Greek convention.

If we take our bearings by textual indications alone, Aristotle clearly indicates an order to his discussion as he takes up the examination of each virtue. After treating courage "first," he suggests that moderation follows "after this one" since the two "seem to belong to the irrational parts" (*NE* 1117b23–4). "Next in order," he notes, is liberality, and then "it would seem to follow next to speak of magnificence," the other, "greater" virtue concerned with money (*NE* 1119b22–3, 1122a18–24). He then connects the discussion of the two subsequent virtues, magnanimity and ambition, with the preceding two by noting that they stand in relation to one another as do magnificence and liberality, but in the sphere of honor (*NE* 1125b1–8). Accordingly, he discusses first magnanimity, which pertains to great honor, and then ambition, which concerns lesser honors. In what constitutes roughly the first

the notion that the *Ethics* is "composed upon a psychological system," then interprets the list as a loosely organized enumeration of common opinion: "[Aristotle] seems to have taken up first the most prominent and striking qualities, according to the common notions of Greece – Courage, Temperance, and Liberality. Liberality suggested to him Magnificence – Magnificence, Great-souledness; and from this he proceeded to distinguish the more ordinary quality of Ambition. He then added, what had hitherto been omitted, the virtue of regulation of the temper; and pointed out that in social intercourse three excellent qualities are produced by bringing the demeanour under the control of the law of balance" (*The "Ethics" of Aristotle*, 2 vols. [New York: Arno Press], I.55–6). See also J. A. Stewart, *Notes on the "Nicomachean Ethics" of Aristotle*, 2 vols. (Oxford: Clarendon Press, 1892), I.213, who sides generally with Grant; R. A. Gauthier and J. Y. Jolif, *"L'Éthique à Nicomaque,"* 2nd ed., 2 vols. (Louvain, FR: Publications Universitaires de Louvain, 1970), p. 153; and W. F. R. Hardie, *Aristotle's Ethical Theory* (London: Oxford University Press, 1968), pp. 116–20, who takes up several of the arguments regarding the order and exhaustiveness of the list of the virtues and who finally sides with Ross. The most systematic treatment of the virtues has been offered by the traditional commentators, and especially by Aquinas, who contends that Aristotle discusses first the virtues and vices pertaining to internal passions, then those pertaining to external goods, and finally those pertaining to external actions. Thomas Aquinas, *Commentary on the "Nicomachean Ethics,"* trans. C. I. Litzinger, 2 vols. (Chicago: Henry Regnery Company, 1964), par. 333–57. For a discussion of Aquinas's innovations on Aristotle, see especially Harry V. Jaffa, *Thomism and Aristotelianism: A Study of the Commentary by Thomas Aquinas on the "Nicomachean Ethics"* (Chicago: University of Chicago Press, 1952), and Frederick Copleston, *A History of Philosophy*, Vol. II: *Mediaeval Philosophy: Augustine to Scotus* (Westminster, MD: Newman Press, 1950).

half of his list of virtues, therefore, Aristotle offers undeniable indications that he is proceeding according to a certain logic. When he discusses the second half of the list, moreover, he also makes explicit statements indicating the relation of each virtue to what has preceded or follows (*NE* 1127a13–14, 17–20, 1127b33–1128a1, 1128b4–9, 35, 1138b13–14), and these statements are supplemented by arguments for studying these virtues. In moving into what proves to be uncharted territory – most of the virtues on the second half of the list are nameless – he insists that it is necessary to coin names for these virtues "for the sake of clarity and understanding" (*NE* 1108a16–19). After ambition, then, he examines the virtue pertaining to anger, which he calls "gentleness," and, subsequently, three virtues having to do with action and speech in our associations ("friendliness," "truthfulness," and "wittiness"). Each of these we must include in order to see whether the virtues are truly means (cf. *NE* 1108a14–16, 1127a14–17). Even as he chooses to innovate, then, Aristotle indicates that the movement of the discussion is guided by its own dynamic; indeed, he predicts, the discussion will make clear not just what the virtues are, what they pertain to, and in what manner, but also how many there are (*NE* 1115a4–5; cf. 1098a16–18). On the basis of Aristotle's own indications, therefore, there would seem to be no firm justification for dismissing the list as haphazard and good reason for examining the order of the virtues.

Yet if we provisionally allow that there is a certain order to Aristotle's list of the virtues, what of the claim that it represents merely the conventions of his time or, at best, the finest distillation of specifically Greek wisdom?[3] Since Aristotle maintains that the moral virtues constitute the habits of one who has been well raised and even that, in

---

[3] See again Joachim, *Aristotle*, p. 111; also Alasdair MacIntyre, *After Virtue: A Study in Moral Theory* (Notre Dame, IN: University of Notre Dame Press, 1981), p. 148. In discussing Aristotle's treatment of slavery in the *Politics*, Malcolm Schofield takes up the question of whether the "endoxic" method – beginning from the "principles" contained in opinion – (a method which Aristotle would appear to employ in the discussion of the virtues) is inherently conservative or ideological. Schofield suggests that at the very least, the method "can offer little resistance to popular ideology" and therefore must be supplemented by reasoned analysis – the method suggested at the beginning of the *Politics*, for example (Schofield, *Saving the City: Philosopher-Kings and Other Classical Paradigms* ([New York: Routledge, 1999], pp. 118–22). Although Schofield may be correct in the case of natural slavery, his suggestion does not address the movement of Aristotle's investigation of the virtues to the "nameless" virtues and vices of the latter half of the list.

an important respect, it is this very upbringing that makes possible the identification of the virtues as virtues (*NE* 1103a31–b25, 1095b3– 8), it seems fair to assume that his account is bound in some way to the conventions of his Greece. To evaluate this assumption, however, one ought also to consider the many signs of his freedom in this regard, beginning with his opening discussion of the cardinal virtue of courage.

To the heirs of Homer, of course, it would come as no surprise that Aristotle should single out courage or "manliness" (*andreia*) as the first virtue to be discussed, devote more time to a discussion of courage than to any other virtue outside of justice, and define courage as noble death in battle. Nevertheless, far from then following Homer's lead, Aristotle first refers to Homeric heroes in a discussion of "political courage," which he dubs a mere appearance of courage, and even here, he mentions not the great hero of the Greeks, Achilles, but Hector, the Greeks' Trojan antagonist (*NE* 1116a15–23) – in fact, Aristotle never breathes the name of Achilles. More significantly, the length of Aristotle's account of courage is governed less by the virtue's conventional importance than by the need to sort out its many confusions (see, for example, *NE* 1108b23–6, 1115b24–30, 1116a15–29, 1116b23–1117a9, 1117a29–b16), and in the end, his attention to courage turns out to have been in an important respect in the service of its demotion. When Aristotle concludes his account, he does so with the strange admission that the truly courageous – those who possess the virtue connected with war and battle – do not actually make the best soldiers (*NE* 1117b17– 20), and in then classifying courage and moderation together as virtues of the "irrational parts," he indicates that with moderation, courage is of a lower rank than those virtues to come (*NE* 1117b23–4). The treatment of courage, moreover, is a harbinger of the later virtues and especially Aristotle's innovations when he begins to do no less than to coin new names.[4] Aristotle's own self-imposed boundary – the perspective

---

[4] As Gauthier and Jolif observe, Aristotle himself points out that the existing language is insufficient, making it necessary for him to invent his own vocabulary (*NE* 1107b30, 1108a16–19; Gauthier and Jolif, *L'Éthique à Nicomaque*, p. 155). Salkever likewise remarks, "Aristotle's pointing to certain names suggests some clear criticisms of Periclean morality: there is no name for excessive virility, no good vocabulary for articulating the virtue of gentleness, and no name for the virtue of everyday honor. These gaps in the language are not surprising for a people not inclined to think of

of the morally serious human being – does not prove to be simply coherent with the conventions of his Greece.[5] How far he moves from these conventions, as well as the grounds of both his restraint and his freedom in this regard, become clearer with his account of the morally serious life.[6]

gentleness as a virtue, or of the possibility that there might be an excess of virility" (*Finding the Mean: Theory and Practice in Aristotelian Political Philosophy* [Princeton, NJ: Princeton University Press, 1990], p. 241). See also Kraut, *Aristotle and the Human Good* (Princeton, NJ: Princeton University Press, 1989), pp. 342–3, n. 27.

5 The absence in his discussion of the cardinal virtue piety is another noteworthy break with the conventional view.

6 Aristotle's treatments of courage (*andreia*, lit. "manliness"), ambition, and anger also raise the question of whether moral virtue as a whole is specifically male. In all three cases, that is, the manly aspect of the virtue is made clear but treated with some ambivalence. Nussbaum thus argues that in the very specification of the virtues, we witness a certain "progress in ethics": "We find argument against Platonic asceticism, as the proper specification of moderation (appropriate choice and response vis-à-vis the bodily appetites) and the consequent proneness to anger over slights, that was prevalent in Greek ideals of maleness and in Greek behavior, together with a defense of a more limited and controlled expression of anger, as the proper specification of the virtue that Aristotle calls "mildness of temper." . . . And so on for all the virtues" ("Non-Relative Virtues: An Aristotelian Approach," in *Midwest Studies in Philosophy, Vol. XIII: Ethical Theory, Character, and Virtue*, ed. Peter A. French, Theodore E. Uehling, Jr., and Howard K. Wettstein [Notre Dame, IN: University of Notre Dame Press, 1988], p. 37). Salkever's ch. 4, "Gendered Virtue: Plato and Aristotle on the Politics of Virility," of *Finding the Mean* lays out what he suggests is the Aristotelian–Platonic critique of the conventional and prephilosophic "politics of virility" and thus ties Aristotle's criticism of such a politics to his criticism more generally of convention. As for the virtues discussed in the *Ethics*, there is clearly a movement away from the kinds of virtues that would be associated with the heroic tradition of Homer, and it could be argued that Aristotle is ultimately concerned with specifically human as opposed to male or female virtue. In the *Ethics* generally, however, he is not immediately concerned with settling the status of sexual differences. An investigation of this question would require a much broader consideration of his works, and projects of this kind include, in addition to Salkever's, Arlene Saxonhouse, *Fear of Diversity: The Birth of Political Science in Ancient Greek Thought* (Chicago: University of Chicago Press, 1992) and *Women in the History of Political Thought* (New York: Praeger, 1985); Nussbaum, "Shame, Separateness, and Political Unity: Aristotle's Criticism of Plato," in *Essays on Aristotle's "Ethics,"* ed. Amélie Oksenberg Rorty (Berkeley: University of California Press, 1987); Jean Bethke Elshtain, *Public Man, Private Woman* (Princeton, NJ: Princeton University Press, 1981); Judith Swanson, "Aristotle on Nature, Human Nature, and Justice: A Consideration of the Natural Functions of Men and Women in the City," in *Action and Contemplation: Studies in the Moral and Political Thought of Aristotle*, eds. Robert C. Bartlett and Susan D. Collins (Albany: State University of New York Press, 1999), pp. 225–47; Darrell Dobbs, "Family Matters: Aristotle's Appreciation of Women and the Plural Structure of Society," *American Political Science Review* 90 (March 1996): 74–89; Harold Levy, "Does Aristotle Exclude Women from Politics?" *Review of Politics* 52 (Summer 1990): 397–416; Thomas K. Lindsay, "Was Aristotle Racist, Sexist, and Anti-Democratic?: A

The discussion of courage is the portal through which we enter into Aristotle's investigation of this life. As he proceeds from courage through the first complete virtue, magnanimity, he elucidates the complex longing behind virtuous action and the elevation of virtue to its status as an independent end and good. This view of virtue as worthy of pursuit for its own sake is reflected in the law's concern to make citizens not only "obedient" but also "noble and good." In his account of courage, Aristotle quickly confirms the horizon of his investigation by explicitly identifying the end (*telos*) of virtue not with happiness but with "the noble" (*NE* 1102a5–7, 1115a4–5, 1115b11–13) – a formulation that recurs frequently throughout the discussion of the first five virtues.[7] This link between virtue and the longing for the noble is frequently overlooked by students of the *Ethics*, yet it is crucial in understanding both the elevation of virtue to its place as an independent end and the tensions within the moral life that result.

COURAGE AS NOBLE SACRIFICE AND SELF-CONCERN

Courage is the virtue that pertains to fear and confidence. Since fear is aroused by and defined as the "expectation of evil," Aristotle first identifies the evil that courage in particular concerns. After eliminating four contenders – disrepute, poverty, illness, and friendlessness – he establishes that death is the greatest evil, for "death is an end, and, furthermore, for the dead there seems to be nothing, neither good nor evil" (*NE* 1115a26–7). In pertaining to the "greatest of the fearful things," then, courage is concerned with death. Nevertheless, just as it does not pertain to every kind of fear, neither is it concerned with every kind of death. Rather, the hope or confidence specific to courage is aroused only when the courageous human being is able "to act like a man" (*andrizesthai*) and "to show his prowess" or when "to die is noble" (*NE* 1115b4–6). Only in the case of these "noblest" of deaths is

Review Essay," *Review of Politics* 56 (Winter 1994): 127–51, which contains a review of the treatment of this question in Salkever's discussion, as well in Judith Swanson's *The Public and the Private in Aristotle's Political Philosophy* (Ithaca, NY: Cornell University Press, 1992) and in Mary P. Nichols's *Citizens and Statesmen: A Study of Aristotle's "Politics"* (Savage, MA: Rowman & Littlefield, 1992).

7 For Aristotle's many references to the noble in this section of the *Ethics*, see *NE* 1116a27–9, b2–3; 1117a7–9, 16–17, b7–9, 13–15; 1119a16–18, b16–17; 1120a13–15, 23–5, b3–4; 1121a1–4; 1122b6–7, 15–18; 1123a6–9.

the confidence proper to courage aroused, and such deaths occur primarily in war because war contains "the greatest and noblest danger" (or risk, *kindunos*; *NE* 1115a30–1). By referring in passing to the honors that cities and monarchs pay to the courageous, Aristotle indicates the perspective from which he speaks (*NE* 1115a31–2). In war, the welfare of the entire city or nation is at risk, and this welfare is a good that is "nobler and more divine" than that of any individual (*NE* 1094b24–32).[8] When Aristotle concludes that "strictly speaking, one would call courageous the one who is fearless with respect to a noble death and any situations that bring death suddenly to hand, and these sorts are especially the ones that occur in war" (*NE* 1115a32–5), we are prepared to think that the nobility of courage is connected with its benefit to the political community.

Indeed, an important, though strangely overlooked, fact is that the noble in the case of courage points first to sacrifice and self-forgetting as the essential aspect of good action.[9] It is nobility in this sense – as manifest in action in behalf of a higher end or good – that first elevates virtuous action as an end worthy of our dedication. At first blush, that is, the nobility of the courageous action is constituted by its selflessness, namely, by the courageous man's service to a good greater than his own: the good of the city or nation. Yet Aristotle elucidates the full complexity of moral motivation and of the longing for the noble by also insisting that the truly courageous individual acts not for the sake of the political community alone or for the honors it bestows. Rather, in showing his prowess as a man or dying nobly, if it is necessary to die, such an individual is willing to suffer death only in an action in which he exercises his own virtue (*NE* 1115a35–1115b6). The courageous

---

[8] Aspasius comes to the same conclusion (*Commentaria in Aristotelem graeca*: Vol. 19, *Aspasii in Ethica Nicomachea*, ed. Gustavus Heylbut [Berlin: G. Reimeri, 1889], sec. 18).

[9] Recent commentators have even been critical of the noble as it is presented in the account of courage, either as encouraging a dangerous "illusion of self-sufficiency" (Lee Ward, "Nobility and Necessity: The Problem of Courage in Aristotle's *Nicomachean Ethics*," *American Political Science Review* 95 [March 2001], pp. 78–80) or as involving an excessive attachment to manliness and honor (Thomas Smith, *Revaluing Ethics: Aristotle's Dialectical Pedagogy* [Albany: State University of New York Press, 2001], pp. 85–91). Jacob Howland suggests that the "love of the noble" is philosophical, a suggestion he does not elucidate ("Aristotle's Great-Souled Man," *Review of Politics* 64 [Winter 2002], p. 30). Grant and Stewart stress the "moral beauty" of the courageous action without explaining the sense in which it is "beautiful" (see Grant, *The "Ethics" of Aristotle*, II.35–6; Stewart, *Notes on the "Nicomachean Ethics" of Aristotle*, I.288).

man is thus distinguished neither by simple altruism nor by the hope of some good extrinsic to the act, but by the dedication to virtue itself. As Aristotle finally observes:

The end [*telos*] of every activity is the one in accord with the characteristic. Furthermore, to the courageous man, courage is noble. Such a sort also, then, is the end, for each thing is defined by its end. For the sake of the noble, therefore, the courageous man endures and does the things that are in accord with courage. (*NE* 1115b20–4)

To the courageous man, it is the deed itself, as well as the characteristic from which it issues, that is noble, and those who act for the sake of any other end possess a courage that is a mere appearance of the true thing (*NE* 1115a32–5, b20–4, 1116a17–21).

This view is not only acknowledged but cultivated by the political community: While the political community may seek its own security through the honors it confers upon courage, these same honors point to courage as the noblest and best aim for a human being.[10] Aristotle treats more fully the relation between honor and true courage in his account of political courage – the characteristic of a citizen soldier – which is the first of five appearances of courage he seeks to dismiss. Political courage is "most like true courage" because the citizen soldier endures dangers "on account of the penalties of the laws and reproaches, and on account of honors" (*NE* 1116a17–19). Both true courage and its political counterpart are products of the education provided by the laws, which punish vice and reward virtue. The similarity between true and political courage reflects the link between virtue and honor Aristotle noted in Book I (*NE* 1095a22–9), a link he reiterates in his opening discussion of fear and courage by saying that the one who fears disrepute is "equitable and modest," whereas the one who does not is "shameless" (*NE* 1115a12–14).

Thus, honor and shame, as well as the penalties or punishments of the law, are the vehicles by which the law educates citizens to virtue. For this reason, it is not surprising, as Aristotle observes, that the most courageous men are found among those peoples who especially honor courage and dishonor cowardice. Citing depictions of the

---

[10] Compare Ward, who draws something of the opposite conclusion ("Nobility and Necessity," pp. 75–6, 78–80).

heroes Hector and Diomedes in the *Iliad*, Aristotle argues that political courage "arises on account of virtue" because it is grounded in the love of honor, which is a "noble thing" (*NE* 1116a27–8). In this sense, citizen soldiers endure in the face of dangers for the sake of the noble, and true courage and its political counterpart are most alike because they share the noble as an end.

There is, nonetheless, an important difference between the particular ends to which the truly courageous man and the citizen soldier attach nobility. For the truly courageous man's end is not finally the honor that redounds to the deed, but the deed itself. In Aristotle's Homeric examples, we begin to see the significance of this distinction. For the same heroes whom he identifies as representative of political courage – of the love of honor and fear of shame – exemplified to the Greeks the dedication to courage as an end that distinguishes the truly courageous man. Indeed, Aristotle refers to Hector later in the *Ethics* as one who represents a virtue that is "heroic and divine" – a virtue of a higher order than moral virtue itself (*NE* 1145a18–22). Moreover, the passages Aristotle cites as illustrations of political courage do not perfectly bear out his claim. It is true that Hector fears the reproach of Polydamas, but he fears reproach precisely because, prompted by his own courage and in opposition to Polydamas's prudent advice, he had led the Trojans into the disastrous battle against Achilles (*Iliad* XXII, 98–110). Fearing not the reproaches of his fellow citizens who are fleeing the Trojan onslaught but the mock of cowardice by Hector, his enemy, Diomedes is barely restrained from a similarly disastrous attack by his compatriot Nestor (*Iliad* VIII, 137–56). In their dedication to their own virtue, these men of political courage are hard to distinguish from those of true courage.

The similarity and link between the two forms of courage is inevitable because the very honors the city establishes with a view to encouraging its defense point to courage itself as noblest and best for a human being. Indeed, although there is a difference between those who act for the sake of honor and those who act for the sake of virtue, there is a very fine line between men who fight and die for the sake of being honored for their courage and those who do so for the sake of the virtue alone. The precise coordinates of this line become clearer when Aristotle observes that one might classify men who possess the courage of a citizen with those who are forced to fight by their leaders, though the latter are worse inasmuch as they act out of fear and flee pain rather than shame (*NE* 1116a29–32). Such reluctant soldiers clearly have no particular hankering for the honors the city bestows, and in whipping them to their posts, their commanders treat them with slightly less harshness than they do the enemy. Yet one might classify these soldiers and their citizen counterparts together because the motivation for both is connected directly to the city, to what it can do for or to them (cf. *NE* 1116b2–3). Citizen soldiers are willing to fight and die if they must because they aspire to the honors of the city and fear its reproach; the worse types are afraid of the punishment the city can inflict. Strictly speaking, therefore, neither aspires to courage for its own sake, and neither attributes to courage a status of its own.[11]

By contrast, although the honor that accrues to courage is originally established by the city with a view to its own security, courageous action ultimately becomes the noble end for the sake of which a virtuous person acts. From the city's point of view, this love of virtue is both honorable and problematic: The courageous man may seek to prove his virtue in less than politically prudent ways – he may wish for "chilling war" among his people (see *NE* 1177b6–12, *Pol.* 1253a1–7) – and he may care more about what his enemies think than about what is best for his city. But no political community would wish for an army that it must whip to its post, even if, in honoring those who fight and die on its behalf, it points to virtue and not itself as the noblest and best end for a human being.

As the portal through which we enter into his inquiry into the morally serious life, then, Aristotle's discussion of courage locates the nobility and goodness of this life in its dedication to virtue in its own right. This discussion thereby preserves the noble as virtue's aim and affirms Aristotle's claim in his introduction to moral virtue that an action is virtuous only if, among other things, it is chosen for its own sake (*NE* 1105a30–4). Indeed, this aspect of the virtue distinguishes it not only from the several appearances of courage Aristotle discusses, including the "natural" courage of *thumos* or spiritedness, but also from

---

[11] Grant and Stewart both observe that there are two kinds of political courage, one that depends on honor and another that depends on fear. Nevertheless, in classifying these two together, Aristotle underscores their similarity: neither type of courage aspires to the deed as a good in its own right (cf. Grant, *The "Ethics" of Aristotle*, II.39; Stewart, *Notes on the "Nicomachean Ethics" of Aristotle*, I.293).

the vice with which it might be mistaken, rashness. As the mean pertaining to fear and confidence, true courage must be confused neither with the complete absence of fear, which Aristotle dismisses as a human possibility, nor with an excess of confidence, which he identifies with those "rash cowards" who boast of their courage, only to turn tail at the first sign of danger (*NE* 1115b32). Because death is the greatest evil, the courageous man reasonably experiences fear; in the face of this fear, however, he remains steadfast, and his confidence is aroused by the prospect of his own noble action. Compared to rash cowards, who appear most willing in advance of the danger but beat a quick retreat when it arrives, the truly courageous "are keen in the deeds but calm beforehand" (*NE* 1116a7–9). The confidence or hope specific to courage can find its fulfillment only in the action of the virtue itself – in an action that, as Aristotle has insisted, offers no reward after death.

Indeed, for all its nobility, courageous action involves a difficulty, the resolution of which will inform the discussion of the virtues that follow. In performing a noble deed, the courageous human being is shown to perform a deed that is at once selfless, in being for the sake of a higher end, and self-regarding, in being for the sake of his own virtue. But in the case of courage, this same action is problematic precisely because it entails the cessation of the activity and life that its presence as virtue makes choiceworthy: "the more a man possesses complete virtue and is happy, the more death will be painful to him, because especially to this sort of man, to live is worthwhile" (*NE* 1117b9–12).[12] As one who is dedicated to virtue above all, nevertheless, the man of true courage will "choose the noble thing in war" instead of his own "greatest goods," and he does this in awareness of his sacrifice and so with pain (*NE* 1117b7–13, 1117a33–4). In contrast to his great medieval interpreter Aquinas, who allows for a courage that finds its reward in the afterlife, Aristotle underscores the sacrifice involved in

---

[12] This tension between courage and happiness prompts Grant to observe that "the most moral of the virtues here named, from a modern point of view, is courage, on account of the self-sacrifice, the endurance of danger, pain, and death, which it implies" (Grant, *Aristotle* [London: William Blackwood & Sons, 1877], pp. 107–8). But compare Stewart: "Aristotle thus gives due prominence in his account of *andreia* to the struggle which some have represented as essential to morality. But we must not allow ourselves to be misled by his remarks here. He is not one of those who make a struggle essential to morality" (*Notes on the "Nicomachean Ethics" of Aristotle*, I.303).

the act by his denial in the discussion of courage of this very possibility (*NE* 1115a27).[13] The same loss that ennobles courage thus makes its action deeply problematic. Its action is so problematic that Aristotle will conclude finally that courageous men, strictly speaking, do not make the best soldiers. The best soldiers, rather, are those willing to exchange their lives "for small profit" (*NE* 1117b19–20). That courage is itself noble, and in this respect a virtue, Aristotle leaves no doubt, but its action raises the question of whether there is a kind of noble action more consistent with self-concern. The concern for our self-preservation and well-being comes so much to the fore in the next virtue, moderation, that the noble as an end almost recedes from view. Yet moderation, which has no action of its own, proves instrumental to the virtue that follows it, liberality, whose noble giving clearly entails a loss, but not a fatal one (*NE* 1121b1–12).

NOBLE DEEDS AND THE ASCENT OF VIRTUE

Aristotle presents in liberality a noble deed consistent with a certain self-concern. Like courage, liberality is hard because it entails a loss for the giver, who gives of his own material goods (*chrēmata*) or money. The liberal person gives with pleasure, nevertheless, because he achieves his end, and he acts entirely in accord with his choice or preference since he prefers noble action to money (*NE* 1120a23–5, 30–3). While the courageous man acts with pain and is even "unwilling," then, the liberal person remains cheerful in the face of his loss (cf. 1117b7–9 with 1115a20–2). He so much loves to give, in fact, that he has a tendency toward prodigality, one of the virtue's associated vices, and he is so easygoing with money that he is vulnerable to being cheated (*NE* 1119b34–1120a4, 1120b4–6, 1121a4–6).

But while the liberal person's noble activity is consistent with self-concern, it raises a new question with respect to virtue: the question of the means needed for its action. The problem in the case of liberality is that in the absence of a lucky inheritance or a winning lottery ticket, a person who seems otherwise unconcerned about money must acquire

---

[13] Compare Aquinas, *Commentary*, I:590: "We must consider, however, that to some virtuous men death is desirable on account of the hope of a future life. But the Stoics did not discuss this, nor did it pertain to the Philosopher in this work to speak of those things that belong to the condition of another life."

and preserve it if he is to have goods to give. Yet, as Aristotle is quick to note, acquisition is governed not by liberality as a virtue but by justice. In observing that liberality pertains to the good use of wealth, he insists that the use of wealth involves giving and spending as opposed to taking and preserving, which have more to do with its acquisition, and his precision is prompted by the fact that justice too pertains to material goods or money and specifically their acquisition (*NE* 1120a4–11, 18–23).[14] The action of giving is governed by liberality, then, but constrained by justice, and the problem of this constraint underlies the abstraction from the requirements and concerns of justice that begins in the discussion of liberality.

Aristotle indicates the problem this constraint presents in a wry digression: "We do not call tyrants prodigal," he observes, "for it does not seem to be easy to exceed in gifts and expenses the amount they possess" (*NE* 1120b25–7). The means of liberal action, that is, are most amply at the disposal of a tyrant, who may be said to own the entire city (cf. *Pol.* 1276a6–16, 1287a1–3). From the point of view of the person who loves to benefit others by giving, and whose specific action and pleasure can be fully indulged only with the requisite means, the tyrant is the most fortunate of men. Liberality is possible, of course, for those of modest means, and Aristotle indicates that a liberal person, who is disposed to give, is not likely to "take from the wrong source" (*NE* 1120a32–3, b28–35). But, as he reiterates at the end of his account of liberality, because the actions associated with acquisition fall under the government of justice, the clearest constraint on a virtuous person who loves noble giving yet has limited means is that obtaining the resources for giving on a grand scale would entail actions that are "wicked, impious, and unjust" (*NE* 1122a3–7). In the case of magnificence and magnanimity – the virtues that follow liberality and that involve great actions – the problem of this constraint will necessarily become more acute, but Aristotle's presentation of these virtues will completely abstract from the activity of acquisition and so from the consideration of justice.

---

[14] That Aristotle is choosing to discuss liberality instead of justice is suggested also by his opening statement in which, as Burnet says, "Aristotle speaks as if *dikaiosynē* had already been treated in its natural place along with *andreia* and *sōphrosynē*" (Burnet, *"Ethics" of Aristotle* [London: Metheun & Co., 1900]; cf. *NE* 1119b22–26).

In the longing for the noble, there is a natural directedness toward great acts that the movement from liberality to magnificence captures: To benefit one person is good, to be sure, but to be the "cause of the greatest good" by benefiting the city as a whole is nobler and even divine (*NE* 1094b7–10; *Pol.* 1253a3031).[15] Like liberality, magnificence pertains to money, but more precisely to giving and spending "on a grand scale" (*NE* 1122a21–3). The one who acts in accord with magnificence longs to produce a noble and great work (*ergon*), and he seeks especially to undertake the "most honorable" works, those of public or common (*koina*) concern (*NE* 1122b19–23, 1122b33–1123a5). In both his private and public expenditures, the one who possesses magnificence acts with pleasure and "for the sake of the noble," which is "common to the virtues," and he possesses a kind of knowledge in doing what is fitting both to the occasion and to his own virtue (*NE* 1122a6–9, b6–8, 34–5). The products of magnificence, therefore, are not only noblest and most honorable, but also the "ornament" (*kosmos*) of their patron's own great virtue (*NE* 1122a6–9).

Because it pertains to great works, however, magnificence is clearly beyond the reach of all but the wealthy. In fact, magnificence is typically contingent on "birth," not least for the money it requires (*NE* 1122b26–35). The problem is that the longing for the noble that ties magnificence to the other virtues is not itself a function of birth, so that the question of acquisition must be addressed. Yet this question has been completely dropped: The virtue of magnificence pertains only to expenditures and not to acquisition on a grand scale. Of the vices associated with such grand acquisitiveness – namely, wickedness, impiety, and injustice – none are extremes associated with magnificence.

---

[15] Kraut makes a similar argument regarding Aristotle's defense of the political life as better than a "private life in which one exercises the virtues by devoting oneself to the well-being of a small circle of friends and family" (*Aristotle and the Human Good*, pp. 345–7). Aristotle indicates that the movement of the virtues to magnanimity as a peak belongs naturally to virtue. Consider Joseph Cropsey's remark: "The *Nicomachean Ethics* is probably the most famous moral treatise that claims no debt to revelation" (*Political Philosophy and the Issues of Politics* [Chicago: University of Chicago Press, 1977], p. 252). See also Larry Arnhart for a discussion of the virtue of magnanimity in the context of the "Christian challenge to ancient naturalism" ("Statesmanship as Magnanimity: Classical, Christian, and Modern," *Polity* 16 [Winter 1983], p. 271), as well as Jaffa's analysis of the Thomistic transformation of Aristotle (*Thomism and Aristotelianism*).

Aristotle presents magnificence, then, in abstraction from the activity on which it depends, and so from the virtue that pertains to this activity, justice. It may be said that as a part of complete virtue, magnificence is necessarily perfected or "completed" by justice, but this suggestion is forestalled by the movement of Aristotle's discussion to magnanimity (*megalopsuchia*, lit. "greatness of soul"), the first peak and completion of the virtues.

MAGNANIMITY AND VIRTUE AS THE HIGHEST GOOD

As a peak and completion of virtue, magnanimity occupies a central place in Aristotle's treatment of the morally serious life. While recent commentators have rightly drawn attention to the ambiguities of Aristotle's account of this virtue, and particularly to its "ironic" or critical aspects, they have tended to ignore the important sense in which magnanimity is indeed a completion of moral virtue.[16] Magnanimity as a virtue is said to pertain to "great things," and especially to great honor, but we quickly learn that magnanimity's relation to honor is mediated by its connection with virtue. Because the magnanimous man possesses "what is great in each virtue," according to Aristotle, he "is worthy of great things" and "regards himself as worthy of great things," especially of "the greatest of the external goods," honor (*NE* 1123b29–30, 20–1, 34–5). Such an individual represents a peak and completion of virtue, then, both in possessing each of the virtues and in assigning to virtue the "prize" of honor as its proper desert (*NE* 1123b16–20). Like the great works of magnificence, the honor that the magnanimous man assigns to his own nobility and goodness (*kalokagathia*) makes magnanimity the ornament (or crown, *kosmos*) of the virtues (*NE* 1123b34–1124a5).

---

[16] Aristide Tessitore (*Reading Aristotle's "Ethics": Virtue, Rhetoric, and Political Philosophy* [Albany: State University of New York Press, 1996]), Howland ("Aristotle's Great-Souled Man"), and Smith (*Revaluing Ethics*) in particular draw attention to this aspect of magnanimity in relation to its defects; more recently, Ryan Hanley has opposed such views by arguing that magnanimity is a civic virtue ("Aristotle on the Greatness of the Greatness of Soul," *History of Political Thought* 23 [Spring 2002]: 1–20). See also Stewart, *Notes on the "Nicomachean Ethics" of Aristotle*, I.355: "The picture of the *megalopsuchos* given in this chapter is a creation of art, intended to present a great philosophical truth with concrete evidence to the imagination."

As virtue's exemplar and champion, moreover, the magnanimous man identifies it not only as his highest end, but also as his greatest good. Even honor, the greatest of the external goods, pales by comparison, for "no honor could be commensurate with perfect virtue" (*NE* 1124a5–9; cf. 1134b6–7). The magnanimous man's singular devotion to virtue is especially manifest in his sense of self-sufficiency and admirable beneficence.[17] He is moderately disposed with respect to every external good and thereby largely undisturbed by the sway of fortune to which they are naturally exposed (*NE* 1124a13–16). He is eager to aid another, but typically declines aid because it belongs to his virtue "to be in need of no one or scarcely so" (*NE* 1124b17–18). He also tends not to dwell upon past evils or to hold grudges; he is not given to flattery or complaints; and he is little concerned with profit or utility (*NE* 1125c3–5; cf. 1124b12–15; 1125a9–10, 11–12). His very deportment reflects his self-possession: He moves slowly, and his voice is deep and steady, "for the one who takes few things seriously is not prone to haste and the one to whom nothing is great is not excitable" (*NE* 1125a12–16).

Indeed, as several commentators have noted, there is a gentle measure of caricature in Aristotle's portrait of the magnanimous man so that we may rightly wonder whether this portrait is in part a fiction rather than a representation of an actual human being.[18] This suspicion might begin to be allayed by the fact that magnanimity is the only virtue for which Aristotle offers examples – except that neither of the examples is of a single great man: The first example is Zeus, and the second, the Athenians (*NE* 1124b15–17). The unusual step of adducing examples, that is, would seem to corroborate our suspicion.

But what, then, are we to learn from this somewhat fictionalized peak of virtue? Is this fiction, as commentators have argued, intended as a critique of the magnanimous man's overweening ambition or of

---

[17] In reconciling self-sufficiency with magnanimity as a civic virtue, Hanley admittedly downplays the magnanimous man's idleness and aloofness ("Aristotle on the Greatness of the Greatness of Soul," pp. 10, 13, 15–19).

[18] Howland, "Aristotle's Great-Souled Man," pp. 31–3; Arnhart "Statesmanship as Magnanimity," pp. 265–7; Hardie, "Magnanimity in Aristotle's *Ethics*," *Phronesis: A Journal for Ancient Philosophy* 23 (1978), p. 74; Joachim, *Aristotle*, p. 125; Burnet, *The "Ethics" of Aristotle*, pp. 179, 181.

his error with respect to his true self-sufficiency?[19] In the first place, Aristotle's portrait of magnanimity and of the magnanimous man's elevation of virtue to the place of the highest human good represents the fullest expression of virtue as an independent end. For in contrast to the courageous man, who still distinguishes virtue as an end from his own "greatest goods," the magnanimous man now wholly identifies virtue as the greatest of his goods. This identification is the logical completion of the morally serious human being's devotion to virtue, with the result that all other goods, including life itself, diminish in significance. In contrast to courage, then, magnanimity represents a more perfect if still problematic union of self-awareness and self-forgetting. Although the magnanimous man will not take small risks, as inappropriate to his greatness, he will take great risks, and when he does so, "he is unsparing of his life, on the grounds that living is not at all worthwhile" (*NE* 1124b6–9).[20] Indeed, Aristotle is intent on drawing our attention to the fact that to the magnanimous man, for whom virtue is best, "nothing is great," a phrase repeated three times. This sense of the insignificance of all but virtue supports the magnanimous man's disinclination to act basely or unjustly: "for the sake of what does he do shameful things, he to whom nothing is great?" (*NE* 1123b31–2). Except when a great honor or work appropriate to his virtue is at stake, his singular dedication to virtue makes him tend toward inaction and idleness (*NE* 1124b24–6). The magnanimous man is unlikely even to fill the time in study or thought: Since "nothing is great to him," he is "not given to wonder" (*NE* 1125a2). In short, the "activity" of magnanimity, about which there is much debate, could be described most simply as the magnanimous man's self-contemplation of his own great virtue.[21]

---

[19] Smith, *Revaluing Ethics,* p. 116–21; Howland, "Aristotle's Great-Souled Man," pp. 32, 46–9; Tessitore, *Reading Aristotle's "Ethics,"* pp. 31–5; MacIntyre, *Dependent Rational Animals: Why Human Beings Need the Virtues* (Chicago: Open Court, 1999), p. 127.

[20] In contrast to my translation "living is not at all worthwhile," most translators render this final phrase as "living at any cost is not worthwhile." The Greek admits of both, but I have chosen the former translation because it makes sense of the suggestion that the magnanimous man is reckless with (*apheidein*) his life. See also Aspasius, *Commentaria,* 212.

[21] Gauthier contends, for example, that the activity of the magnanimous man is philosophy (*Magnanimité: L'ideal de la grandeur dans la Philosophie Païenne et dans la Théologie Chrétienne* [Paris: Librairie Philosophique J. Vrin, 1951], pp. 55–118), Jaffa argues that it is largely political (*Thomism and Aristotelianism,* pp. 134–8), and Aspasius

But Aristotle thus shows that in reaching its peak in magnanimity, moral virtue also reaches an impasse that reflects the abstraction from the requirements and concerns of justice. For even if most things are not worth doing, let alone pondering, at this high point of virtue, the greatest and noblest of actions – the great risks on behalf of which the magnanimous man is willing to throw away his very life – remain most choiceworthy. As Aristotle will insist in Book IX, the serious man (*spoudaios*) would prefer "to live nobly for one year than lead an indifferent existence for many, and to do one great and noble deed than many insignificant ones" (*NE* 1169a22–5; cf. the account of Dion at *Pol.* 1312a21–39). And, as we have seen, the action of the virtues from courage through magnanimity issues from an admirable longing on the part of the virtuous person to exercise his virtue. Even in the face of death on the battlefield, the truly courageous man longs to perform a courageous deed, and at the peak of the virtues, the magnanimous man will "throw away" his life in a great deed that accords with his great virtue. Yet, in the absence of the necessary "resources," the longing for noble action that distinguishes the morally serious human being requires him either to remain idle or to acquire the means to exercise his virtue.[22]

The problem that this choice presents has already been pointed to by Aristotle's discussion of liberality: The means to the greatest scope of noble action are open only to the tyrant. In explicitly confronting this problem in his introduction to the best regime in the *Politics*, Aristotle suggests that it might indeed cause us to wonder whether, for the person who loves noble action, "having authority over all is best, for in this way one would have authority over the greatest number and noblest of actions" (*Pol.* 1325a34–7). The argument Aristotle marshals in support of this view insists that the only clearsighted course for the one who believes that the most choiceworthy life is the life of noble

suggests that it is perhaps theology (*Commentaria*, 114). Stewart observes that "he [the magnanimous man] 'contemplates' the *kosmos* or beautiful harmony of his own nature, and allows nothing external to it to dominate his thought or conduct," but he then insists also that the magnanimous man "is a man of the highest *speculative* power" (*Notes on the "Nicomachean Ethics" of Aristotle*, I.336–7).

[22] Compare Smith, *Revaluing Ethics*, pp. 118–19, who, following from his criticism of magnanimity, argues that the magnanimous man's idleness is a kind of "sloth" that points up the emptiness of a life devoted to "virtue-as-virility" and honor.

action is to forgo all obligations of justice, and even of family and friendship, in order to rule over others (*Pol.* 1325a36–41).[23]

But as Aristotle also indicates in the discussion of liberality and explicates more fully in the *Politics*, this argument leaves the virtuous person in a terrible quandary. Obtaining the conditions of his own activity will require deviations from virtue that he could never make up for later. In particular, the one who would seek the greatest scope of noble action would need to deviate so far from justice – in wresting rule from those who possess it and who may have an equal claim to it – as to degrade his own virtue. For justice too is a virtue; it is, more importantly, the other complete virtue, understood as "the sum of the virtues" and as "directed toward another" (*NE* 1129b29–33).

Aristotle's complex picture of moral virtue is made still more complex by the presence of two complete virtues. Magnanimity is in part a fiction because it wishes for a self-sufficiency and superiority that abstracts from the demands and concerns of justice.[24] Indeed, the magnanimous man demands as virtue's prize the honor that Aristotle reserves in Book I for the truly self-sufficient and divine things: the gods and happiness (*NE* 1101b13–27, b35–1102a4). By contrast, as human beings, we live in community with others, and our perfection must therefore also take account of justice – as a matter of moral or right action and not simply, as current students of Aristotle emphasize, of our happiness or flourishing.[25] Aristotle indicates that even in the case of less than perfect regimes, the weight of law and the importance of the common good are such that some consideration of justice must be made (*NE* 1128b21–6, 1129b11–19, 1134a24–32; *Pol.* 1253a30–9, 1269a12–24, 1276b27–35, 1282b14–18). Yet, as he also suggests in

---

[23] Here the discussion of magnanimity in the *Eudemian Ethics* is illuminating: The magnanimous man would be pained not only by being dishonored, especially by other good men, but also by being "ruled by someone unworthy" (*EE* 1132b10–14). See also *Posterior Analytics* 97b15–20 and Jaffa, *Thomism and Aristotelianism*, pp. 122–3, 128–130.

[24] Contrary to the suggestions of Howland ("Aristotle's Great-Souled Man," pp. 46–9) and Tessitore (*Reading Aristotle's "Ethics*," pp. 31–5), the horizon within which Aristotle is critical of magnanimity is not "true greatness of soul" understood as philosophy, but moral virtue itself. Thus, the magnanimous man's error is not primarily intellectual – an error of reasoning – but moral, and can be described as a deep tension between his love of virtue for its own sake and the considerations that attend justice.

[25] Compare Smith, *Revaluing Ethics*, pp. 153, 211–16, 225–9; Howland, "Aristotle's Great-Souled Man," pp. 50–3; Ward, "Nobility and Necessity," pp. 80–2.

the *Politics*, perhaps there is one regime – the best – in which the virtues of the good man will coincide with those of the good citizen (*Pol.* 1278b1–5). To formulate this possibility in terms of justice: In the best case, perhaps our full moral perfection is truly to be found in community with others and in action "toward the good of another." Aristotle's discussion of the second completion of virtue explores the full scope of this possibility and, in doing so, confronts the problem of its limits.

3

Justice as a Virtue

As a principle of the political order, justice is the focus of much scrutiny in contemporary political theory, yet even among neo-Aristotelians, little attention is paid to justice as a characteristic or virtue of the individual.[1] Aristotle, by contrast, begins his inquiry by emphasizing that justice is like the other virtues in constituting a characteristic that disposes us to act well, namely, "to do just things, act justly, and wish just

---

[1] Thomas Smith and David O'Connor are exceptions that prove the rule and share much common ground with one another; see Smith's *Revaluing Ethics: Aristotle's Dialectical Pedagogy* (Albany: State University of New York Press, 2001) and O'Connor's "The Aetiology of Justice" in *Essays on the Foundations of Aristotelian Political Thought*, eds. Carnes Lord and David O'Connor (Berkeley: University of California Press, 1991). My argument will diverge on several important points, not the least of which is the question of justice as a perfection. Pierre Aubenque takes up some aspects of justice as a virtue, but finally offers a modern, even Christian, rendering of *isonomia* as "equal dignity" grounded in "the logos inscribed on [human] essence" (Pierre Aubenque, "The Twofold Natural Foundation of Justice According to Aristotle," in *Aristotle and Moral Realism*, ed. Robert Heinamen [Boulder, CO: Westview Press, 1995], p. 38). Bernard Williams looks at the question of "motives" instead of "characteristics," arguing that Aristotle erred in attempting to tie acts of injustice to character traits ("Justice as a Virtue" in *Essays on Aristotle's "Ethics,"* ed. Amélie Oksenberg Rorty. [Berkeley: University of California Press 1980], p. 194). As for the school of virtue ethics, Rosalind Hursthouse's comment is informative: "An obvious gap [in *On Virtue Ethics* (Oxford: Oxford University Press, 1999)] is the topic of justice, both as a personal virtue and as the central topic in political philosophy.... Although I acknowledge the existence of the gap, it would be premature to assume that this gap cannot be filled. In their introduction to *Virtue Ethics*, Crisp and Slote, admitting that virtue ethics needs to meet the challenge... look forward to the day when there will be an 'Oxford Readings in Virtue Politics'" (pp. 6–7).

things" (*NE* 1129a3–11). His first task, then, is to examine justice as a virtue that constitutes our perfection. The immediate complication is that justice has two meanings that are similar but not the same: "the lawbreaker is thought to be unjust," but so too is "the one who takes more than his share [*pleonektēs*] and is unfair [lit. "unequal," *anisos*]" (*NE* 1129a32–4). In short, justice may mean either "lawfulness" or "fairness," alternatives that Aristotle classifies under the respective headings of general and particular justice (*NE* 1129a34–b1). Accordingly, there exist two different, though related, characteristics in the case of justice. General justice as lawfulness is complete virtue, understood as the sum of all the virtues directed toward the good of another (*NE* 1129b26–30). Particular justice as fairness is the proper disposition concerning the good things – security, money, and honor – in which all who belong to the political community must share (*NE* 1130a32–b5).[2]

In exploring the full range of justice as a virtue, Aristotle addresses the question raised by magnanimity: whether the devotion to the common good can be reconciled in the best case with the dedication to one's perfection in virtue simply. The limits of justice in this regard first become apparent in the discussion of particular justice. In brief, the requirements of particular justice understood as fairness prove to be grounded in a standard other than the one that Aristotle himself establishes as that by which an individual ought to choose the good things. This standard is one's true benefit or harm – in the best case, the possession and activity of the virtues that pertain to the good things simply. One ought to choose the goods that contribute to one's perfection in this sense and avoid those that are detrimental (*NE* 1129b3–6; see also 1124a26–31). Aristotle's discussion of particular justice shows that, in contrast to the other virtues, justice as a mean is not defined in relation to our good condition or perfection, but in terms of a

---

[2] I employ the usual English translations, "general" and "particular" justice, but Kraut objects: "Many scholars call justice as lawfulness 'universal' or 'general' justice, and justice as equality 'particular' or 'special' justice. I find these tags misleading, and prefer to describe Aristotle's distinction as one between a broad and narrow sense of the word. To speak of one type of justice as 'universal' or 'general' and the other as 'particular' or 'special' might suggest that the former is observed in all or most communities, whereas the latter is more restrictive. But that is not at all what Aristotle's distinction is meant to suggest" (*Aristotle: Political Philosophy* [Oxford: Oxford University Press, 2002], p. 102, n. 6.)

principle of equality that establishes what is equal or fair in relation to the common good and that accords with the equality constituting the "regime" (*politeia*). For this reason, Aristotle will settle the question of justice as a virtue only after he has investigated the "proportionate reciprocity" at the origin of the political community. After setting forth Aristotle's accounts of general and particular justice as perfections, I turn to his discussion of reciprocity for the light it sheds on the limits of justice as a virtue.

JUSTICE AS THE LAWFUL

General justice is complete virtue in being all the virtues "summed up in one" and "directed toward another," and complete virtue in this sense is properly understood as justice first in its connection with the law (*NE* 1129b26–30).[3] As Aristotle observes, "all the lawful things are somehow just" not only because they have been "laid down by the lawgiver" but, more importantly, because they have a comprehensive scope and end: The laws "make pronouncements on everything," and they seek the common advantage, understood in terms of the variety of regimes as "the advantage for all in common or for the best or for those who hold power in accord with virtue or in some other such way" (*NE* 1129b14–17). Complete virtue is justice, then, because the law commands the deeds of virtue and forbids bad acts in order to "produce and preserve happiness and its parts for the political community" (*NE* 1129b17–19). With this end in view, for example, the law commands courage in requiring that soldiers not break ranks in battle; moderation, in prohibiting adultery or outrage; and gentleness, in forbidding assault or slander (*NE* 1129b19–24).[4]

---

[3] See again *NE* 1138a5–11. Grant observes: "The view given here of law, which is expressed still more strongly below, ch. xi § 1, is quite different from modern views. Law is here represented as a positive system . . . aiming at the regulation of the whole of life" (*The "Ethics" of Aristotle*, 2 vols. [New York: Arno Press, 1973], II.101–2).

[4] For recent liberal versions of the virtues understood in terms of the regime, compare Galston's account (*Liberal Purposes: Goods, Virtues, and Diversity in the Liberal State* [Cambridge: Cambridge University Press, 1991], pp. 213–327) with that of Macedo (*Liberal Virtues* [Oxford: Oxford University Press, 1996], 265–77). See also Berkowitz's discussion of the relation between liberalism and virtue in *Virtue and the Making of Modern Liberalism* (Princeton, NJ: Princeton University Press, 1999), especially chs. 1–4, and Salkever, *Finding the Mean: Theory and Practice in Aristotelian Political Philosophy* (Princeton: Princeton University Press, 1990), pp. 178–90. In "Justice and

The law thus strives to instill all the virtues or general justice in every citizen.

The orientation of general justice toward another constitutes its unique power – "justice *alone* of the virtues is thought to be the good of another" (*NE* 1130a3–5; my emphasis) – and as a result of its orientation, justice attracts very high praise as "the greatest [*kratistē*] of the virtues" (*NE* 1129b27–9). Indeed, the case for justice as the best or highest of the virtues is the one Aristotle offers here. Citizenship in a community means that any action, including a virtuous action, has a dual aspect: It can be understood from the point of view of either one's own perfection or another's benefit. Justice would appear to be the most complete of the virtues, then, because, in obvious contrast to the pride and self-sufficiency of magnanimity, it comprises both the sum of the virtues and the "use" of this perfection in its orientation toward the good of another.[5] General justice, by this account, constitutes both another's good and our true perfection, a conclusion Aristotle encourages in saying that virtue and justice are the same, but "in their being [*to einai*]," they differ: "in being in relation to another, it [the characteristic] is justice, but in being a certain characteristic simply, virtue" (*NE* 1130a10–13).[6]

The tenor of Aristotle's account of general justice becomes clearer in light of the attack on justice to which it alludes: the attack by the sophist Thrasymachus in Plato's *Republic*. Thrasymachus attaches blame to justice understood as the advantage of another, arguing that justice is simply the advantage of the stronger: the ruling group that establishes laws for its own advantage and then declares that it is just for the ruled to obey them (*Republic* 338c–339a). In celebrating the greatness of justice understood as "another's good," Aristotle recalls Bias's saying that "ruling will show the man [*anēr*]" (*NE* 1130a1–2); it

---

the Dilemma of Moral Virtue" (*Aristotle and Modern Politics: The Persistence of Political Philosophy*, ed. Aristide Tessitore [Notre Dame, IN: University of Notre Dame Press, 2002], pp. 105–29), I offer a general comparison of Aristotle and contemporary liberal thought on the question of virtue and justice.

5 See Aquinas, *Commentary on the "Nicomachean Ethics,"* 2 vols., trans. C. I. Litzinger (Chicago: Henry Regnery Company, 1964), I:910: "The law-abiding just man is most virtuous and legal justice is the most perfect of the virtues."

6 This is a notoriously difficult statement in the *Nicomachean Ethics*. For further discussion, see Stewart, *Notes on the "Nicomachean Ethics" of Aristotle*, 2 vols. (Oxford: Clarendon Press, 1892), I.401, and O'Connor, "The Aetiology of Justice," p. 141). See also Smith on equity (*Revaluing Ethics*, pp. 151–5).

will show the man in the best sense as one who is "a guardian of the just" and not, as Thrasymachus recommends, as a tyrant (*NE* 1134b1–8).[7] Far from condemning justice as the advantage of another, Aristotle distinguishes between the best and worst human beings in a manner heavily weighted on the side of justice: "the one who uses wickedness both toward himself and toward his friends is the worst, but the best is the one who uses virtue not toward himself but toward another, for this is a difficult task" (*NE* 1130a5–8). By identifying the best of actions with definitively just acts at the same time as he singles out the difficulty of such acts, Aristotle captures a side of justice that Thrasymachus's attack obscures. Justice does indeed require us to act with a view to another's good, and this is exactly why it is admired.

Having bestowed such praise on general justice, Aristotle turns to particular justice, which he tells us is the true focus of our investigation (*NE* 1130a14, 1130b18–20). Like the other virtues, particular justice is a part of the law and so of general justice: It is therefore its own perfection as a virtue and a part of that complete virtue commanded by the law with a view to the common advantage (*NE* 1130b8–16). Like general justice, however, particular justice is also distinguished from the other virtues in having its specific character defined by its orientation "toward another," and the investigation of particular justice begins to illuminate the problematic consequence of this orientation for justice as a mean and a virtue.

JUSTICE AS FAIRNESS

Whereas commentators who treat particular justice in the *Nicomachean Ethics* tend to focus on its technical terms – the proportional equalities of its two forms, commutative and distributive justice – Aristotle's own first order of business is to prove that particular justice is in fact like the other virtues in being a characteristic and a specific perfection.[8]

---

[7] See also *NE* 1125b11–14 as well as *Republic* 359b1. As Aristotle notes, the ruler is thus the "guardian of the just," but as a result, "there seems to be nothing left for him" (*NE* 1134b1–3).

[8] Smith, Tessitore, and O'Connor tend either to focus on general as opposed to particular justice or to collapse the discussion of particular justice into the consideration of general justice. See Smith, *Revaluing Ethics*; Tessitore, *Reading Aristotle's "Ethics": Virtue, Rhetoric, and Political Philosophy* (Albany: State University of New York Press, 1996); and O'Connor, "The Aetiology of Justice."

His very efforts in this direction suggest room for doubt, and his case in favor of this view begins to bring out the difficulties with particular justice. He argues that certain bad actions, even some that may appear to issue from a vice other than injustice, actually stem from the desire "to get the larger share" (*NE* 1130a16–22). The coward may flee from danger, for example, a stingy person may begrudge a loan, or an immoderate human being may commit adultery. But none who act from these specific vices do so with a view to profit or gain strictly speaking; indeed, they may even suffer a loss as a result of their deeds (*NE* 1130a24–8). By contrast, the one who is unjust in wanting more of the good things without consideration for others would do all these same deeds simply from the desire for gain. Particular justice is thus distinguished both from the other virtues and from complete justice as the perfection that pertains specifically to gain (*NE* 1130a24–5, 32–3).

As virtues that both "possess their power in being in relation to another," general and particular justice are similar, but as the perfection pertaining to gain, particular justice consists more narrowly in the proper disposition toward the goods of another (*NE* 1130a32–b5). The just human being in this sense stands in relation to another in being disposed to take only his own fair or equal portion of the goods that human beings necessarily share as members of the same political community (*NE* 1130b4). The crucial question for particular justice, then, is how to define the equality in accord with which one must choose, and it is in connection with this question that the difference between justice and the other virtues begins to emerge.

The formal definition of particular justice is offered in Aristotle's discussion of its two kinds: distributive and commutative justice. Aristotle presents a mathematical account of these equalities, each of which involves a minimum of four terms: the shares of the good to be allotted and the persons to whom these shares are to be assigned (*NE* 1131a15–20). Distributive justice is concerned with equality in the distribution of the common goods understood as "honor, money, or any of the good things of which there is a part for those who share in the regime" (*NE* 1130b30–2), and it employs a geometric proportion to measure all the terms of the equation because it assigns goods in accord with a principle with which "everyone" agrees, which is merit or desert (*NE* 1131a25–6). Commutative justice pertains to contracts or transactions, "voluntary and involuntary," and because it is blind to the differences with respect to merit, it employs an arithmetical proportion to restore the parties involved in an unjust transaction to the correct equality by compensating the plaintiff and imposing a penalty (or punishment, *zēmia*) on the wrongdoer (*NE* 1131b32–1132a18).[9]

The crucial difference between justice and the other virtues emerges, then, as Aristotle links the assignment of the equal in particular justice with the definition of justice as a mean and virtue. For the just mean represents not our good condition with respect to two extremes, deficiency and excess, but the principle of equality established by law in relation to which the excess and the deficiency – taking more and receiving less than this equality – are then defined (*NE* 1131a10–15). Moreover, in its distributive form, this equality is the object of a dispute that points to the problematic significance first of distributive justice and finally of the regime in defining justice as a mean and a virtue (cf. *NE* 1130b30–2). For, Aristotle acknowledges, there exist deep divisions concerning what constitutes desert or merit in the distribution of the common goods: "democrats say it is freedom; oligarchs, wealth; others, noble birth; aristocrats, virtue" (*NE* 1131a27–9). The "fights and accusations" that break out when there is a perceived inequality extend not only to the distribution of security, money, and honor (*NE* 1131a22–4), but also, as Aristotle will indicate in his discussion of reciprocity, to the regime itself as the defining distributive principle of the political community. As the distribution of ruling offices determined by the authoritative element of the city and by the end for the sake of which this element rules, the regime reflects the fundamental equality in accord with which one is just (*Pol.* 1278b10–15, 1279a25–1279b10).

Aristotle leaves the full resolution of the dispute connected with ruling offices to his *Politics* (*Pol.* 1280a7ff.), but his discussion of reciprocity points to the necessary and problematic role of the regime in establishing justice as a mean and a virtue. As Aristotle's final step in clarifying the limits of justice in this regard, this discussion also begins to illuminate a tension within moral virtue between the two ends that demand our devotion as morally serious human beings: the common good, on the one hand, and our perfection in virtue as an end in itself, on the other.

---

[9] On the question of the assessment of this penalty, see Burnet, *The "Ethics" of Aristotle* (London: Metheun & Co., 1900), pp. 218–9.

RECIPROCITY AND THE REGIME

Aristotle's discussion of reciprocity presents itself largely as an analysis of the conditions for economic exchange necessary for the common life of individuals seeking the good. Yet this analysis also raises the more fundamental question concerning the foundation of political rule.[10] While rejecting the "Pythagorean" view that simple reciprocity (or "retaliation," *antipeponthos*) – suffering what one has done to another – is justice, Aristotle insists that a certain proportionate reciprocity is necessary if human beings are to come together in a political association (*NE* 1132b21–34). There is the necessity of "exchange" in the case of both evils and goods, since if people cannot requite evil for evil, they are regarded as slaves, and without an exchange of goods, there is no community (*NE* 1132b34–1133a2). Accordingly, reciprocity in the form of an original equality among individuals must exist if a community is to exist. Indeed, this equality, however it is ultimately elaborated, is the ground of law, since law is natural only among those "for whom there is equality in ruling and being ruled" (*NE* 1134b14–15).

Now, in the case of economic exchange, the natural standard by which goods are valued is "need," and the "measure" – the term that represents need, makes the value of goods comparable, and acts as a "guarantee of future exchange" – is, by general agreement or

---

[10] Even the most careful treatments of justice devote little attention to Aristotle's discussion of reciprocity. See D. G. Ritchie's "Aristotle's Subdivisions of Particular Justice," *The Classical Review* 8 (May 1894): 185–93, on ill-conceived efforts to absorb the discussion of reciprocity into the accounts of commutative and distributive justice. Miller briefly surveys efforts of this kind (*Nature, Justice, and Rights in Aristotle's "Politics"* [Oxford: Clarendon Press, 1995], p. 73, n. 14). Keyt is correct in noting that "distributive justice for Aristotle is concerned primarily with the distribution of political authority (*politikē archē*) and only secondarily with the distribution of wealth" (David Keyt, "Aristotle's Theory of Distributive Justice" in *A Companion to Aristotle's "Politics,"* eds. David Keyt and Fred D. Miller, Jr. [Oxford: Blackwell, 1991]). But this fact is made clear in particular in his discussion of proportionate reciprocity. In *A Democracy of Distinction: Aristotle and the Work of Politics* (Chicago: University of Chicago Press, 2005), Frank emphasizes the voluntary nature of economic relations in Aristotle's discussion of reciprocity in order to argue for a notion of "reciprocal justice" that will lead to "social harmony" and even "friendship" among classes, but while Aristotle affirms the importance of economic exchange in uniting a political community, he also points to the necessity of equality in the capacity to requite evil for evil – an aspect of reciprocity that largely drops out of Frank's analysis (see especially pp. 83–92).

convention, money (*NE* 1133a19–31, 1133b10–12). By equalizing goods in this manner, money thus makes possible a relation of exchange that, as the ground of a common advantage and life, holds the community together as a community. But every political association must agree also on the distribution of political goods, the most fundamental of which are ruling offices. The arrangement of these offices is determined by the distributive principle with which everyone agrees: to each in accord with merit. Not need but merit, then, establishes commensurability, and honor, not money, is the currency when it comes to the distribution of political offices (cf. *Pol.* 1278b8–17, 1279a22–32, 1280a7–21, 1281a28–39).

In determining what or who is to be honored in the matter of ruling, however, we are thrown back on the dispute over what constitutes merit: freedom, wealth, noble birth, or virtue. With respect to the question of rule, the fights and accusations that break out concerning the distribution of shares are the most pressing issue for justice, as Aristotle reveals in the example he offers as evidence against the Pythagorean view that simple reciprocity is justice. For if a ruler strikes one who is ruled, the ruler should not be struck in return; if the reverse were to happen, however, then the one who is ruled should not only be struck in return but "punished in addition" (*NE* 1132b28–30).[11] As this example pointedly recalls, justice must preserve rule and account for the compulsion and punishment necessary for ensuring the obedience to law. In acknowledging the necessity for such coercion, in fact, Aristotle draws our attention to his general reticence to speak of force and punishment throughout the account of justice. His mathematical treatment of distributive and commutative justice not only downplays the dispute over rule but also virtually ignores the role of anger and retribution in the punishment of harms.[12] Even as he acknowledges the need for the "exchange of evil for evil" in his analysis of proportionate reciprocity, he focuses on the exchange of goods and thereby

[11] As Aquinas remarks, "Obviously, worse damage is done when someone strikes a ruler, by reason of the fact that injury is done not only to the person of the ruler but also the whole commonweal" (*Commentary*, I:960). See also Burnet, *The "Ethics" of Aristotle*, p. 224.

[12] See Delba Winthrop, "Aristotle and Theories of Justice," *American Political Science Review* 72 (December 1978), pp. 1203–4, and Ritchie, "Aristotle's Subdivisions of Particular Justice," p. 190.

on the more voluntary pursuits that bring human beings together in community. Nevertheless, the role of reciprocity at the origin of the political community reminds us that justice involves an agreement or convention concerning the most fundamental question of rule, and even Aristotle's studied avoidance of the issue of force cannot fully cover over the partly compulsory character of this "agreement" and so of the defining principle of the political community, the regime, in accord with which justice is a mean and a virtue.

Once he has clarified the origin of the political community in proportionate reciprocity, Aristotle acknowledges that justice is not a mean with respect to two vices. Rather, justice "belongs to a mean," and the person whose "choice accords with the just" is one who "does not assign more of the *choiceworthy* to himself and less to his neighbor, or the reverse of harm, but assigns *equal shares in accord with proportion*" (*NE* 1134a1–6; my emphasis). As a characteristic and a part of general justice, therefore, particular justice disposes a person to abide by the mean established in law, and the law itself accords with the equality consistent with the common advantage of those who "share in the regime" (cf. *NE* 1130b30–2).

JUSTICE AND THE DUAL ENDS OF MORAL VIRTUE

In light of the conclusion that the just choice accords with the mean established in law and more fundamentally the regime, we are now in a position to consider the status of justice with respect to the other standard for choice pointed to by Aristotle. This standard was the good – in the best case, the possession and activity of virtue. In the best case, that is, it would seem that one ought to choose the things necessary for the perfection of one's character and the exercise of virtue. Yet the difficulty now appears to be that the requirements of the good in this sense would entail particular injustice. For the law must also meet another standard: It must care for the common advantage and therefore require that we abide by the mean established by distributive and commutative justice for the sake of the common advantage. Aristotle's analysis of justice as a virtue has therefore raised the question of whether, even in the best case, the law can reconcile the two ends to which it demands our devotion as morally serious human beings:

the common good, on the one hand, and our perfection in virtue as an end in itself, on the other.[13]

Aristotle proposed a preliminary answer to this difficult question in his discussion of particular justice as a characteristic: Justice is the specific perfection that pertains to the desire for gain (see again *NE* 1130a16–32). To choose in accord with the just and the law, by this account, is to act in accord with the virtue with respect to gain. But in the course of providing evidence that there is a characteristic we identify with particular justice, Aristotle reminded us that there are other characteristics pertaining to gain. In the case of the good that human beings tend to love most, money, the obvious one is liberality (cf. *NE* 1130a16–19, 1121b31–1122a3, 1122a7–13, 1122a3–7), and Aristotle has also identified courage and magnanimity as the respective virtues pertaining to security and honor, the other goods associated with particular justice. In light of these other virtues, then, how can it be said that justice constitutes the proper perfection pertaining to gain?

Aristotle suggests an answer to this question by making particular justice a part of complete justice: Particular justice constitutes the proper mean pertaining to gain in relation to the common good. But this answer, we can now see, merely begs the question.[14] For justice's

---

[13] The difficulty is that the law seeks two aims – our perfection and the common good – that it cannot reconcile, and therefore it requires guidance concerning the proper order of ends for a human being. But compare Tessitore, who suggests that the difficulty is that the law "does not look toward virtue from the point of view of virtue itself (i.e., the noble or what befits the noble), but rather from the point of view of political justice" (*Reading Aristotle's "Ethics,"* p. 39). Smith takes a similar view: "law does not in truth aim at comprehensive excellence" (*Revaluing Ethics*, p. 150).

[14] Kraut notices the problem: "Since injustice is caused by a great desire for money, honor, or some other good, why cannot Aristotle treat all cases of injustice as the manifestation of one of the vices he has already discussed in Books II–IV of the *Ethics?*" (*Aristotle's Political Philosophy*, p. 137). But Kraut's solution – "Aristotle takes *pleonexia* to be a distinct vice because he tacitly assumes that it involves a desire to have more *at the expense of others*" (p. 138; emphasis in the text) – does not resolve the difficulty that the standard of more and less is set by the law and not the good. Moreover, Kraut goes quite far in claiming that the "unjust person is glad that his gain comes at the expense of another, because causing that suffering is part of his motive" (p. 138). Although Aristotle indicates that an unjust person takes pleasure in his gain, he nowhere clearly suggests that pleasure in another's suffering is a part of such a person's motive (cf. pp. 138–40).

status as a virtue is on the table precisely because the mean in the case of justice is established not by reference to our good condition regarding gain – not, that is, by the standard Aristotle pointed to in saying that one ought to take those of the good things that are necessary for the education to and exercise of virtue (*NE* 1129b1–11). Rather, the mean in the case of justice is determined by the equality or proportion established by law concerning parties contending for the good things. If, in its connection with the common good, particular justice is not a mean with respect to two vices, then by this very fact, it is also not like the other virtues in being an "extreme in accord with the best and that which is done well" (*NE* 1107a6–8).[15] Just action accords with what is fair or equal, and not with the good judged by any other standard.

We are confronted by the difficulty, then, that particular justice as a mean is necessarily defined by a standard other than the good condition of the individual with respect to moral virtue. For in determining the distribution of goods among equals, justice must guard the good of the community as a whole, and even in the best case – the regime in which merit is defined by virtue – there not only are competing claims of merit, but the goods human beings generally pursue, including those necessary for the education to and exercise of virtue, are limited and must be shared.[16] Indeed, by definition, the "equal" as a measure for particular justice, and as the necessary ground of law, exists to adjudicate competing claims with regard to the good, and the very "nature of justice" is to be this principle of equality by which limited goods are distributed and are not the property of one

---

[15] Compare O'Connor, "The Aetiology of Justice," pp. 148–55.

[16] Aristotle's discussion of justice thus opens up the question, raised in the *Politics*, of whether the virtue of the good citizen and the good human being are the same. For although scholars often assert that according to Aristotle, in the best regime the virtue of the good citizen and the good human being are the same (see, e.g., Burnet, *The "Ethics" of Aristotle*, p. 212), Aristotle's statements to this effect are highly qualified (*Pol.* 1277a20–5, b4–1278a5, 1293b1–7) and called into doubt by other statements (e.g., *Pol.* 1276b35–1277a5) and by his insistence, on the one hand, that citizenship necessarily involves "ruling and being ruled in turn" (*Pol.* 1277a25–7, 1278a35–40, 1283b42–1284a3, 1287a16–25) and, on the other hand, that the "regime" in which "the truly best" rule would have to be a kind of permanent kingship (*Pol.* 1284b24–34, 1288a24–39). In this regard, consider Robert Bartlett's discussion of the choiceworthy life and the best regime in "The 'Realism' of Classical Political Science," *American Journal of Political Science* 38 (May 1994): 381–402.

(*NE* 1134a14–16, 1134a24–b2).[17] It is for this reason also that justice can never be wholly separated from compulsion.

The problem presented in the case of particular justice mirrors the problem for justice generally, since in being oriented toward the general advantage of the community, the virtues as complete justice must take their bearings from an end other than themselves. The difficulty for the virtuous individual is most striking in the situations in which the community's good and the activity of moral virtue are most at odds: for example, when the common good requires ignominious surrender rather than noble action in battle; when a generous or magnificent act would mean robbing one to give to another; when the defense of the country calls for deception or fraud or even the betrayal of a friend; or when justice demands punishments at which reason balks. In seeking to handle this difficulty, and to preserve the law's full moral authority and goodness, one might be tempted to redefine virtue solely in terms of the common good: If surrender is necessary for the preservation of the community, for example, then surrender is the truly courageous or noble act. Yet Aristotle's own investigation of moral virtue indicates that this temptation should be resisted. For, in addition to his insistence that each virtue, such as courage, has its precise definition and is an end in its own right, he shows that the law also looks to more than the requirements of the political community in defining our perfection and that the morally serious person understands this perfection not simply in terms of the common good, but in terms of his or her own nobility. Even in the case of a community as intimate and grounded in affection as the family, Aristotle suggests, should a base act be required for the "noble end" of its preservation, the act itself does not cease to be base, and the action of a virtuous person in such a situation is therefore "chosen" under compulsion (*NE* 1109b35–1110a19). Although the law and a decent human being may bow to the necessity of actions that preserve the common good, then, neither would wish to redefine as virtue such deception, fraud, or betrayal that the common good may require but moral virtue itself abhors.

In general, the deepest difficulty that Aristotle points to in his account of particular justice is the tension between moral virtue's

---

[17] Compare Ritchie, "Aristotle's Subdivisions of Particular Justice," pp. 191–2; Winthrop, "Aristotle and Theories of Justice," p. 1205.

orientation toward the common good and its requirements and activity as an independent end. Accordingly, when he cautions early in his discussion of justice that the education of the citizen (the education "with a view to the community [*koinon*]") may not be the same as the education of the good man (*anēr*) simply (*NE* 1130b25–9), he is pointing in the first place not to a tension between moral virtue and some other possibility, but to a tension *within* moral virtue.[18] He thus clarifies the problem at the heart of civic education: The two ends that necessarily demand our devotion as morally serious human beings cannot be fully reconciled.[19] In this way, Aristotle's account of the virtues both describes the political community's noblest pedagogic aim and, on the basis of this community's own aim, establishes its limits.

LAW AND RIGHT REASON

Having completed his investigation of justice as a virtue, Aristotle indicates that he has sufficiently treated the "nature of justice and injustice" and "the just and unjust in general" (*NE* 1134a14–16), but his discussion does not end here. He proceeds with brief accounts of political and natural justice, a complex consideration of just and unjust action and their relation to choice, an account of equity, and a final statement on the connection between law and right reason. Among the difficulties that remain is the question raised by the discussion of justice as a virtue: what the law and the morally virtuous human being look to in determining right action (cf. *NE* 1103b31–4, 1138b18–34). Aristotle's investigation of the tension within moral virtue has revealed that although the law and moral virtue seek to be authoritative with respect to human action, neither on its own terms can provide full guidance concerning the correct hierarchy of ends for a human being (*NE* 1145a6–11, 1152b1–2; see also 1137b34–1138a3). This problem

---

[18] Compare Smith, *Revaluing Ethics*, pp. 60–2; Tessitore *Reading Aristotle's "Ethics,"* pp. 39–42; Burnet, *The "Ethics" of Aristotle*, p. 212.

[19] In Smith's account of the law and moral virtue, this tension is obscured by his argument that equity, understood as a "sense of fairness" and "a persistent willingness to render to others what is their due," is "comprehensive moral virtue" and even the "whole of virtue," and therefore the "standard for law itself" and the end toward which practical wisdom, "the single existential virtue that is required to order all our actions," directs us (*Revaluing Ethics*, pp. 35, 50, 151–5, 265).

persists through the second half of his discussion of justice and is carried forward into his account of the intellectual virtues in Book VI, in which he immediately takes up the subject he had postponed in his introduction to moral virtue: the subject of right reason.

In his introduction to moral virtue, Aristotle had noted that right reason (*orthos logos*) underlies the particular virtues, and at the end of the discussion of justice, he reiterates the law's role as the voice of right reason. Because the city and the law represent right reason, they have as their aim more than the lawful things in a partial sense – more than simply the preservation of the "equal."Just as, for example, the law commands moderation, which produces and preserves our health and well-being, so it forbids any action that contravenes the right reason informing the virtues. It is as the representative of right reason that the law is comprehensive and that Aristotle makes the sweeping claim, so foreign to modern liberal ears, that "what the law does not command, it forbids" (*NE* 1138a7).[20] By way of example, he observes that the law does not command suicide and therefore imposes a penalty on the person who, in a fit of anger, kills himself. The law imposes this penalty despite the fact that acts done out of anger are not thought to have been done from forethought and that this penalty is neither retributive nor remedial (cf. *NE* 1135b25–6). In harming himself, in fact, this person suffers no injustice because, as Aristotle will establish, it is impossible to do an injustice to oneself voluntarily. Since the one who kills himself in a fit of anger acts contrary to right reason, however,

[20] Compare Hobbes, *Leviathan*, ed. Edwin Curley (Indianapolis: Hackett Publishing Co., 1994): "As for other Liberties, they depend on the silence of the law. In cases where the sovereign has prescribed no rule, there the subject hath the liberty to do, or forbear, according to his own discretion" (p. 271). Aristotle's statement is so foreign to modern ears that Ostwald observes that "it hardly seems likely that Aristotle meant to say that every action not explicitly ordered by the law is implicitly forbidden" (*Nicomachean Ethics*, trans. Martin Ostwald [Upper Saddle River, NJ: Prentice Hall (Library of Liberal Arts), 1999], p. 143) and Irwin thinks nothing of simply dropping the phrase (*Nicomachean Ethics*, trans. Terence Irwin [Indianapolis: Hacket Publishing Co., 1985], p. 238). Burnet's refutation of Victorius's oft-cited tautology that *ou keleuei = apagoreuei* is helpful in emphasizing the example Aristotle uses, suicide: "The law forbids us to kill anything which it does not expressly enjoin us to kill" (*The "Ethics" of Aristotle*, p. 244). But the larger context is made clear from the immediately preceding statement: "Of the just things, one set are those that have been established by the law in accord with the whole of virtue" (*NE* 1138a5–7). Cf. also Stewart, *Notes on the "Nicomachean Ethics" of Aristotle*, I.533–4 with Grant, *The "Ethics" of Aristotle*, II.141.

he does injustice to the city, and consequently, the law inflicts a penalty, dishonor, on him (*NE* 1138a12–14). The city seeks in such a case not to mete out justice in the strict sense but to assert its authority regarding right reason.

Now, as Aristotle argues in his discussion of political justice, "the just exists among those for whom there is also law in relation to one another," and justice "is found in a life which is in common with a view to being self-sufficient, among people who are free and equal, either in accord with a proportion or arithmetically" (*NE* 1134a26–31). The discussion of reciprocity has made clear that the political community is constituted first by an established equality with respect to the common goods of the regime among human beings who, in being capable of the "reciprocal exchange of evils," are not slaves to one another (*NE* 1130b30–3; 1132b4–1133a1). In this respect, law naturally exists among those "to whom ruling and being ruled equally belong" (*NE* 1134b14–15; cf. *Pol.* 1287a8–18). But the discussion of political justice underlines the fact that the political community is constituted also by a common life that aims at "self-sufficiency" – not simply at living, but at living well (*Pol.* 1252b27–1253b1). The law seeks to preserve the political community, therefore, by preserving the regime, including both the principle of equality underlying the regime and the good life its members hold in common.

It is with a view to preserving this equality and the common life of the city that we prefer the rule of law to that of a single man. The difficulty is that a man seeks his own good and, in distributing "more of the simply good or less of the simply bad" to himself, takes the law into his own hands and becomes a tyrant. By contrast, the ruler who acts in accord with law is a "guardian of the just" and thus "also of the equal" (*NE* 1134a33–b2). Indeed, precisely as a result of his justice, "there is nothing left" for him, and he "labors for another" (*NE* 1134b2–5). As the example of the just ruler illustrates, because justice is clearly "the good of another," some recompense in the form of honor or privilege is necessary, and there are still those potential tyrants for whom even such recompense is insufficient. At the same time that Aristotle points to the primacy of the good for human beings, therefore, he indicates the need for coercion of those whose ambition the political community cannot accommodate. The primacy of the good undergirds the necessity of both law and force.

Aristotle presents justice as the disposition to act "in accord with the choice of the just," and choice is so central to just action that he returns to the subject repeatedly throughout this second half of the account, including in his preface to political justice (*NE* 1134a17–23; see also 1134b11–13, 1135b8–11, 1136a1–4, 1136b3–9, 23–9).[21] In short, since justice consists in choosing the just share, the character of one's choice determines whether an action is truly unjust or incidentally so. A person can perform an unjust act through either passion or ignorance, for instance, without being unjust: "a man could have intercourse with a woman, knowing who she is, not on account of a principle of choice but through passion," just as one can steal and not be a thief (*NE* 1134a1–21; see also 1130a24–7, 1136a1). One can perform an unjust action, then, without wishing to do harm or injustice to another, and on this basis, Aristotle contends that only acts in which a person deliberately chooses his own good over that of another are truly unjust: "if a person does harm from choice, he is unjust," and likewise "he is just when he does a just action, having chosen to do so" (*NE* 1136a3–4).

In connection with the consideration of choice, however, we must ask not only whether one does harm or injustice to another, but also whether one does harm or injustice to oneself – whether, as Aristotle puts it, the same holds for the suffering as for the doing (*NE* 1136a24–5). In his longer discussion of which unjust acts are truly or incidentally unjust, Aristotle generalizes the question: Does anyone ever choose to do harm or injustice to himself? It is by way of a denial of this possibility – "no one chooses to harm himself, and on account of this, there is not injustice toward oneself" (*NE* 1134b11–13) – that he first distinguishes political justice from what is just for a master and a father, and he reiterates this denial in his discussion of suicide (*NE* 1138a12). When he takes up the question directly, he points to the

---

[21] Stewart notes that the passage on choice prefacing the discussion of political justice seems out of place: "I believe, with Rassow (p. 38), Jackson (p. xvii, & c.), and Ramsauer that these sections are foreign to the present context; but I do not venture to designate any other context in the Fifth Book as their original locus" (*Notes on the "Nicomachean Ethics" of Aristotle*, I.476–7). The passage does seem disconnected from the discussion of political justice that follows, except that it is immediately preceded by Aristotle's summary of justice as a "choice" of the just share, and the question of the choice of the good as compared to the lawful is central to the issue of political justice.

example of an "incontinent" human being (*akratēs*, intemperate, lacking in self-control), who might seem to harm himself voluntarily. But the example itself proves that no one voluntarily seeks to be treated unjustly, since the incontinent person does what he believes he ought not to do and thus "acts contrary to his wish." "No one," Aristotle concludes, "wishes what he does not believe to be a serious [*spoudaion*] thing" (*NE* 1136b5–8).

In leading to this conclusion and thus to the view that no one chooses to be treated unjustly, Aristotle's analysis of just action and choice suggests that human beings act with a view to their own desert or merit, namely, the good we suppose we deserve. Because human action is shot through with considerations of the good in this sense – both the good that is owed another and that which is owed oneself – it inevitably raises the question of the true merit of each and all.

By what standard, then, do we judge this merit? First, Aristotle locates the "just things" by looking "among those [beings] who share in the good things simply and who can have an excess and deficiency of them" (*NE* 1137a26–7). On this basis, he eliminates two groups: the gods, for whom there is no excess of goods, and the incurably bad, whom the good things only harm (*NE* 1137a27–30). Because there can be such an excess and deficiency among the rest of humankind, however, justice must be a "human thing" (*NE* 1137a30). As the examples of the gods and of the incurably bad illustrate, this excess and deficiency are determined not by the mean established by law but by a consideration of the harm and benefit of each. In saying that justice exists only for those for whom good things may be in excess or in deficiency, Aristotle recalls his observation early in the account of justice that human beings ought not to pray for and pursue the good things simply but ought to pray that these things also will be good for them and choose what is good for them (*NE* 1129b4–6). If harm and benefit are taken into a consideration of justice, then the truly just share is not the mean established by law, but the share that will benefit and not harm its recipient.

The problem presented by this distinction between law and benefit is connected in a complicated way with one of the main controversies that have divided commentators regarding Aristotle's brief account of natural justice: whether we can infer from this account the existence of a natural law or immutable principles of action.[22] The immediate problem is that he classifies natural justice as a part of political justice. Hence, political justice itself is derivative not of nature, which is always the same, but of particular regimes, which vary; conversely, the natural justice of which he speaks is a part of political justice.[23] Nevertheless, against those who would argue that *all* the just things are just by law or convention – that there are no naturally just things – since what is by nature is unchangeable and the just things are changeable, Aristotle insists that there are just things by nature. In his most puzzling statement, he acknowledges that "what is by nature is unchangeable and has the same force everywhere," only then to assert that "among us [human beings], there is something that is in fact by nature, yet all is changeable," and that the just by nature and the just by convention

---

[22] The school of natural law that traces its roots back to Aristotle, of course, has its origin in Thomas Aquinas, and Jaffa's *Thomism and Aristotelianism: A Study of the Commentary by Thomas Aquinas on the "Nicomachean Ethics"* (Chicago: University of Chicago Press, 1952) and Frederick Copleston, *A History of Philosophy, Vol II: Mediaeval Philosophy: Augustine to Scotus* (Westminister, MD: Neuman Press, 1950) each offers an analysis of Thomas's transformation of Aristotle's discussion of natural right. But the history of commentary on Aristotle's short and puzzling discussion presents little agreement. My treatment of the passage and this commentary is cursory. For longer accounts, see Jaffa and Copleston, as well as R. A. Gauthier and J. Y. Jolif, *"L'Éthique à Nicomaque,"* 2nd ed., 2 vols. (Louvain, FR: Publications Universitares de Louvain, 1970), II.391–6; Stewart, *Notes on the "Nicomachean Ethics" of Aristotle*, pp. 492–7; Grant, *The "Ethics" of Aristotle*, II.126–9; Hardie, *Aristotle's Ethical Theory*, (London: Oxford University Press, 1968), pp. 204–5; Strauss, *Natural Right and History* (Chicago: University of Chicago Press, 1953), pp. 156–64; Joachim, *Aristotle: The "Nicomachean Ethics"* (Oxford: Clarendon Press, 1951), pp. 154–6; Richard Bodéüs, "The Natural Foundations of Right" in *Action and Contemplation: Studies in the Moral and Political Thought of Aristotle* (Albany: State University of New York Press, 1999), pp. 79–86, Yack, *Problems of a Political Animal: Community, Justice, and Conflict in Aristotelian Political Thought* (Berkeley: University of California Press, 1993), pp. 140–9; Richard Kraut, *Aristotle: Political Philosophy*, (Oxford: Oxford University Press, 2002), pp. 125–32; Fred D. Miller, Jr. "Aristotle on Natural Law and Justice" in *A Companion to Aristotle's "Politics,"* eds. David Keyt and Fred D. Miller (Oxford: Blackwell, 1991), pp. 279–308.

[23] Commentators typically acknowledge that conventional or legal justice derives from the "regime" (constitution or state); see, e.g., Jaffa, *Thomism and Aristotelianism*, p. 181). Aristotle's previous statement that political justice (and perhaps the just simply) "is found in a life which is in common with a view to being self-sufficient, among people who are free and equal, either in accord with a proportion or arithmetically" makes clear that political justice too is derivative of the regime (1135a26–8; see also 1135b12–15). As Strauss observes, however, the statement that natural right is a part of political right "does not mean that there is no natural right outside the city or prior to the city" (*Natural Right and History*, p. 157).

and agreement "are likewise changeable" (*NE* 1134b24–32). If the fundamental question raised by justice is the true good of human beings, then among the puzzles Aristotle's discussion of natural justice presents is the one with which he concludes: "the things that are just not by nature but among human beings are not the same everywhere, since the regimes are not, but there is one regime that is everywhere the best in accord with nature" (*NE* 1135a3–5). However Aristotle's notion of natural justice is understood, his conclusion underlines the difficulty that the naturally best is not always and everywhere just.

In the face of this problem and of the centrality of choice in just action, it is not surprising, as Aristotle observes, that contrary to what "people suppose," it is not easy either to act justly or to know what the just things are (*NE* 1137a4–12). Acting justly requires that one not only do the just things but do them "having a certain characteristic" (*NE* 1137a6–9). Moreover, people suppose that it is not a matter of wisdom to know the just and unjust things, since it is not difficult to understand what the laws say. But Aristotle insists to the contrary that "the laws are not the just things, except incidentally" (*NE* 1137a9–12). Rather, knowing how "the just things are done and distributed" is a greater task than understanding what is involved in bringing about health, "seeing that in this also it is easy to know honey and wine and hellebore and cautery and surgery, but how they ought to be applied with a view to health and on whom and when is no less a task than to be a doctor" (*NE* 1137a14–17). Indeed, Aristotle's earlier discussion of justice as a virtue raises the question of the relation between the characteristic or habit instilled by law and the knowledge by which action is guided. For if, even in the best case, the law does not supply the guidance we require, then to what do we turn for this guidance?

Aristotle follows this difficulty through his account of equity and the equitable. Equity, to which we turn when the law requires correction, is not the same thing as justice, but it is also not different generically. Yet, in sometimes praising what is equitable and the equitable person, we make it clear that equity is better than justice (*NE* 1137a33–b2). There is, accordingly, a tension in our claims, since "it appears strange that if the equitable is something contrary to the just, it is a praiseworthy thing" (*NE* 1137b2–4). Our speech points to several different possibilities: "If the equitable is better and praiseworthy, then the just is not a serious thing; or if the equitable is different from the just, then it is not just; or if both are serious things, then they are the same" (*NE* 1137b4–5). The problem of the relation between equity and justice, Aristotle says, leads to near perplexity concerning the equitable.

He resolves this perplexity in the following way. Seeing that the equitable is something better than the just (or a "certain" just), but not in a different class, and therefore also that the just and the equitable are the same and both are serious things, we come to understand that "the equitable is just, not in accord with law, but as a correction of the legally just" (*NE* 1137b8–13). Such correction is necessary because "all law is general, but concerning some things, it is not possible to speak correctly in general terms" (*NE* 1137b13–14). Where it is necessary but not perfectly correct to speak in general terms, "the law takes the majority of cases" – it accepts what is correct "for the most part" – but it is also "not ignorant of the element of error" (*NE* 1137b14–16). The law thus presents itself as just and authoritative and, at the same time, as aware of its own deficiency. "The error," Aristotle insists, "is not in the law or in the lawgiver but in the nature of the matter, for such is simply the stuff of actions" (*NE* 1137b17–19).

As a result of its necessary generality, therefore, the law must take account of its own imperfection by looking to equity as a means for its correction: "when a case arises under it which is contrary to its general statement, then in that which the lawgiver neglects and errs as a result of speaking generally, it is correct to rectify the omission" (*NE* 1137b19–22). In such a case, the omission is rectified by looking to "what the lawgiver himself would have said if he were present and would have legislated if he had known" (*NE* 1137b22–4). By this account, the need for equity does not impugn the law's justice since the error is not in the law and there is provision for its correction in those circumstances that the law could not foresee. Justice and equity fall within the same class: "the equitable is just and better than a certain justice, not than justice simply but than the error that is due to its absoluteness" (*NE* 1137b24–5). Aristotle calls the correction of law "the very nature of the equitable" (*NE* 1137b26).

Yet, a second problem that equity must address reveals the inadequacy of this resolution: Not everything can be regulated by law

because some things are singular instances and must be handled by
a decree (*NE* 1137b27–8). Aristotle compares the application of a
decree to the use of the leaden rule in Lesbian house building, arguing that "of a thing which is indefinite, so also the rule [by which it is
measured] is indefinite" (*NE* 1137b29–30). More precisely, the "indef-
initeness" of the rule in such an instance would appear to consist in its
flexibility, which enables it to take the proper measure of any matter
not amenable to law: Just as the leaden rule is not rigid but adapts
itself to the shape of the stone, so too does the decree to the matter at
hand (*NE* 1137b31–2).

But this suggestion raises a question that Aristotle does not address
except to say that the rule is indefinite: Even though there is no general
rule or law, is there not a standard by which one who issues decrees
takes his bearings? This same question, moreover, must be addressed
also to the correction of the law. To use one of Aristotle's favorite
examples: Just as the doctor looks to health as his end, to what does
the lawgiver look in deciding singular cases or in correcting the law?
Aristotle has referred several times to "the just simply" or to "the just in
the first sense," but since he never supplies a clear account of either, we
depart his discussion of equity still with this puzzle before us (see *NE*
1132b22–3, 1134a25–6, 1136b33–4, 1137b24–5; see also 1134a30–1,
1137a11–12).[24]

Indeed, Aristotle concludes with an equally puzzling description of
the equitable man. Contending that it is apparent from the discussion
of equity who the equitable man is, he describes him as one who is
"disposed to choose and to do these sorts of things" (*NE* 1137b34–5).
In light of the discussion of equity, the equitable man would seem to be
the one who possesses the knowledge to correct the law and issue just
decrees.[25] Yet Aristotle proceeds to describe him as one who is "not

---

[24] In "The Natural Foundations of Right," p. 79, Richard Bodéüs assimilates the "simply
just" to "political justice," reading the phrase at 1134a23–6, *kai to haplōs dikaion kai to
politikon dikaion*, as placing the two in apposition. But this assimilation obscures the
problem presented especially by equity, and there is no necessity to read the phrase as
placing the simply just and political justice in apposition. Compare Tessitore, *Reading
Aristotle's "Ethics,"* p. 39 and Stewart, *Notes on the "Nicomachean Ethics" of Aristotle*,
I.479–80.

[25] This is the meaning that Kraut attributes to equity as a virtue: "A juror must call
upon the virtue of 'equity' (*epieikeia*), a skill that enables him to see how to correct

insistent to a fault upon justice but disposed to less, even though he has the law on his side," and concludes by calling equity a "characteristic" and "a certain sort of justice and not a different sort of characteristic" (*NE* 1138a1–3; cf. 1136b19–21). Given the equitable man's "flexible" stance toward the law, however, what is the characteristic that distinguishes him? Can his flexibility be grounded in a disposition or habit, or does it require knowledge? If it is grounded in knowledge, then by what, if not the law, does the equitable man take his bearings when he chooses and acts? The equitable man is thought to merit an "equal share" established in accord with the law, yet he clearly looks to some other principle or end in his own action.

When describing the equitable man in his earlier discussion of choice, Aristotle notes that while he may be thought to do injustice to himself, by taking less than he merits, "it may happen that he takes more of another good, for example, of repute or of the noble simply"; at any rate, Aristotle insists, because "he suffers nothing contrary to his wish," the equitable man does no injustice to himself (*NE* 1136b21–4). We might then expect an account of the relation between the law and the good, but Aristotle's vagueness regarding the principle or end that guides equitable judgment seems of a piece with his ambiguity concerning whether justice, and likewise equity, is a characteristic or some kind of knowledge.[26]

In light of these difficulties, Aristotle's return to the subject of right reason as he concludes the account of justice is understandable. For the law is not and cannot be our guide simply – it is not absolute in determining action. By recalling the subject of right reason, Aristotle prepares us for the discussion of intellectual virtue with the problem of the law and moral virtue still fully in play. After outlining his treatment

those deficiencies of the laws that result from their over-generality" (*Aristotle: Political Philosophy*, p. 109). But this suggestion does not accord with Aristotle's own description of the equitable person; nor does it resolve the question of what a juror looks to in deciding a case, if not the law. The significance of the difficulty is noted by Kraut most simply: "Paradoxically, lawfulness can occasionally require violating the law. Little wonder, then, that being a lawful person and doing what is lawful are no easy matters" (p. 110).

[26] In raising this question, Aristotle also notes the possibility raised in the *Republic*: If justice is an art, then the clever guardian is also the clever thief (*Republic* 333e–334b). He denies this possibility by emphasizing justice as a characteristic (*NE* 1137a17–26).

of this problem in his account of prudence in Book VI of his *Nico-machean Ethics* – how this treatment leads to his investigation of the good in the latter half of this work – the next chapter follows Aristotle's turn to his *Politics* and his consideration in particular of the regime as the source of the law.

4

Prudence, the Good Citizen, and the Good Life

THE PROBLEM OF PRUDENCE

When Aristotle concludes the account of the particular moral virtues to turn to intellectual virtue, the question of the standard to which the morally virtuous person and the law look in determining right action forms a new horizon in the *Nicomachean Ethics* (*NE* 1138b13–14). That this question remains is indicated immediately by the fact that he returns to the subject of right reason he had earlier postponed (*NE* 1138b18–20). The investigation of right reason is inseparable from a consideration of the target (*scopos*) at which the virtues aim and the boundary (or limit, *horos*) within which the mean is identified (*NE* 1138b21–5, 32–4). In the absence of such a consideration, the definition of virtue – as the mean defined by the prudent human being (*phronimos*) – is true but unclear (*NE* 1138b25–6).

Despite the apparent urgency of this task, Aristotle does not approach it directly, instead undertaking a lengthy treatment of the characteristics of the rational or intellectual parts of the soul. While we might then expect his discussion of prudence, the rational characteristic that governs deliberation in the realm of action, to shed light on the question of right reason, this discussion proves first to complicate rather than illuminate the matter. A simple sketch brings out the central difficulty.[1] In short, we learn that prudence is required for perceiving the right thing to do in a particular situation. But in tackling the question of how prudence makes this perception, Aristotle concludes both that prudence requires moral virtue to set the end and that it completes moral virtue by bringing right reason to bear on the means to achieve the end and on the end itself (*NE* 1144a28–b1, 1145a2–6, 1144b14–25).[2] He thus leaves unclear the most urgent matter: what right reason is and what the standard is by which the end is determined.

Nevertheless, in concluding the discussion of intellectual virtue, Aristotle begins to lay the groundwork for clarifying this standard by redrawing the terrain within which it will be explored in his continuing investigation of the good in the *Ethics*. For he reiterates that moral virtue must finally be understood not in terms of itself, but in terms of its contribution to the proper target or end: the highest human good understood as the perfection of a human being. But now Aristotle no longer defines this target in terms of moral virtue, as he did in adopting the political perspective in Book II. Rather, he insists that the highest good necessarily includes, if it is not wholly constituted

[1] Like Aristotle's account of natural justice, his treatment of prudence or practical wisdom (*phronēsis*) presents several interpretive difficulties; as Sarah Broadie observes, "This [Aristotle's discussion of practical wisdom] more than most is a rough terrain for commentators, being densely thicketed with controversy" (*Ethics with Aristotle* [Oxford: Oxford University Press, 1991], p. 179). Richard Bodéüs offers an analysis of some of the key disputes, and in particular the complicated question of the relation between moral virtue and prudence. At the heart of this dispute is a disagreement about whether prudence is dependent on moral virtue, deriving its "principles" from proper habituation, or whether it is "an intellectual operation assigned to the discursive search for principles of action" (see Bodéüs, *The Political Dimensions of Aristotle's "Ethics,"* trans. Jan Edward Garrett [Albany: State University of New York Press, 1993], p. 35; see pp. 27–38 for his overall analysis). In addition to the traditional commentators Bodéüs surveys, C. D. C. Reeve's *Practices of Reason: Aristotle's "Nicomachean Ethics"* (Oxford: Clarendon Press, 1992) is a more recent treatment of prudence that differs from Bodéüs's view on several important points.

[2] This difficulty informs Hardie's remark: "Commentators have sometimes involved themselves, and their readers, in needless perplexities about Aristotle's doctrine of practical wisdom, and about the so-called practical syllogism, as a consequence of not attending to the limited scope of Aristotle's remarks in particular parts of the discussion. Thus they have felt bound to try to explain away the fact that Aristotle describes *phronēsis* both as discerning means to an end determined by moral virtue (1145a5–6) and as involving a true understanding of an end (1142b31–3)" (*Aristotle's Ethical Theory* [London: Oxford University Press, 1968], p. 213).

by, wisdom (*sophia*). He is even so bold as to claim that it is wisdom that constitutes the health of the soul and happiness and that has authority over moral virtue, which seeks to bring wisdom into being (*NE* 1144a3–7; cf. 1137a9–17; 1145a6–9).

Now these are claims Aristotle must more fully elucidate and defend, but to do so, he must also step outside of the horizon of the law and moral virtue. His account of the morally serious life has justified such a move first by acknowledging the authoritative status of the law and moral virtue and then by showing that they nevertheless require guidance in establishing the hierarchy of ends for a human being. When Aristotle turns to Book VII of the *Ethics*, therefore, he explicitly begins anew (*NE* 1145a15), and this new beginning points to the "political philosopher," as compared to the law, as the "architect of the end toward which we look in calling one particular thing bad and another good simply" (*NE* 1152b1–3; cf. 1094a22–8 and 1141b23–7). In the investigation that follows, Aristotle expands the range of characteristics that pertain to action and, in contrast to the easy dismissal of the life of pleasure as slavish in Book I, he here investigates it as potentially the highest human good (Bk. VII); he also offers a lengthy treatment of friendship as the community, in contrast to the *polis*, within which the good works most deserving of praise are done (Bks. VIII, IX); and he explicitly defends the view that the contemplative or theoretical life, and not the political or moral life, is the best one for a human being (Bk. X). This fuller account of the human good and the emergence of the theoretical life as best is the new terrain within which virtuous action must find its final end and definition.

This expansion of the investigation does not by itself resolve the question raised by Aristotle's elliptical statements regarding the relation between moral virtue and prudence: whether, in short, prudence is dependent on moral virtue and thus on habituation to set the end of action or whether it derives its principles from a discursive analysis of the good.[3] Aristotle's account of moral virtue suggests that action issues

---

[3] See again Bodéüs, *The Political Dimensions of Aristotle's "Ethics,"* pp. 27–38. Bodéüs himself argues that prudence is clearly dependent on moral virtue and habituation and that it must be understood within the realm of political science or expertise: "Aristotle's man is above all a political man, prudence above all an excellence of political life, and the good man a leading citizen" (p. 44). Bodéüs's conclusion refutes the prevailing notion, given weight by the commentary of Gauthier and Jolif (*"L'Éthique à Nicomaque,"*

from the proper disposition of the desires and longings and therefore that habituation is primary.[4] Moreover, in determining right action, prudence cannot ignore the authoritative character of the political community and especially the law, which is this community's voice of command. The most that can be said at the conclusion of Book VI is that the law and moral virtue have been shown to seek a self-sufficiency they cannot fully attain. Against the claims of the law, not to say its divine origins, Aristotle is thus able to suggest the necessity of political philosophy as a guide and to posit the possibility of wisdom as our final end.

If the need for or significance of Aristotle's investigation of moral virtue and law seems at first opaque to us, a modern liberal audience that professes to view politics and law with much less reverence, the current debate about citizenship suggests that we are not so free of authority or reverence as we assume. In fact, especially for us, Aristotle's account of the virtues is necessary in illuminating the authoritative place of moral virtue with respect to the human good and in clarifying the deepest problem of law and civic education. This problem

2nd. ed., 2 vols. [Louvain, FR: Publications Universitaires de Louvain, 1970]) that "Aristotle's ethical works expound an 'autonomous moral science'" (see the discussion of P. A. Vander Waerdt, "The Political Intention of Aristotle's Moral Philosophy," *Ancient Philosophy* 5 [Spring 1985], p. 77). But in placing the account of prudence and political science more generally in the larger context of Aristotle's treatment of the human good, Bodéüs also concludes that Aristotle's statements regarding the relation between virtue and leisure "permit us to establish exactly the purpose of the Aristotelian ethics. If it had been addressed to the particular individual, rather than to the lawgiver, the 'philosophy' and 'speculative' excellence which Aristotle as a moralist locates above the level of action would appear to be an ideal which the human being must reach apart from the city and apart from every form of political life. But nothing of the sort is being proposed" (p. 125). This conclusion is more difficult to sustain. Cf. Reeve, *Practices of Reason*, which argues that the primary audience of the *Ethics* is the philosopher (pp. 189 and 195), as well as Tessitore's criticisms of Reeve in *Reading Aristotle's "Ethics": Virtue, Rhetoric, and Political Philosophy* (Albany: State University of New York Press, 1996), pp. 131–3.

4 John Cooper insists that it is "not open to reasonable doubt that in the *Nicomachean Ethics* Aristotle held that the practically intelligent person knows by some kind of intellectual intuition what the correct ultimate end is. This is something he knows, but he does not know it either by having worked it out by deliberation or by having deduced it from the first principles of any theoretical science" (*Reason and Human Good in Aristotle* [Cambridge, MA: Harvard University Press, 1975], p. 64). The difficulty remains, however, that Aristotle has not supplied the account of "right reason" he promised and that moral virtue, which is to supply the "correct ultimate end," is sometimes inadequate to the task.

is not, as much of the current debate suggests, the tension between the common good and individual flourishing,[5] but the tension within moral virtue between its orientation toward the common good and its independence as an end in its own right. It is precisely out of a consideration of this problem, Aristotle helps us to see, that the question of the human good, first answered by the political community, reemerges as a matter of investigation, and that wisdom proves necessary and potentially constitutive of the good. From the point of view of the political community, then, the most fundamental difficulty connected with its own education is the possible tension between the end it authorizes as our perfection, justice, and the end Aristotle posits at the conclusion of Book VI, wisdom.

In positing wisdom as our good, of course, Aristotle has not made the case for its claim; nor has he concluded that justice and wisdom are simply in tension with one another. Wisdom emerges as a contender for the best way of life first from the problem presented by moral virtue and, consequently, from a certain necessity: our need for guidance concerning action. It does not reduce the complexity of the question concerning the relation between justice and wisdom, or moral and intellectual virtue, to note that they constitute different

---

5 The core issue of this debate is captured by a division among neo-Aristotelians themselves. While Aristotle's current students generally agree that virtue's aim or end is the good, they disagree fundamentally about the scope of civic education and the relation between the common good and individual happiness or "flourishing" (*eudaimonia*). On the one side, liberal Aristotelians circumscribe civic education by distinguishing the virtues required for the common good and perpetuation of the constitutional order from those that constitute diverse forms of individual flourishing (e.g., Galston, *Liberal Pluralism: The Implications of Value Pluralism for Political Theory and Practice* [Cambridge: Cambridge University Press, 2002], ch. 1; *Liberal Purposes: Goods, Virtues, and Diversity in the Liberal State* [Cambridge: Cambridge University Press, 1991], pp. 140–3, 172–3, 301–4; Nussbaum, *The Fragility of Goodness: Luck and Ethics in Greek Tragedy and Philosophy*, rev. ed. [Cambridge: Cambridge University Press, 2001], pp. xvii–xxiv; "Human Functioning and Social Justice: In Defense of Aristotelian Essentialism," *Political Theory* 20 (May 1992), pp. 202–46. Communitarian Aristotelians, by contrast, seek to show that in the well-ordered community, the virtues that constitute individual flourishing also serve or achieve the common good (e.g., MacIntyre, *Dependent Rational Animals: Why Human Beings Need the Virtues* [Chicago: Open Court, 1999], chs. 9–11; Smith, *Revaluing Ethics: Aristotle's Dialectical Pedagogy* [Albany: State University of New York Press, 2001], ch. 8). But the division among neo-Aristotelians mirrors a split more generally among scholars concerned about civic education, including those who take their bearings from classical or liberal republicanism, progressive liberalism, and deliberative democracy.

ends and activities and take their bearings from different authorities. Whether the life of wisdom is a "radical alternative" to the ethical life, as some suggest, or consistent and coherent with it, as others argue, is a related but separate question to which Aristotle's investigation of the morally serious life opens the door without resolving.[6]

Indeed, Aristotle devotes two of the four remaining books of the *Ethics* to a discussion of friendship, a mere sketch of which shows that this question remains fully in play. For friendship is a community that is so cherished a good that "*no one* would choose to live without friends, even if he had all the rest of the goods" (*NE* 1155a5–6; my emphasis). At its best, moreover, friendship would seem not only conducive to the pursuit of wisdom but to promise a perfect common good or "justice in the fullest sense" that legislators seek to emulate in instilling a common vision of the good (*homonoia*) in citizens (*NE* 1155a22–8). In such a community of friends, therefore, justice and wisdom would appear to be potentially coherent. On the other hand, in contrast to the political community, the primary question for friendship is not whether its end or activities are just – done with a view to another's good – but whether they accord with the true health and happiness of a human being.[7] As such, friendship can be grounded in "self-love," the good human being will seek as his true friends only those who are truly good for him, and, in the end, Aristotle will not hold the "wise man's" essential self-sufficiency – the fact that he is "able to contemplate even by himself" – against him but, to the contrary, will count this self-sufficiency as a mark of his superior virtue (*NE* 1168b28–34, 1169a3–6, 1172a8–14, 1177a27–b1).[8]

---

[6] Compare, for example, Tessitore, *Reading Aristotle's "Ethics,"* p. 50, and Smith, *Revaluing Ethics*, pp. 272–84.

[7] Even for Smith, who treats friendship as a model or "analogy" for the just political community and the good life, the aim is finally one's own flourishing: "practically wise activity entails ... viewing other people as necessary for one's own happiness because they help one both know oneself and acquire the qualities such as wisdom that make flourishing possible" (*Revaluing Ethics*, pp. 265–6); moreover, "contemplation – the activity associated with philosophy – is most practical because it is most in our interest" (p. 245).

[8] There is growing interest in Aristotle's treatment of friendship, a sign of its significance in his political philosophy and for ethics and politics generally. See Lorraine Smith Pangle, *Aristotle and the Philosophy of Friendship* (Cambridge: Cambridge University Press, 2003); Michael Pakaluk's commentary on Books VIII and IX of the *Nicomachean Ethics* (Oxford: Oxford University Press, 1998); A. W. Price, *Love and Friendship*

The final books of the *Ethics* thus grapple with the question that is most serious for Aristotle and at the heart of civic education and virtue: the question of the best way of life. The account of the virtues makes clear that a complete consideration of this question requires an examination of the political community's highest and noblest pedagogic aims. By undertaking this examination, we come to see both why the question of the best life is central to politics and why the full examination of this question is necessarily bound up with an investigation of justice and wisdom. Aristotle is more explicit in the *Ethics* than he is in the *Politics* that the philosophic or contemplative life is the best life for a human being. His investigation of moral virtue – the virtue at which the political community's education aims – presents the initial justification for the continued investigation of the good in the *Ethics*, but it would require a systematic examination of Books VI through X of the *Ethics* to illuminate the full grounds for and significance of the work's final conclusion concerning the best life.

By thinking through the demands of good action, nonetheless, we understand better the political community's relation not only to wisdom but to moral virtue itself. For even if the political community is not perfectly self-sufficient as an educator, it remains, in a crucial sense, the home of the human good. Aristotle echoes the opening claims of his *Ethics* regarding the political community's authoritative power in the introduction to his *Politics*. He also links the two works with his final statement in the *Ethics* that the next step is to undertake an examination of legislation and of the regime in general "so that, as best as we are able, we may complete our philosophy of human affairs" (*NE* 1181b14–15). As he introduces this transition to the subject matter of the *Politics*, Aristotle recalls his earlier observation that in the current inquiry, we are seeking not theoretical but practical knowledge: "not to contemplate and understand each thing, but to

---

in Plato and Aristotle (Oxford: Oxford University Press, 1989); Suzanne Stern-Gillet, *Aristotle's Philosophy of Friendship* (Albany: State University of New York Press, 1995); Paul Schollmeier, *Other Selves: Aristotle on Personal and Political Friendship* (Albany: State University of New York Press, 1994); and David Konstan, *Friendship in the Classical World* (Cambridge: Cambridge University Press, 1997). In different ways, Smith and Frank use aspects of Aristotle's treatment of friendship to model a just community, and both find support for forms of pluralism (see Smith, *Revaluing Ethics*, ch. 8 and Frank, *A Democracy of Distinction: Aristotle and the Work of Politics* [Chicago: University of Chicago Press, 2005], ch. 5).

do it... for, surely concerning virtue, it is not sufficient to know it but one must try to possess and use it" (*NE* 1179a35–b3; cf. 1103b26–30). At the forefront of Aristotle's consideration and turn to the *Politics*, then, is again the problem of how we are to become good and act well. Having now an adequate "outline" of the best life, the virtues, friendship, and pleasure, we must complete our inquiry by examining not simply legislation but also the source of legislation, the regime.

EDUCATION, LAW, AND COMPULSION

It is in the context of the practical problem of legislation that the concluding chapter of the *Ethics* returns to the question of education and law.[9] For we know that the highest pedagogic aim of the political community, moral virtue, entails the habituation of the desires and longings, and that the law is said to be the voice of command concerning this habituation. With regard to education, Aristotle points first to certain necessities: Because reason or speeches (*logoi*) alone are insufficient in making people good (*epieikēs*, equitable), law is required as a form of constraint. More precisely, speeches have the power to persuade only those who are already well disposed – those who are "liberal," "well-born," and lovers of the noble – and the same speeches have no power over those who "by nature obey not out of awe [*aidos*] but out of fear" and "are swayed not by shame but by punishments" (*NE* 1179b7–9). Some human beings can be brought to virtue if they receive the proper training from youth on. Indeed, such training is absolutely necessary for the young, whose inborn love of pleasure requires checking and pruning lest it overrun their reason, and whose nurture and pursuits must therefore be "arranged by the laws" (*NE* 1119b7–11, 1179b32–5). For others, law is required

---

[9] Of this final chapter of the *Nicomachean Ethics*, Bodéüs writes, "Two thousand years of scholarship have not exhausted this chapter's richness" (*The Political Dimensions of Aristotle's "Ethics,"* p. 47). As the transition to Aristotle's treatment of politics in the obvious sense, this chapter underlines the practical matters connected with virtue, in particular, the obstacles to its acquisition, but as Bodéüs indicates, such concerns raise the kinds of difficult questions that Plato addresses in his *Laws* and *Meno* regarding the limits of reason and the teachability of virtue (pp. 48–57). See also Stewart, *Notes on the "Nicomachean Ethics" of Aristotle*, 2 vols. (Oxford: Clarendon Press, 1892), II.466–7.

with a view to deterrence or coercion simply: Because most people are obedient only through compulsion, they are moved not by arguments or by the noble, but by punishment alone; there are those, in fact, who are so "incurable" that the laws cannot educate or retrain them, and they must therefore be "banished" (*NE* 1180a5–10).

It seems a sober realism on Aristotle's part that now presents the law less in terms of its highest aims and more in terms of its deterrent force and remedial effect. His presentation contrasts with his careful avoidance of the question of coercion and punishment in the discussion of justice. If the controlling metaphor in his discussion of corrective or retributive justice is mathematics – the calculation involved in restoring an aggrieved party to "equality" – Aristotle now speaks more bluntly of punishments and penalties and, in general, of the application of pain as a form of chastisement or remedy. Although the law is "drawn from a certain prudence and intelligence," it must have "compulsive power" if it is to oppose effectively the "impulses" (*hormai*) of the many (*NE* 1180a21–2). As a common concern, then, the law comes to sight in light of the need for coercion. To be sure, in being drawn from a certain prudence and intelligence, the law wishes to use its compulsive power in the service of right reason, and because "the law is not oppressive when it commands what is equitable," it attracts less enmity than does the command of a single human being (*NE* 1180a22–4). Yet, even though the laws are "speeches," they are speeches that must carry a big stick.

Aristotle acknowledges that most political communities badly neglect nurture and education as a common concern. For most are "utterly careless" and even reflect a kind of barbarism, "each man living as he wishes, like the Cyclops laying down what is right for his children and wife" (*NE* 1180a26–9; cf. *Pol.* 1253a22–3). In the light of this actual experience, Aristotle is led to consider education as a private matter, saying that in most cities, those who care to bring their children or friends to virtue must do so, as well as they can, in their capacity as parents and friends. Yet moral education can never be a wholly private affair. The obvious difficulty, for both political communities and private educators, is that in pertaining to our associations and common relations, such education ultimately falls under the purview of justice and the law. It matters not, Aristotle observes, whether the laws are written or unwritten, or whether they educate one person or many; they necessarily superintend the common concerns connected with virtue. For this reason, among others, there is no way to evade the influence of the laws and, more fundamentally, the regime. To be truly effective, the one who cares about education would have to become a lawgiver (*NE* 1180a32–b2).[10]

In a concession to private education, however, Aristotle allows that it has two advantages: It can command obedience on the basis of "affection" and "kinship," and it can take account of what is fitting with regard to each individual (*NE* 1180b2–14). By contrast, the law may not attract enmity, but neither does it inspire love, and by its very nature, law speaks only to what is general or "for the most part," and not to the individual or to particular circumstances. This latter fact leads Aristotle to consider whether there is a science that pertains to education or whether one can learn all one needs to know by way of experience alone, without rising to the level of general principles and so science. Yet he quickly, if tentatively, dismisses the latter idea: If it is through the laws that human beings become good, then one must proceed to the general principle and comprehend this as far as possible (*NE* 1180b20–5). If, in fact, we become good through law, then regardless of the advantages of private education or its necessity, we must still undertake an examination of law. We must investigate the possibility of a science of law.

Accordingly, Aristotle's consideration of education and law returns him to the question raised at the beginning of the *Ethics*: What is the capacity, art, or science that superintends the human good? But he now reformulates the question: From what or how, he asks, does one become a lawgiver if not through the political art (*politikē*, *NE* 1180b28–30)? This question proves immediately complicated. While law is the "product" of the political art, politics itself contrasts with other arts and sciences in presenting a dichotomy between its actual practitioners, the

---

[10] In part for this reason, Richard Bodéüs understands Aristotle's ethics as having as its primary purpose "the instruction of the lawgiver." He argues, "for Aristotle, as for Plato, legislation is the tool required for the realization of the ends pursued by life in the city, that is, not only political life but life in general as lived in the framework constituted by the political organization. . . . Put into perspective in this way, Aristotelian ethics, far from describing an individual ethics alien to politics, presents, on the contrary, the essential body of learning with which the lawgiver must fortify himself when legislating" (*The Political Dimensions of Aristotle's "Ethics*," p. 123).

politicians, who practice politics but seem incapable of transmitting their capacity, and the "knowers" or the Sophists, who do not practice politics but profess to transmit its art or science. Aristotle is critical of both groups. Although the politicians would seem to know what they are doing on the basis of a "certain power and experience rather than thought," they nevertheless prove incapable of transmitting their capacity even to their own sons and friends, and thereby of supplying their community with this very great good (*NE* 1180b35–1181a9). The Sophists classify politics with rhetoric or some inferior art, and in wrongly supposing that one can legislate simply "by collecting the well-regarded laws," they neglect the fact that the very selection of the best laws involves "an act of understanding" – that "to judge correctly is a great thing," which requires knowing both what is noble and what suits a particular circumstance or individual (*NE* 1181a12–18). Consequently, neither the politicians, who practice the political things, nor the Sophists, who profess to teach them, possess that art or science by which one becomes a legislator.

In light of these difficulties, Aristotle concludes the *Ethics* by suggesting that it is necessary to begin again (*NE* 1181b24). We seek what has not yet been discovered, if indeed it exists: a political science. The completion of our philosophy of human affairs is undertaken in recognition of the complex nature of such an undertaking, which involves the apprehension of general principles as well as of particulars that can be known only on the basis of experience and may be covered by no general principle. Moreover, Aristotle's treatment of education and law has indicated that, compared with his investigation of the good in the *Ethics*, this new beginning and the political science at which it aims are not primarily concerned with the question of the best simply, and so with a peak or possibility that may be in a crucial respect beyond the law. Rather, from an awareness of the necessities, pedagogic and otherwise, that impinge upon political life, the investigation of the *Politics* seeks to discover the education that is "in common." A complete understanding of citizenship and especially of the education that the law, well or badly, supplies requires a study of politics from the ground up.

At the end of the *Ethics*, Aristotle offers an outline of this study that corresponds loosely to the plan of his *Politics* (*NE* 1181b15–23). Yet, he opens the *Politics* with an issue not included in this plan: the

naturalness of the city or political community.[11] Although he introduces this issue in connection with the question of the good, the naturalness of the city finally proves bound up with the necessary existence
of law – with "adjudication" (*dikē*) and justice (*dikaiosynē*) – and thus
with the arrangement of the political community understood as the
"regime."

THE POLITICAL COMMUNITY AS NATURAL END

Aristotle begins his *Politics* by appealing to evidence we can "see" –
that seems self-evident: Every community or partnership (*koinonia*) is
constituted "for the sake of some good." He quickly posits that the city
(*polis*), understood as the political community, is the one that aims
at the most authoritative good and embraces all other associations
(*Pol.* 1252a1–7). This supposition immediately calls to the fore a difficulty: What is the nature of a city's authority or rule? Some people
suppose that there is no essential difference among political expertise,
the expertise of a king, household management, and mastery. Or they
suppose that the only significant difference among them is the number of those ruled in each case, and therefore that there is no essential
difference between a "great household" and a small city or between
a king and a political man (*Pol.* 1252a7–17). Aristotle rejects this

---

[11] Simpson offers a helpful overview of the commentary on this plan (*A Philosophical
Commentary on the "Politics" of Aristotle* [Chapel Hill: University of North Carolina
Press, 1998], pp. 11–14). As for the inclusion of Book I of the *Politics*, he observes,
"The topic of investigation for the *Politics* (as the last chapter of the *Ethics* has just
shown) is legislation and regimes. But what legislation legislates and what regimes
arrange is the city.... Consequently the city must be the focus of the present study
since it is the object of both legislation and regimes (see 3.1.1274b32–38)" (p. 14).
See also Aquinas, *Commentary on the "Nicomachean Ethics,"* 2 vols., trans. C. I. Litzinger
[Chicago: Henry Regnery Company, 1964], II.2180, who treats the first book of the
Politics as a "connecting link": "he [Aristotle] sets down in the first book certain
principles from which he says we must begin. This will serve as a connecting link
with the work on the *Politics* and as a conclusion to the whole work of the *Ethics*." But
compare Vander Waerdt's objections: "It is generally agreed that the outline at *EN*
1182b12–24 does not introduce the extant *Politics*. It alludes only to books ii (b15–
17), v–vi (b17–20; cf. 1289b23–26, 1301a19–25, 1316b31–36) and vii–viii (b20–21).
Moreover, the further investigation of how each of the regimes is ordered and what
laws and customs it uses (b22) is absent from our *Politics*" ("The Political Intention of
Aristotle's Moral Philosophy," [*Ancient Philosophy* 5 (Spring 1985)], p. 80). Simpson's
argument in favor of reordering the books of the *Politics* – placing Books VII and
VIII after III and before IV, V, and VI – offers some response to Vander Waerdt's
objections (see pp. xvii–xx and p. 10, n. 10).

view – it is neither nobly said nor true – and he indicates that the grounds of his rejection will become clear to those who proceed using the "usual method." The usual method is to break a compound whole, such as the city, into its constituent parts.[12] Proceeding in this way will allow us to see how the types of rule differ from one another and whether there is an art or expertise that can be acquired concerning each (*Pol.* 1252a17–22).

In investigating the political community, and the view of those who deny a fundamental distinction between mastery and political rule, then, Aristotle proceeds as if seeing the political community develop "naturally from the beginning" (*Pol.* 1252a24).[13] The elementary associations – the associations without which each partner cannot exist – are two. The first is the union of male and female, who come together not through choice but through the natural striving imbued in all animals and plants to procreate and so "to leave another like oneself." The second is the association of ruler and ruled, whose common advantage, preservation, is achieved by the foresight of the former and the labor of the latter (*Pol.* 1252a26–b1).[14] From these two "communities" begins the evolution to the city, first from the household, which is "constituted in accord with nature" for the sake of satisfying "daily needs" or mere life, then to the village, which is a natural outgrowth of our desire not simply for mere life but for living well. But the evolution of human communities goes beyond the household and the

---

[12] See again Schofield's discussion of method in *Saving the City: Philosopher-Kings and Other Classical Paradigms* [New York: Routledge, 1999), pp. 118–22.

[13] For a thorough analysis of Aristotle's treatment of the naturalness of the city in Book I, chs. 1 and 2, see Wayne H. Ambler, "Aristotle's Understanding of the Naturalness of the City" *Review of Politics* 47 (Winter 1985): 163–85. As Ambler points out, Aristotle's contention about the naturalness of the city would have been a challenge to both the orthodox (pious) view and the Sophistic view (pp. 163–4). Ambler goes on to show, however, that Aristotle presents a complicated challenge to his own initial assertions concerning the naturalness of the city. Frank offers a far-reaching argument regarding Aristotle's view of nature, especially its mutability, and the naturalness of the city in ch. 1 of *Democracy of Distinction*.

[14] Ambler notes, "The simplicity and abstractness of the first two associations thus serve this general purpose: they are examples of associations which are natural without qualification. They establish a standard of what a natural association is, or at least of what one kind of natural association is" ("Aristotle's Understanding of the Naturalness of the City," pp. 167–8). But Ambler offers a specious ground for the "naturalness" of these first two associations – that each partner could not exist without the other. At least in the literal sense, this is true in neither case. Nevertheless, Ambler is correct in suggesting that Aristotle holds up these associations as models of a kind.

village because the fully self-sufficient association with respect to living well is the city or *polis*, the properly constituted political community. The city is a "termination point of full self-sufficiency," which, as the completion of an evolution from the first communities, would appear to be wholly natural (*Pol.* 1252b27–9).

In the course of this evolutionary tale, however, Aristotle indicates some doubt concerning the original claim that the first associations are themselves wholly natural; indeed, the household itself must be "constituted" and the Cyclops must "lay down" a law for his wife and children (*Pol.* 1252b12–13, 22–3). Moreover, Aristotle points up the inadequacy of the evolutionary account by treating more fully the question of the city as an end. Human beings, properly speaking, are in need of the city and incomplete outside of it, and the city is self-sufficient and natural as the community that completes or perfects the human being. But what this completion consists in – in what sense a human being is, in Aristotle's famous phrase, "by nature a political animal" – needs much clarification. As he indicates, since bees and any of the herd animals would appear also to belong to communities, there may seem to be little difference between a herd, a hive, and a city. In the face of this difficulty, he proposes that the distinctive aspect of a human community is connected with our capacity for speech. For all animals can make their "perception" of the pleasant and the painful known through the voice, but speech, which belongs to human beings alone, can make clear the "advantageous and the harmful, and so also the just and the unjust." Through speech, human beings are capable of more than the perception of pleasant and painful – "they alone have perception of the good and the bad, and the just and the unjust, and the rest." It is a "community of this sort," Aristotle insists, that "makes a household and a city" (*Pol.* 1253a1–2, 7–18).[15]

---

[15] In parsing this passage of the *Politics* in his *Finding the Mean: Theory and Practice in Aristotelian Political Philosophy* (Princeton, NJ: Princeton University Press, 1990), Stephen Salkever first emphasizes the role of *logos* and interest: "Human beings are unique in having the capacity to perceive what is best for them ('living well') and to order their lives according to that perception rather than responding to each moment as if it were a new world. Justice is such an ordering, and it is like politics neither simply natural nor desirable in itself, but desirable only as a way in which 'living well' or simply 'our interest' can be brought into being" (p. 75). But then Salkever acknowledges the role of law: "The sense in which we are political animals can now be formulated in this way: Human beings are uniquely capable of, and uniquely in need of, a reasonable perception of their interest, and such a perception

If Aristotle's first outline of the city's development suggests that the city is natural in being the termination point of a natural evolution from the original associations, the incompleteness of this outline alone sheds doubt on its conclusion. Nevertheless, the discussion prepares the ground for the claim that the city is naturally more than an aggregation of individuals or even families – that it is, rather, a whole of which human beings are the "parts."[16] As such a whole, he insists, the city is necessarily prior to each of its members, and it defines the function and power of each in accord with his or her contribution to the whole. In making this argument, Aristotle speaks from the perspective of the political community: The city may be the termination point of an evolution driven by the human desire to live well – in this sense, "every city is natural" (*Pol.* 1253b30–1) – yet the highest end proves to be not the good life of any single individual, but the good of the city as a whole. It is in speaking from this perspective that Aristotle introduces the consideration of justice and argues that the good of the city and that of the individual coincide in the way of life that the political authority establishes through law (*nomos*) and adjudication (*dikē*) (*Pol.* 1253a30–4).[17] That law and adjudication are necessary

(and therefore a good life) is somehow dependent upon the presence of *nomoi*" (p. 77). This dependence on *nomos*, however, cannot be captured wholly by an appeal to interest. Moreover, while most commentators point to the capacity of speech to bring human beings together, it is equally important to see that speech has also the capacity to divide us. Speaking of the "double-edged faculty of speech," Paul Rahe observes, "According to the peripatetic philosopher, *logos* serves initially to clarify the advantageous and the harmful; only thereafter and 'as a consequence (*hōste*)' of this essentially private concern is the faculty of rational speech applied to the just and the unjust as well" (Paul H. Rahe, *Republics Ancient and Modern: The Ancien Régime in Classical Greece* [Chapel Hill: University of North Carolina Press, 1994], p. 42; see also pp. 21, 209, 215).

[16] As Ambler observes, the first argument regarding the naturalness of the city "implies that man should serve the city, for it is a superior natural being of which he turns out to be a part, while the second [argument regarding the naturalness of the city] indicates that it is the city's responsibility to bring man to his natural end" ("Aristotle's Understanding of the Naturalness of the City," p. 170). By the account at the end of I.2, however, this "natural end" is justice, which, as the *Nicomachean Ethics* has underlined, is "another's good."

[17] Arguing against Arendt's version of Aristotle, Catherine Zuckert observes: "Although it is true that the *Politics* begins by showing that the *polis* does not emerge until or unless the necessities of life are provided by the *oikos*, it is not true, as Arendt claims, that the *polis* is characterized by a sharp distinction between public and private. On the contrary, Aristotle shows that the regime (*politeia*) shapes and so infuses all aspects of private life, especially the family" (Catherine H. Zuckert, "Aristotle on the Limits and Satisfactions of Political Life," *Interpretation* 11 [May 1983], p. 186).

for our preservation alone, not to say our full flourishing, is evidenced by the fact that in their absence, human beings are "without virtue," and so "most unholy and savage" and "the worst with respect to sex and eating" (*Pol.* 1253a35–6). Through law and adjudication, the political community becomes educator, and justice (*dikaiosyne*) emerges as the definitive virtue of a human being (*Pol.* 1253a37–8).[18]

But justice is, as Aristotle observes, a "political thing": "adjudication is an arrangement of the political community, and justice is a judgment concerning the just" (*Pol.* 1253a37–9). A political community, strictly speaking, entails an "arrangement" of offices and powers – a regime – that reflects its view of justice. It is this arrangement, therefore, that is prior to every part, individuals and associations alike, and defines the function and power of each. As such an arrangement, moreover, each political community represents an answer to the question that the family and village settle naturally on the basis of kinship and age: the question of who should rule. The political community, by contrast, cannot take for granted the claims of age, or even wisdom, and it cannot rely on the ties of kinship. When it comes to ruling, it must adjudicate or decide among various claims and determine the best or most authoritative one.

We thus begin to see the outlines of Aristotle's answer to those who assert that there is no distinction between political rule and simple mastery, for distinctively political rule requires an arrangement and a judgment concerning the just. The city is prior to all its parts in this regard, and even the household, which may seem natural, is ultimately

---

[18] One sees the concerns of the final chapter of *the Nicomachean Ethics* – education and compulsion – come together also at end of ch. 2 of the *Politics*. Paul Rahe observes: "Though much may separate Plato from Aristotle, on this fundamental point they were agreed: To understand the ancient Greek *polis*, one must be willing to entertain two propositions – that the political regime (*politeia*), rather than economic or environmental conditions, is the chief determinant of what one acute, ancient observer called 'the one way of life of a whole *polis*' and another dubbed 'the city's soul,' and that education in the broadest and most comprehensive sense (*paideia*) is more important than anything else in deciding the character of the regime" (*Republics Ancient and Modern*, p. 10). Nevertheless, as Rahe adds, "The ancients were by no means naïve.... Though they insisted on the primacy of *paideia*, they recognized that there is a strong case to be made for institutional balances and checks; and though they made a point of judging human affairs from the perspective of the best regime, they conceded that, in politics, one must nearly always settle for the lesser evil" (pp. 10–11).

constituted in accord with the view of justice of the city; indeed, the gods themselves prove to be made in the city's image (*Pol.* 1252b24–7). From this point of view, Aristotle's "natural beginning" is a bit of a red herring: The city presents its justice as the natural completion of a human being, yet the city is not simply natural in one respect: It must be constituted.[19] For this reason, when Aristotle returns to the question of the city in Book III of the *Politics*, he begins from the "citizen" as its most elementary part.[20]

If, in fact, citizens achieve their completion or perfection as human beings through obedience to law and justice, then the one who first constituted the political community is clearly "the cause of the greatest goods" (*Pol.* 1253a30–1). As it is now presented, this good or perfection is inseparable from the preservation and perpetuation of the political community that is its cause and the highest object of our reverence. Insofar as Aristotle's introduction to the *Politics* points to a best life for the individual, then, it points to a life of action consistent with

[19] See Nichols, *Citizens and Statesmen: A Study of Aristotle's "Politics"* [Savage, HD: Rowman & Littlefield, Publishers, 1992), p. 18: "If the city has two ends, must it not also have two beginnings? The city is indeed a strange being, for it has a second beginning, and yet its second beginning cannot be simply a beginning, for its first beginning continues in part to define its end. Like human beings themselves, who are unlike other parts of nature, the city both goes beyond its origins and remains limited by them."

[20] In *Nature, Justice, and Rights in Aristotle's "Politics"* (Oxford: Clarendon Press, 1995), Fred Miller makes what Malcolm Schofield rightly calls an "heroic attempt to make the concept of rights central to Aristotle's political philosophy" (Schofield, *Saving the City*, p. 141). Miller's argument has several important premises, among which are the following: (1) "When the polis is in a natural condition, it is governed according to natural justice and its citizens possess rights 'based on nature' (*kata phusin*)" and (2) "rights have a central place in Aristotle's politics because he understands justice as the virtue permitting co-operation for mutual advantage. As a co-operative association a just polis must recognize the claims of each of its contributing members. To recognize 'rights' in Aristotle is to acknowledge the respect for individuality which is a central theme of his political theory" (p. 17). Miller concedes that Aristotle has no robust notion of rights as derivative from man's natural or "prepolitical" state – such as in Hobbes or Locke – but the preceding premises raise two questions: (1) what is Aristotle's understanding of "natural justice"? and does it support a conception of rights?, and (2) is "the respect for individuality" indeed a central theme of Aristotle's political theory? Acknowledging that Aristotle's discussion of natural justice "suffers from a high degree of abstractness" (p. 75), Miller seems finally to define natural justice and rights in terms of each other; see especially his summary of his four main premises on pp. 137–8. See also Scholfield's criticisms in *Saving the City*, pp. 141–59, and John M. Cooper, "Justice and Rights in Aristotle's *Politics*," *Review of Metaphysics* 49 (June 1996): 859–72.

justice and in service to the community's preservation and perpetuation, not to say its very founding.[21] The education provided by the
political community accordingly presents the virtue of a citizen, and
particularly of a ruler, as the most complete human virtue, and this
is the perspective from which Aristotle begins when he takes up the
definition of the citizen in Book III.

Yet, as the *Nicomachean Ethics* shows, the question of the best or most
choiceworthy life is more complicated than Aristotle here suggests.
Consequently, when he returns to the question of the choiceworthy
life in his introduction to the best regime, he recasts the question in
such a way as to give the political perspective its due without wholly
conceding its position. By doing so, he is able to underscore the political community's own necessary commitment to law and justice, but
also the limits and dangers in elevating the activity of citizenship as the
highest activity of a human being. Before turning to Aristotle's analysis
of citizenship and law in Book III, therefore, we can gain a fuller sense
of the issues at stake in this analysis and the limits placed upon it by
turning first to his treatment of the best life in his introduction to the
best regime.

RECASTING THE QUESTION OF THE GOOD LIFE

Aristotle begins Book VII of the *Politics* by insisting that the investigation of the best regime requires first an investigation of the most
choiceworthy life (*Pol.* 1323a14–17). His early examination of this
question in the *Nicomachean Ethics*, undertaken in acknowledgment
of the political community's priority as educator and architect of the
human good, posits that the best life is the one in accord with moral
virtue, at the peak of which is the activity of ruling. In his introduction
to the *Politics*, Aristotle similarly indicates that this life is constituted

---

[21] Simpson argues that "the city is the human beings who together compose it
(3.1.1274b41)" and "the regime is the way human beings arrange themselves so
as to live together well (4(7).8.1328a35–b2)" (*Philosophical Commentary*, p. 25). But
these suggestions need to be established and, on the face of it, assume that the city
as a whole does not have a good beyond the good of each of its aggregate parts. In
short, these suggestions assume, as Simpson seems to proceed to argue, that justice
is, in the best case at least, perfectly equivalent with the good of the individual, a
question of no little dispute (see pp. 25–7).

by the city in accord with adjudication and justice and with a view to the city's own founding and perpetuation. But as he approaches the study of the best regime, it proves necessary to confront the question of the end at which the city as a whole aims and whether, indeed, there is an end higher than the city itself. In returning to a discussion of the most choiceworthy life in the context of the best regime, Aristotle proposes that the city does not order the highest end but is ordered by it, and therefore that each individual and the city as a whole must be "organized" with a view to the "better aim" (*Pol.* 1324b33–5). Yet the immediate difficulty is not simply that the most choiceworthy life is in dispute, but that this life, whatever it may be, may not be the same for all in common and for each individual. Aristotle's effort to sort through these matters begins to clarify the limits of an inquiry into the best life in connection with the city and the regime.

Aristotle seeks first to establish that the choiceworthy life, properly understood, is the one in accord with virtue.[22] Beginning from the tripartite division of goods outlined in the *Ethics* – external goods, goods of the body, and those of the soul – he argues that while all these goods belong to a truly blessed life, the goods of the soul or the virtues are most essential. His opening appeal is to the utility of virtue: No one could live well who "is afraid of the flies buzzing around him, abstains from none of the excesses when he desires to eat and drink, destroys his dearest friends for the sake of a pittance, and likewise concerning thought, is as senseless and deceived as a child or madman" (*Pol.* 1323a27–34). Moreover, the "facts" seem to support this claim,

---

[22] Aristotle includes in his consideration of the best life some propositions of the "exoteric speeches," which he considers "adequate" for his purpose (*Pol.* 1323a21–3), and there is debate over the meaning of the reference. See Newman, who questions whether Aristotle refers even to speeches of his own, though he suspects that he does (*The "Politics" of Aristotle*, 4 vols. [Oxford: Oxford University Press, 1902], III.308), as well as Lord, who inclines to J. Bernays's view that the reference is to one of Aristotle's lost dialogues (*Education and Culture in the Political Thought of Aristotle* [Ithaca, NY: Cornell University Press, 1983], p. 181), and Simpson, who emphasizes that such "external" discourses would be more popular in character (*Philosophical Commentary*, p. 197). The simplest point seems to be that Aristotle does not undertake a systematic treatment of the question of the best life but one adequate to his immediate purpose, which is to establish agreement about the most choiceworthy life for all. See also Bodéüs, who undertakes a longer discussion of the meaning and history of "exoteric" and "esoteric" works (*The Political Dimensions of Aristotle's "Ethics,"* pp. 88–92).

inasmuch as we see that "people do not gain and preserve the virtues by way of external things, but the latter by the former" (*Pol.* 1323a38–41). This appeal to the utility of virtue, however, proves inadequate. From the utilitarian point of view, that is, the virtues – Aristotle mentions courage, moderation, justice, and prudence – may be necessary, but they are not ends or goods in their own right. Some other good – wealth or power, for example – is the higher end.[23] In short, the utilitarian argument may be the most common or accessible, but we cannot establish its adequacy or truth if we do not know what the good life consists in: whether it consists in the actions of virtue for their own sake, or simply requires virtue as a means to those things that people typically desire "without limit," namely, wealth, material goods, power, and repute (*Pol.* 1323a36–8).

In moving toward the view that virtue is good in itself and the end of the best life, Aristotle offers a somewhat more subtle argument, which he prefaces with an apology for having raised utilitarian considerations in the first place: The argument from utility cannot resolve the question of the best life because the highest end has to do not with "the useful," but with "the noble" (*Pol.* 1323b11–12). Accordingly, we must determine what is most "honorable" in the threefold division of goods and the end that orders our choices. Regarding this ranking, Aristotle supposes that the soul is "more honorable than both a possession and the body" (*Pol.* 1323b16–17). If this is the correct view – and he presents it in conditional terms – then the end at which the city ought to aim is the good arrangement of the soul. In support of this conclusion, Aristotle makes two more appeals. He looks first to "the god" as a "witness" since the god is "happy and blessed not on account of the external goods but on account of himself and in being a certain sort with respect to his nature" (*Pol.* 1323b23–6). Second, he appeals to the sense that happiness must be distinguished from good fortune and suggests that because justice and prudence, unlike external goods, are not subject to chance, they are more to be identified with happiness (*Pol.* 1323b26–9; cf. *NE* 1100a35–b4, b11–22). By this account, the case for virtue relies on opinions about the soul, the god,

---

[23] As Newman points out, Aristotle later notes that "external goods are the gift of fortune" (*Pol.* 1323b27), further undermining the argument from utility (*The "Politics" of Aristotle*, III.312).

and happiness – opinions that are not argued for but clearly frame the consideration of the best life as a concern of the best regime.

Nevertheless, Aristotle seems satisfied for the moment that the first question – the most choiceworthy life for the individual – is settled, and he takes up the second question: whether this life is the same for the city. He offers several prefatory statements. The happy city is the one that is best and acts nobly since it is "impossible for the one who does not do the noble things to act nobly" (*Pol.* 1323b31–2). Although this apparent tautology raises the question of whether the city "acts" in the same way that an individual does, Aristotle presses forward with his argument by insisting also on the identity of the city's virtues with those of the individual. Because the "courage, justice, and prudence of the city have the same power and form [or shape, *morphē*] as those shared by human beings who are called just, prudent, and moderate," the best life – the one "so furnished with virtue as to share in the actions that accord with virtue" – is the same for each and for all in common (*Pol.* 1323b29–36). Acknowledging that there are those who dispute this conclusion, Aristotle promises to address their objections later (*Pol.* 1324a2–4).

It may come as a surprise, therefore, that he continues his consideration of the identity of the happiness of a human being and the city, though he asks a slightly different and more limited question: whether "it is necessary" to assert this identity. For an answer, he highlights the agreement by "everyone," or, at least, all those who ascribe living well to wealth, tyrannical power, or virtue, that the best life is the same for individual and city. On the basis of this consensus, he claims that the identity of the individual's happiness and that of the city is settled, noting that those who approve virtue as the end of the good life assert also that the happy city is the "morally serious" one (*Pol.* 1324a12–13). It is these proponents of virtue and the morally serious city that Aristotle now addresses. In particular, he arbitrates a debate within the camp of virtue lovers by way of which he arrives at the radical view that the best city is the one whose "actions" are "complete in themselves" – actions that he describes as "theoretical studies [*theoriai*] and ways of thinking [*dianoēseis*] that are for their own sake" (*Pol.* 1325b16–23).

Among the champions of virtue and the morally serious city, there are two matters of disagreement. The first concerns the character of the virtuous life: Is the more choiceworthy the life in which one lives as a "fellow citizen" and "shares in the city," or the life of a "stranger" and of one who is separated from the political community? Second, regardless of this distinction, which regime and disposition of the city "ought to be regarded as best" (*Pol.* 1324a14–19)? This latter question in particular is the "task of political thought and contemplation" and the focus of the "present inquiry," whereas the question of the choiceworthy life is a secondary or subordinate task (*parergon*) (*Pol.* 1324a19–23).

Yet Aristotle immediately takes up the secondary question of the choiceworthy life. The dispute over this question begins from a fundamental agreement that the best regime is the arrangement under which anyone would act well and live blessedly and that the life of virtue is the best life. Nevertheless, as their disagreement has already indicated, those who hold this position then dispute whether the most choiceworthy way of life is the "political" and "active" one or the one that is "released from all external things." The latter way of life is a "certain theoretical one, which some assert belongs to philosophy alone." Evidently, there are "pretty much" only these two lives as choices for those who are "the most ambitious [*philotimotatoi*, lit. "greatest lovers of honor"] with a view to virtue," and Aristotle confirms that he himself means by these lives the political and the philosophic (*Pol.* 1324a25–32). Thus, although he had sought to drop the question of which life is best for the individual simply, or to relegate it to a subordinate place in the inquiry, Aristotle proves unable to do so.

Indeed, the question of the best life and its relation to the city is at the forefront of the debate between those who otherwise agree that the best city is the morally serious one. The immediately curious fact is that while they champion the morally serious city as best, those who argue that the most choiceworthy life is a certain theoretical one reject political action as a good altogether. For they contend not only that despotic rule over one's neighbors is necessarily accompanied by the "greatest injustice," but that even political rule, while just, is an "impediment to one's own well-being" (*Pol.* 1324a35–7). On the other side, those who choose the political life insist that this life is "the only one for a man [*anēr*]" and that there are no virtuous actions that belong more to the individual or private life than to the life of the city in common. Despite their own approval of the morally serious city, however, this second group's argument leads finally to the claim that mastery and the tyrannical regime is the "only happy one"

(*Pol.* 1324a37–b3) – a claim that finds support in the experience of actual regimes, among which "the standard [*horos*] of both the laws and the regime" is the exercise of mastery over their neighbors (*Pol.* 1324b3–5). Whereas the laws among most peoples are a confused "heap," the regimes that possess some organization *all* aim at domination, and their laws and customs, which encourage prowess in war, are directed toward the virtue of courage in particular. Aristotle offers examples of several peoples, Greek and non-Greek, whose distinct practices are nonetheless alike in honoring the courageous in war against their enemies (*Pol.* 1324b5–11). Thus, some of those who are ambitious regarding virtue accord with the usual practice in pursuing conquest and domination, whereas others of this same camp disdain this practice and reject the active and political life, even when it is just, as truly choiceworthy.

In considering the views of these two groups, Aristotle begins by questioning whether the usual practice presents the full picture, noting that "it might seem very strange" that the task of political expertise is to acquire mastery over "those nearby, both those who wish it and those who do not." In this context, he recalls the claim that political expertise and lawgiving are intertwined: How could conquest belong to political expertise when it is not even lawful (*Pol.* 1324b22–7)? Although the unique character of political science has already been noted, Aristotle here points to the example of the "other sciences," such as medicine and piloting, whose proper expertise does not consist in either persuading or compelling their patients or passengers to accept their rule, but in bringing them to health or safety. It is true that "the many" identify political expertise with mastery, even as they reject the idea that they themselves ought to suffer what is not just or advantageous. But if there is by nature "that which is suited to being mastered and that which is not," this fact alone requires that one not seek "to master everyone." Aristotle has recourse to a rather chilling example to make his point: One ought not to hunt human beings with a view to making them one's feast or sacrifice, but only those creatures – wild edible animals – that are by nature suited to this end (*Pol.* 1324b29–41).

Moreover, he also hypothesizes, "if it were indeed possible for a city to be settled by itself somewhere," it would not be arranged with a view to war or the conquest of neighbors, since neither possibility would exist. If such a city were to establish "morally serious laws," then, it would be "nobly governed" (*Pol.* 1324b41–1325a3). Barring the problem of civil war, a city settled in such fortuitous circumstances would be free to aim at an end higher than war, and although Aristotle indicates that all the concerns connected with war are to be regarded as noble, he insists that they are not the highest. The highest end for a city, a family, and every community is "the good life and the happiness that is possible for them" (*Pol.* 1325a5–10). While a lawgiver must take account of the problem of war, this sad necessity ought not to be confused with the political community's best aim.

If war or conquest is not the highest end of the city, how does one settle the debate between the two sides who are ambitious with a view to virtue but clearly differ with regard to its use or practice? Those who reject the holding of political offices as the proper practice of a virtuous life believe that "the life of a free person is something other than that of a political expert." By contrast, their opponents insist that "it is impossible for the one who does not act to act well, and that good action is happiness" (*Pol.* 1325a18–23). The debate turns, accordingly, on the relation between virtue and action.

On the one side, Aristotle agrees that the life of a free man is better than that of a master because "there is nothing holy in using a slave as a slave" and "command with respect to the necessary things in no way shares in the noble" (*Pol.* 1325a25–6). But he seems willing to go only this far in favor of the side that rejects the active life, in the first place because he rejects the idea that all rule is identical with mastery. Referring to his treatment of master and slave in Book I of the *Politics*, he suggests that just as there is a distance between a master and a slave, so there must be a distance between the rule over free men and the rule over slaves. More importantly, he agrees with those who insist that "happiness is a certain action" and that the ends connected with actions of justice and moderation involve many noble things (*Pol.* 1325a32–4). Nevertheless, as the proponents of this position acknowledge, this argument without qualification leads to the conclusion that tyranny or "to rule over all" is best, for only in such a case does one have "authority over the greatest number and noblest of actions" (*Pol.* 1325a34–7). But, as Aristotle proceeds to show, those who champion the political life err most grievously in this matter. For by their own account, their happiness consists in the actions of virtue, yet significant deviations from virtue would be entailed in the transgressions of nobility and justice involved in conquest.[24] Particularly among those who are "similar" and "equal," absolute rule, as opposed to ruling and being ruled in turn, is "against nature" (*Pol.* 1325b3–10). As for the one who has both superiority in virtue and the power to practice the best things, Aristotle observes that it is noble for others to follow such a person and just to obey him (*Pol.* 1325b10–12). Yet, even in such a case, one requires not only virtue but also the power to act – one may possess the virtue appropriate to ruling but meet resistance that must be put down.

The education to virtue that places the political community and the life connected with it in the place of highest reverence also assumes that the greatest and noblest of actions belong to the statesman or ruler. Nevertheless, Aristotle now shows, these actions are not simply available to the one who seeks and may even deserve to undertake them. In the absence of a revolution to a kind of permanent kingship, citizenship in a regime and therefore under the law always involves ruling and being ruled in turn. Only perhaps in a situation in which the law has broken down and must be reconstituted might it be possible for the most ambitious regarding virtue to achieve their aims. When the law is primary and preeminent, however, a ruler is properly under the law and a guardian of it.

The difficulty Aristotle thus illuminates is that especially for those who love virtue and seek its activity as best, such a subordination to law is never wholly satisfactory. Moreover, the education supplied by the political community in no way resolves – indeed, it creates – the tension between the demands of citizenship and the greatest aims of the virtuous. As Aristotle suggests in his discussion of citizen virtue in Book III of the *Politics*, it is perhaps because the virtue of the ruler and that of the citizen are not the same that "Jason said he was hungry except when he was tyrant" (*Pol.* 1277a23–5), and the portrait of magnanimity in the *Ethics* shows that in the absence of fortuitous circumstances, the

---

[24] It is important to see that this argument is framed in the terms set by the proponents of the active life, since Aristotle shows that their own understanding of virtue establishes the limit of the argument in favor of this life. Cf. Darrell Dobbs's suggestion that this argument is the "philosopher's," a claim that he uses to attack the view that Aristotle is willing to tolerate slavery under certain conditions (Dobbs, "Natural Right and the Problem of Aristotle's Defense of Slavery," *Journal of Politics* 56 [February 1994], p. 70.)

love of virtue that distinguishes the morally serious human being leads not to activity but to inaction and idleness. Without the aid of fortune, it seems, the one who longs for noble action must either undertake conquest or become idle, and whereas the former action would constitute a stain upon his virtue, the alternative, idleness, is hardly the measure of a happy life.

Aristotle nonetheless insists that if the considerations he has laid out are "nobly said" and "happiness is assumed to be good action," then the active life is indeed the best life in common for the whole city and for each (*Pol.* 1325b14–16). How, then, is the political community to confront the difficulty created by its own education to virtue? Aristotle's solution is neither to lower the aim of this education – happiness understood as the virtue of the human being – nor to insist on the absolute or inviolable character of the law. Rather, he suggests, the problem presented by this education points in the direction of a more fundamental fact about human nature: As a part of the human quest for happiness, the longing for virtue involves the desire for self-sufficiency. It is on these grounds, and by way of a consideration of human action itself, that Aristotle suggests the radical view with which he concludes the argument between those who prefer the active and political life and those who prefer a certain theoretical one or philosophy. For he reinterprets action and the active way of life to include thought – study and thinking that are "complete in themselves" and "for their own sake" – and suggests that the political community may be organized so that its highest aim is action understood in this sense (*Pol.* 1325b16–23).

The education Aristotle lays out in his account of the best regime presents this possibility in the form of a life of leisure in which the arts and music figure most prominently. This life is neither wholly political nor wholly philosophic – neither wholly devoted to the city nor separated from it.[25] Rather, as a middle ground between the two,

---

[25] In my analysis of the debate that Aristotle adjudicates, I emphasize the difficulties and impasses that each side confronts, and therefore especially the problems that the education of the best regime poses. More must be said about the character of the life at which this education aims. I take up this question more fully in Chapter 6, but for different views on the character of this life, and especially its connection with philosophy, compare Simpson, *Philosophical Commentary*, pp. 206–10, 237–43 and Bodéüs, *The Political Dimensions of Aristotle's "Ethics*," ch. 2 with Lord, *Education and Culture in the Political Thought of Aristotle* (Ithaca, NY: Cornell University Press, 1983), pp. 188–92, P. A. Vander Waerdt, "Philosophy and Kingship in Aristotle's Best

it manages to preserve the political community as a community of free persons under the law and to redirect those most ambitious with respect to virtue to higher and more self-sufficient actions than those to which the political community on its own terms would point. Aristotle's program of education in the best regime, accordingly, is a solution to a problem.

We see, moreover, the complementarity of his *Nicomachean Ethics* and *Politics*, for the full investigation of the good requires the study Aristotle undertakes in the *Ethics*, especially his accounts of prudence, friendship, pleasure, the contemplative life, and happiness. Aristotle's brief mention of philosophy as one of the virtues of the best regime may well hold out the life of wisdom as a possibility other than tyranny for some of those who long to exercise their virtue (*Pol.* 1334a22–5), but in the *Politics* we see most clearly the necessities and limits that shape political life even within the best regime. We can therefore appreciate better the practical and theoretical significance of the life of leisure as the political expression of the life Aristotle himself calls best.

As the highest in Aristotle's ranking of lives, the life of wisdom is in some tension with the rule of law, not least because the law cannot wholly tolerate a competitor to its authority as right reason. Aristotle's careful treatment of law and justice in the *Nicomachean Ethics* – the deftness with which he deflects the Thrasymachean attack on justice and his accounts of natural justice and equity, for example – is matched by a similar discretion in his *Politics*. Nevertheless, it is clear that however necessary law is for political stability and moral education, it is not simply wise and must find its place within a broader horizon than the political community can supply. The law must be open to guidance even as it guards against the usurpation of its authority. In this respect, Aristotle's treatment of the best regime is both radical and sober; it does justice to the highest aim of political life while tempering the hopes of those devoted to this aim.

Our understanding of the education of the good citizen and especially the status of law in this education is further deepened by Aristotle's treatment of the citizen in Book III of his *Politics*. For in Book III, Aristotle not only undertakes to identify or define the citizen,

Regime," *Phronesis: A Journal of Ancient Philosophy* 30(3) (1983), pp. 255–64; and Bartlett, "The 'Realism' of Classical Political Science," *American Journal of Political Science* 38 (May 1994), pp. 382–4, 393–5.

but also explores the fundamental political question: Who should rule? To address this latter question, he must finally arbitrate the dispute regarding merit, which he mentions in his account of distributive justice in the *Ethics,* only to put it aside. The difficulties involved in arbitrating this dispute underline its explosive character – its connection with the deepest concerns of justice – and, accordingly, the need for the extraordinary evenhandedness with which Aristotle treats all the claims to rule. These difficulties eventually point also to another crucial political question: whether it is better, or more advantageous, for the best man or the best laws to rule. In coming to a clearer understanding of this question, especially of its significance for the demands of law upon citizens and the limits of those demands, we are better prepared to appreciate the fine line Aristotle will ultimately draw between our necessary obedience to law and our freedom from it.

5

Citizenship and the Limits of Law

THE IDENTITY OF THE CITIZEN

Aristotle's consideration of the dispute over rule is preceded and made necessary by the problem with which he introduces Book III and presents first as a practical and legal matter: the problem of the city's identity (*Pol.* 1274b32–4). He indicates that he will proceed by dividing the city, a composite whole, into its component parts (*Pol.* 1274b38–41; cf. 1252a17–20). This is formally the procedure he employed at the beginning of the *Politics* when he divided the political community into the natural associations that form for the sake of some good and then established the city as the natural whole that completes the human quest for the good. In Book III, by contrast, Aristotle begins from a part of the city whose identity is an object of dispute: the citizen.[1] By

---

[1] The use of the same method but different elements in analyzing the city already suggests that the question of its identity cannot be resolved deductively (cf. Schofield, *Saving the City: Philosopher-Kings and Other Classical Paradigms* [New York: Routledge, 1999], pp. 118–22) or rest on apparently "self-evident" premises (cf. the beginning of the *Politics*); the resolution of the question, rather, requires the arbitration of this dispute. Simpson offers a way of reconciling Books I and III, which are considered by some commentators to evidence Aristotle's confusion regarding the "parts" of the city. Simpson suggests, in short, "The city... *comes to be* out of households, but it *is* a multitude of citizens" (*A Philosophical Commentary on the "Politics" of Aristotle* [Chapel Hill: University of North Carolina Press, 1998], pp. 133–4; emphasis in text). He goes on to argue that the arguments of Books I and III clarify the sense in which the city is prior to the individual and the citizen to the city: "the city... is prior as the whole to the parts that it perfects, but the citizens are prior as the parts to the whole that

Book III, the question of the political community has become a part of a larger investigation of the regime, and Aristotle is considering the city not as a natural whole but first and foremost as an arrangement of offices having an authoritative ruling element and directed toward the end established by that element (*Pol.* 1274b36–8, 1279a25–7, 1289a15–18). In this context, the city acquires its identity, as does the citizen, through the institution of a particular regime, and the identity of the city becomes most obviously a question when it must be constituted – when it is founded or undergoes a revolution.

In defining the citizen, Aristotle confronts the immediate difficulty that just as in times of crisis and revolution, people dispute whether it was the city that acted, or the oligarchs or tyrant, so they argue over "whom one ought to call a citizen, and what a citizen is" (*Pol.* 1275a1–2; cf. 1274b23–6). As the disagreements regarding distributive justice and rule will illustrate, whom one ought to call a citizen may differ from what a citizen is in practice. Although the identification of a citizen varies across regimes, Aristotle first seeks a generic definition. That there exist common criteria is suggested by the fact that ordinary usage typically rules out certain possibilities: Aliens, slaves, and children are not considered citizens in the full sense; nor does being subject to adjudication and law make one a citizen. Rather, the "citizen in the unqualified sense is defined by nothing so much as by sharing in judgment and rule" (*Pol.* 1275a22–3). In fact, the consensus that citizenship involves sharing in rule anchors the dispute over the identity of the citizen, for this dispute concerns the different principles of merit that regimes employ in identifying those entitled to share in rule.[2]

As a consequence, when this generic definition is given substance, we see that it describes most broadly democratic citizenship since the

they define. Individuals as individuals thus exist for the city (since it perfects them), but the city subsists in the individuals as citizens (since it *is* them)" (p. 134; emphasis in text). Yet, it must be added – and is added by the considerations of Book III – that the regime is prior to both city and citizen.

[2] Following Grote, Newman distinguishes between "wholes" that are mere aggregates of their parts – "aggregates like a heap" – and those that possess an "essence" or "First Cause" of their own and are more than their constituent elements – "aggregates like a syllable (organic or formal)" (*The "Politics" of Aristotle*, 4 vols. [Oxford: Oxford University Press, 1902], III.131). If, in Book I, Aristotle attempts to present the city as a natural whole in this latter regard, in Book III he underscores the conventional character of the city's "essence" or, more simply, definition.

other regimes reserve the offices involving deliberation and rule for progressively fewer numbers, and in some cases have no recognized assembly or *demos* (*Pol.* 1275b7–8).[3] The definition may therefore apply across regimes but only by abstracting from more significant differences.[4] Aristotle concludes, nevertheless, by identifying the city as a "multitude" of those who share in the office of deliberation and – a multitude that is "adequate with a view to a self-sufficient life" (*Pol.* 1275b18–21). How the requirements of the city's self-sufficiency bear on citizenship remains to be considered. In particular, it is not yet clear whether those who perform the functions necessary to the city's existence and those who perform the functions belonging to its highest end or purpose have equal claim to rule.

By drawing out the component of office-holding or rule in citizenship, however, Aristotle confirms the crucial role of the regime in defining a citizen and therefore the necessity of an agreement concerning who should rule. Accordingly, he underscores the seemingly conventional as opposed to natural character of citizenship. In practice or standard usage, he acknowledges, a citizen is defined as one born of citizen parents, but this emphasis on the natural principle of birth obscures the basic "agreement" regarding rule required at every political community's founding. With respect to the view that citizens are made and not born, Aristotle concurs with the sophist Gorgias's witticism that "just as mortars are made by mortar-makers, so also Lariseaeans are made by craftsmen, for some are Larisa-makers" (*Pol.* 1275b26–30). The institution of citizenship by the "first households"

---

3 Curtis Johnson argues that Aristotle's first definition or "first revised definition" – "one who shares in indeterminate office" – is the one that is most applicable to democracies. This definition is then revised, he suggests, to become "he who enjoys the right of sharing in deliberative and judicial office" or "authority" because public juries and popular assemblies ("indeterminate offices") are not present everywhere: "This definition is obviously superior to the earlier ones, for it succeeds, as they do not, in making citizenship dependent upon a universal element in constitutions, a certain kind of authority rather than a certain kind of office" (see Curtis Johnson, "Who Is Aristotle's Citizen?," *Phronesis: A Journal for Ancient Philosophy* 29(1) (1984), 73–9.

4 See again Johnson, "Who Is Aristotle's Citizen?": "Different states have different constitutions, some nearer, some further removed from the best. And, as constitutions differ, so too do the citizens within them. One must, therefore, not only show who citizens are 'in the absolute sense'; one must also take account of the variety of practices found in different states and how the difficulties raised by these various practices can themselves be resolved by reference to the ideal definition" (p. 81).

or "founders" may seem to have a natural beginning, but the conventional and controversial character of citizenship clearly emerges in a time of regime change, when those who were not citizens are made citizens; Aristotle offers as an example Cleisthenes' reforms after the fall of the tyrants in Athens.[5]

The dispute in such cases centers on the question of justice – people disagree "not about who is a citizen, but whether one is a citizen justly or unjustly" – and therefore seeks to establish the just grounds of citizenship: "supposing that 'unjust' and 'false' have the same power," is one who is not a citizen justly truly a citizen (*Pol.* 1275b37–1276a2)? In confronting this question, however, Aristotle simply reasserts the distinction typically made in practice between the requirements of justice and the identity of the citizen, and he thus insists that the citizen is defined "by a certain office," whether the office is held justly or unjustly (*Pol.* 1276a3–4). For all practical purposes, this argument holds, since we see that in fact some rule, even if unjustly. Consistent with such purposes, Aristotle tries to drop the question of justice. Yet this is a move that becomes less tenable as his investigation continues. The effort to find a generic definition of a citizen simply underscores the significance of the dispute regarding distributive justice, which Aristotle will eventually have to address.[6]

CITIZENSHIP, REVOLUTION, AND THE REGIME

Having raised the problem of justice, Aristotle returns to the original question: "when the city acted and when it did not" (*Pol.* 1276a8–9).

---

[5] Harvey Mansfield offers this qualification: "He [Aristotle] does not merely adopt the perspective of the sophisticated Gorgias; he tries to combine the citizen's perspective with it in order to show how the citizen is both conventional and natural. The citizen is in part conventional as the product of his city; he has been 'socialized,' as we say. But he is also a contributor to the city. He brings his natural capacities to the city, and moreover, his unsophisticated belief that his city is natural is not altogether wrong according to Aristotle, because it contains a greater truth about the citizen's responsibility which the sophisticated perspective hides from view" (Harvey C. Mansfield, *Responsible Citizenship Ancient and Modern* [Eugene: University of Oregon Books, 1994], p. 7).

[6] As Johnson notes, "It is thus by means of this 'difficulty' about the rightful claims of citizenship that Aristotle connects the discussion of citizenship with the rest of Book III ... the identity of the state is thus really a question about the rightfulness of political rule" ("Who Is Aristotle's Citizen?," p. 82).

In times of revolution, when disputes arise over whether, for example, the city is obligated to honor contracts entered into by a former ruler, the question of the city's identity needs to be settled. Although he first frames this question in terms of justice – one may disavow the actions of those regimes that exist by mastery and not for the sake of the common advantage – Aristotle notes only that on these grounds, one could as easily disavow the actions of a democracy as those of an oligarchy or tyrant. Instead of pursuing this distinction between mastery and the common advantage, then, he presents the path to resolving the problem of the city's identity as "somehow" conformable to a theoretical puzzle: what makes the city "the same and not the same" (*Pol.* 1276a17–19)? By proceeding in this way, Aristotle would appear to avoid the controversy connected with justice. Although the adequacy of this tack is finally called into doubt when this controversy returns with a vengeance, his efforts and subsequent failure to establish a formal definition of the city help to clarify the relation between the concern for justice and the limits of any definition of the citizen.

Aristotle approaches the theoretical puzzle by a process of elimination: By what criteria is a city not properly defined, or what is not the "cause" (*aitia*) of the city? Among the possibilities he dismisses, the most "superficial" are "the place and the human beings" (*Pol.* 1276a19–20). For a city may remain a single political entity while geographically divided, and it may be geographically unified while politically disjoined – indeed, as exemplified by Babylon, this latter case sheds some light on the relation between political unity and size.[7] The "sameness" of the city's inhabitants also does not provide an adequate ground of identity since human beings come into being and perish, but the city itself remains. The fact that the place and its inhabitants do not suffice as criteria – that as the "matter" of the city, they can change and the city remain the same – points Aristotle back in the direction of the regime as the cause of the city's identity: "If indeed the city is a certain community, and it is a community of citizens in

---

[7] Newman explains with the aid of Herodotus: "Herodotus (I.191) says that owing to the size of Babylon, when the outer part of it had been taken, the inhabitants of the center were unaware of the fact and continued to celebrate a festival till they learnt it" (*The "Politics" of Aristotle*, III.150).

a regime, then if the regime becomes other in form and different, it would seem to be necessary also for the city not to be the same" (*Pol.* 1276b1–4). It follows, then, that we can discover what constitutes the city by looking to the cause of its change, which is its regime. But we thus return to the problem that a citizen in a democracy differs from a citizen in an oligarchy, and Aristotle's attempt to establish the identity of the citizen by looking to its formal cause is in this regard a failure. We wish to know, as Aristotle has indicated, not simply who is a citizen in this formal sense but whom one ought to call a citizen.[8]

Moreover, as he acknowledges, the generic definition of the citizen as one who shares in judgment and rule in no way settles the question of whether it is just to release a city from contracts entered into by the former regime. This question belongs to "another argument," and it remains a legal and practical concern (*Pol.* 1276b13–15).[9] Rather than turning to the question of justice or to this other argument, however, Aristotle next examines "whether the virtue of a good man [*anēr agathos*] ought to be regarded as the same as that of a morally serious citizen [*spoudaios politēs*]" (*Pol.* 1276b16–18). That he discusses this question before addressing the dispute over justice already suggests that his investigation of the virtue of a good man and citizen will be a partial one. One would expect the virtue of these two to coincide only in a regime that is just, but the question of the justice of every regime remains unsettled.

THE GOOD CITIZEN AND THE GOOD MAN

Aristotle's investigation of the relation between the virtue of the good man and that of the morally serious citizen is complex, but the traditional view of its conclusion is that of W. L. Newman: The virtue of the good citizen and human being is the same for the ruler in the best

---

[8] For this reason also, contra Simpson, the question of the identity of the city is not yet resolved (*Philosophical Commentary*, p. 139, but see his qualification on p. 140).

[9] Simpson argues that since Aristotle "understands justice as the common good (3.12.1282b16–18), his answer would presumably be that previous agreements should be kept if keeping them would serve the common good" (*The "Politics" of Aristotle* [Chapel Hill: University of North Carolina Press, 1997], p. 80). But this suggestion skirts the question of whether there is a "common good" or for whom the good is common.

regime.[10] This view tends to overlook Aristotle's many equivocations as well as the frame within which the question is discussed. To be sure, Aristotle ultimately confines his examination of virtue to the capacities required for ruling, including the virtues of moderation, justice, and prudence, but he is fully aware of the consequent limits of his examination. One sign of his awareness is that in speaking of the good or morally serious man, he uses exclusively the strong sense of man, *anēr*, thus recalling also those virtues explicitly identified in the *Ethics* as manly and distinctive of rule: ambition and "correct anger" (*NE* 1125b8–12; 1126a36–b2). There is no doubt that ruling and its virtues constitute a peak for human beings in Aristotle's view, but that they constitute the highest human peak is borne out neither by his discussion of the virtues in the *Nicomachean Ethics* nor by his investigation of the good citizen and morally serious man in the *Politics*.

Aristotle's opening effort in this investigation concludes first in the negative: There is "not a single virtue for a citizen and a good man" (*Pol.* 1276b40–1277a1). Yet he leaves open the possibility that the virtue of the morally serious citizen and man is the same in the case of the ruler, and he begins from a simple fact. The virtue of a citizen is necessarily defined in terms of the works or functions (*erga*) that pertain to the

---

[10] See Newman, *The "Politics" of Aristotle*, III.155; also John Burnet, *The "Ethics" of Aristotle* (London: Methuen & Co., 1900), p. 212 who cites *Politics* 1276b34 and 1293b5 and observes that in the *kat' aretēn politeia*, the true *aristokrateia*, the good man and the good citizen will coincide in the ruler. See also Joachim, *Aristotle: The "Nicomachean Ethics"* (Oxford: Clarendon Press, 1951), p. 135; Rackham, trans., *Aristotle: Nicomachean Ethics* (Cambridge, MA: Harvard University Press [Loeb Classical Library], 1982), p. 266; Apostle, *Aristotle's "Nicomachean Ethics,"* (Grinell, IA: The Peripatetic Press, 1984), p. 261. Most contemporary students of Aristotle accept the traditional view, even those who emphasize the many necessities that impinge upon the good individual in political life. Bernard Yack offers a compelling account of moral conflict in Aristotle's thought but nonetheless concludes: "Aristotle sums up the basis for moral conflict in ordinary political life in his famous distinction between the good man and the good citizen (*Pol.* 1276b–78b). Only in the best regime will the good man and the good citizen have exactly the same virtues (*Pol.* 1278b)" (*The Problems of a Political Animal: Community, Justice, and Conflict in Aristotelian Political Thought* [Berkeley: University of California Press], p. 262). Thomas Smith details clearly and without compromise the political limits of the common good, but suggests that in the best case – when individuals are properly oriented toward the good – the problem of the common good can in principle at least be solved. He supports this suggestion by treating relationships of *philia*, the family and friends, as "analogical communities" to the political community (*Revaluing Ethics: Aristotle's Dialectical Pedagogy* [Albany: State University of New York Press, 2001], ch. 8).

preservation of the community and regime, "on account of which, it is necessary for the virtue of a citizen to exist with a view to the regime" (*Pol.* 1276b30–1). Given the multiplicity of regimes and of functions pertaining to the preservation of each, however, it would seem that the virtue of the morally serious citizen cannot be the same as that of the good man because it cannot be the single or complete virtue we attribute to the latter (*Pol.* 1276b31–4). Proposing another way of resolving this difficulty, Aristotle attends to the case of the best regime, yet he shows that even in the case of the best regime, the city is formed from dissimilar things. As analogies of such complex wholes, he points to a living being, the soul, the household, and property, each of which is also formed of dissimilar parts: a living being, of the soul and body; the soul, of reason and longing; the household, of male and female; property, of master and slave. Just as each of these parts must possess the virtue appropriate to its function within the whole, so even in the best regime, each citizen's perfection is defined in terms of his function in the city. The proviso of this claim, Aristotle observes, is that the best regime or morally serious city need not be constituted only of good men. Indeed, it is unclear whether any city could be constituted of a single type, a difficulty he will confront when he turns finally to the dispute over rule (*Pol.* 1277a1–5).[11]

Having distinguished among the functions of citizens, Aristotle proposes that perhaps for a "certain citizen" – the one who has the work of ruling – virtue is the same unqualifiedly for the good citizen and man (*Pol.* 1277a20–3). The argument in favor of this view requires that another unexamined proposition be true: that the virtues of a good man are properly defined in terms of the activity of ruling. Suggesting that the education of a ruler is necessarily different from that of a citizen, because a morally serious ruler is good and prudent, whereas a citizen is not necessarily prudent, Aristotle notes that the discussion reveals something additional about education. It reveals in particular the difference between the education appropriate to a master, which is concerned with the "necessary things," and the education appropriate

---

[11] But compare 1332a32–6, where Aristotle argues that the morally serious city is one in which the citizens who share in the regime are morally serious. Simpson notes the "conflict" (*Philosophical Commentary*, p. 142), as does Newman, *The "Politics" of Aristotle*, III.158).

to a ruler, which is "for himself and for the sake of his own use" and does not use another as a slave (*Pol.* 1277a33–6, b2–7). In light of this distinction, Aristotle further proposes that there is a form of rule, "political rule," which exists among those who are "similar in kind and free," and which, as such, involves the knowledge and power both to rule and to be ruled. Insisting that this knowledge and power are the virtue of the citizen, he adds that they belong also to the good man (*Pol.* 1277b14–18).

As it turns out, however, virtue connected with political rule in this sense has a dual character, which conflicts with Aristotle's initial insistence that the virtue of a good man is single and complete. As he notes regarding moderation and justice, there are "forms" of these virtues "in accord with which one will rule and be ruled," such that "there would not be a single virtue for the good one" (*Pol.* 1277b18–19). But how is such duality tenable if the virtue of the good man must be single and complete? And how is a "different form" of moderation or justice not, in essence, a different virtue?

These difficulties become all the more pressing in the case of the virtue Aristotle identifies as distinctive of the ruler, saying that prudence belongs only to a ruler, whereas "true opinion" belongs to a citizen (*Pol.* 1277b25–9). By the measure of the former, however, the latter hardly qualifies as a virtue (compare Aristotle's discussion of shame in *NE* 1128b10–35). Indeed, the two qualities differ so much with respect to the crucial criterion, knowledge, that one wonders how there can be an alternation between them: When one is ruling, one possesses prudence, and when ruled, only true opinion?[12] Hence,

---

[12] Simpson attempts the following resolution: "First, it does not follow from this that the good man is only a good man when ruling, as if, absurdly, he were to lose prudence when he left office. Rather what follows is that the virtue by which he is a good man will only be the same as the virtue by which he is a good citizen when he is actually ruling. When he is ruled his virtue as a good citizen will be different, and his virtue of prudence will not be exercised (at least not in ruling the city)" (*Philosophical Commentary*, p. 145). But this resolution leaves three serious problems: (1) the virtue of the good citizen is not single and complete, (2) the virtue of the good citizen when ruled is a lesser virtue, and (3) the life of the good citizen when ruled is not a happy life insofar as he is not exercising his highest virtues. See also Nichols, *Citizens and Statesmen: A Study of Aristotle's "Politics"* (Savage, MD: Rouman & Littlefield, Publishers, 1992), pp. 60–1, who argues that "Aristotle's discussion of the case in which the good citizen and the good man are the same constitutes a rebuke to the one who claims absolute rule for himself. Aristotle defines human goodness so that he excludes those

when Aristotle concludes that it is now apparent whether and how virtue is the same for a good man and a morally serious citizen, we are left at something of a loss.

Most apparent are the questions that the investigation has failed to address. Among these is the one central both to Aristotle's account of the good in the *Nicomachean Ethics* and to his discussion of the best regime in the *Politics*: What is the best "work" (*ergon*) or "activity" (*energeia*) of a human being? The assumption of the present discussion would appear to be that ruling is this work or activity, but the dubiousness of this assumption is indicated both by the conclusion of the *Ethics* and by Aristotle's complex treatment of the political life in his introduction to the best regime in the *Politics*. Most immediately, this assumption is called into doubt by difficulties in the current investigation. The best form of rule, Aristotle has suggested, is "political," but the distinctive work of political rule – of "ruling and being ruled in turn" – leads to a duality of virtue that fails Aristotle's earlier test that the virtue of a good man be single and complete. Moreover, political rule, properly speaking, involves only work that is free, which Aristotle has defined as for oneself and for the sake of one's own use. Yet the activity of ruling looks above all to the good of another and the community (see again *Pol.* 1276b30–1). The virtues of a ruler, like those of one who is ruled, are thus defined by their usefulness to the regime, and Aristotle himself emphasizes the moderation and justice in accord with which one would rule with a view to the good of one's fellow freemen and accept their rule in turn. Even the intellectual virtue of prudence, which he identifies as peculiar to the ruler, must be measured by this standard: As a ruler of the free, one does not employ another as a slave, but one's own action and thought are necessarily circumscribed by the requirements and needs of "another" and the community in general.

who act as if they are self-sufficient, unable to be ruled along with others, as if they have no need for moderation or justice" (p. 61). This argument is connected with the following one: "Human beings are commensurable; justice and friendship can therefore exist among citizens (*NE*, 1161a32–34); political rule is the just alternative to despotism; and law, in spite of its deficiencies, is an appropriate political standard" (p. 61). The connection of these two arguments is crucial in Nichols's analysis, but at least two problems remain: whether any regime is wholly just and whether law is an appropriate standard simply.

But if, by the very standard of freedom he lays down, rule is not the best work of a human being, then this investigation of the good citizen and man must be understood in terms of its limitations. As he wraps up the investigation, Aristotle both confirms these limitations and indicates the need to return to the dispute over justice. He begins by noting a remaining puzzle: "Is a citizen in truth one for whom it is possible to share in rule, or ought we to regard the vulgar as citizens?" (*Pol.* 1277b33–5). Each of the possible answers to this question complicates rather than resolves the problem of citizenship. If the vulgar are not citizens, it is not clear how or whether they are a part of the city, but if they are citizens, then not all share in citizen virtue. The reason for the latter difficulty is that only some members of the community will be able to undertake the work with which this virtue is associated, and Aristotle expands upon his earlier claim that the virtue of a citizen belongs only to those "who are free from the necessary things." He contrasts those who are free in this sense with slaves, who work for the sake of one man, as well as with the vulgar and laborers, who work for the community. By this measure, in fact, he notes that the virtue of a citizen does not belong "even to every free person" (*Pol.* 1278a9–10). In contrast to those who labor for the sake of another, then, the truly free labor for themselves and for their own sake. But what is the nature of such activity, and would ruling fit the criteria Aristotle lays down? These are questions he does not address in this context.

Moreover, by establishing rule and the virtues associated with it as the measure of citizenship, his definition circumscribes the political boundaries of the city, excluding in particular many who labor for the city's preservation and prosperity. By what right, however, does such an exclusion occur? Is there not a just claim to citizenship by all who work in the political community's behalf?[13] As Aristotle reiterates, the regimes represent different claims in this regard. Consequently, some who would be citizens in one regime would not be citizens in another: In an aristocracy, citizens are those who, free from necessary work, "pursue the things of virtue"; in an oligarchy, only those who meet the

---

[13] This is the concern behind many scholarly efforts to broaden Aristotle's definition of citizen. See Donald Morrison, "Aristotle's Definition of Citizenship: A Problem and Some Solutions," *History of Philosophy Quarterly* 16 (April 1993): 143–65 for an overview of such efforts.

established property assessment qualify; and in other cases, necessities
of the city may call for less exclusive criteria (*Pol.* 1278a15–29). Yet,
for all this variation, Aristotle nevertheless insists that "what is meant
most by a citizen is the one who shares in honors [or prerogatives,
timai]," and that whenever this fact is "concealed" – presumably when
the ones who are called citizens do not share in rule – a "fraud" (*apatē*)
is perpetrated upon the members of a community (*Pol.* 1278a34–40).

It is with a view to ruling as the essential and best work of citizenship
that Aristotle concludes his investigation, saying that "it is clear from
what has been said" that the virtue of the good man and morally serious
citizen is the same for "the political man and one who has authority
[*kurios*, or "control"] or who is able to have authority, either by himself
or with others, over the care of the common things" (*Pol.* 1278b3–5).
This emphasis on the care of the common things underlines the nature
of the work that such a virtuous human being would undertake (cf.
again *Pol.* 1278a9–14). Whereas in his introduction to the best regime,
Aristotle indicates that it is necessary finally to evaluate the end of the
city on the basis of the most choiceworthy life simply, and likewise to
evaluate the virtue instilled by the city's education, he here reverses
the equation. The virtue of a good human being – of a good man in
the strong sense – is defined in terms of ruling. The limitations of this
view are now evident in the current discussion. For the work of a good
citizen must be subordinated to the requirements of the political community as a whole, and in the case of rule, this work must care for the
common things. Moreover, because distinctively political rule eschews
mastery among those who are equal in freedom, it must respect this
equality and so allow for "ruling and being ruled in turn." Such equality with respect to rule, Aristotle will later say, is "already law," and the
law, both in this regard and in general, aims at the common advantage (*Pol.* 1287a14–16). Citizenship is accordingly distinguished by its
orientation toward the common advantage. Hence, by Aristotle's own
definition, its work is not simply "free," even though it may rightly be
said to belong to those who do not use one another as slaves. Citizenship's natural link with law and the common advantage necessarily sets
the terms within which its virtues are understood.

One might say, of course, that in the best case, there is no opposition between the common advantage – the advantage of the city as a

whole – and the advantage of the good ruler: Good action in behalf of the city is the best action of a human being.[14] Yet here it is important to return to the fact that the dispute regarding the principle of merit in accord with which one is entitled to rule – to be a citizen in the full sense – remains unresolved, and its resolution involves the question Aristotle raised and abruptly dismissed: Whose advantage is served (see again *Pol.* 1276a10–13)?[15] As he will show, the problem is that every claim to rule is just but partial, for each looks to the claimants' advantage but not to the common advantage of all who might be citizens; especially with regard to the "ruling offices," that is, all claims are "oligarchic" (*Pol.* 1281a32–4). The seriousness of this kind of exclusion is highlighted by the fact that the denial of the honors or prerogatives of ruling to those who are called citizens is a form of fraud.

In seeking next to determine whether there is one regime or many, Aristotle looks in particular to the end for the sake of which the city is established and argues that this end is the common advantage, understood as both life in the literal sense and living nobly. Insofar as each "governing body" (*politeuma*) – the one, the few, or the many – seeks the advantage of both ruler and ruled, it constitutes a "correct regime," whereas deviant regimes seek only the advantage of the rulers. Whether the common advantage in this full sense is possible, however, proves to be the rock upon which the resolution of the dispute over rule founders. Aristotle's failure to resolve this dispute precedes and informs his exploration of the rule of law – an exploration that clarifies the political necessity of law and its inherent limits and that ultimately recalls the central concern of the best regime: education.

[14] A recent version of this argument is that of Smith, who emphasizes equity as "the whole of virtue" (*Revaluing Ethics*, pp. 35, 50, 153, 257), but it is implicit in the traditional view that the virtues of the good citizen and human being coincide in the ruler in the best regime.

[15] Keyt rightly observes, "In Book III at least there is a central idea threading its way through his [Aristotle's] labyrinthine discussion, an idea that he wishes to develop and to which most of the topics in Book III are tied. This idea is distributive justice (see III.9. 1280a9–25, 12. 1282b14–23). Aristotle explains it in a brief chapter of his essay on justice in one of the common books of the *Nicomachean* and *Eudemian Ethics* (*EN* V = *EE* IV), and then uses it as the foundation of an argument in *Politics* III" (David Keyt, "Supplementary Essay" in *Aristotle: "Politics" Books III and IV*, trans. with Introduction and comments by Richard Robinson [Oxford: Clarendon Press, 1995], p. 127).

CITIZENSHIP AND THE RULE OF LAW

Before he turns to the exploration of law, then, Aristotle investigates several questions associated with the dispute over rule. In brief, after clarifying the grounds upon which we may identify the various regimes and their correctness, he sorts through the principles of merit that each governing body espouses in establishing its just claim to rule. Out of the resulting dispute emerges a discussion of kingship in which the question of "whether it is more advantageous to be ruled by the best man or by the best laws" is "the beginning point of the inquiry" (*Pol.* 1286a7–9).

Aristotle introduces the dispute over rule by first raising a question that seemed settled: whether there is one regime or many. At the very least, the discussion of the citizen proceeded on the assumption that there are many regimes, and Aristotle now returns to this assumption by pointing to the "governing body" (*politeuma*) as the difference in accord with which regimes vary – in a democracy, the many or the *demos* governs, and in an oligarchy, the few. Hence, as he will later say, "regime and governing body signify the same thing" (*Pol.* 1279a25–6). But he now emphasizes in addition that regimes differ regarding the end toward which they are directed and, in clarifying this difference, reiterates his claim in Book I that "a human being is by nature a political animal" (*Pol.* 1278b17–19). Regimes differ, that is, also in the extent to which they achieve the end for which the city comes into being or is established (*Pol.* 1278b15–17). The natural striving that brings human beings together in a political community involves more than the need for mere assistance. Rather, "the common advantage" also brings us together "insofar as it confers upon each a share in living nobly": "especially this" – living nobly – "is the end, both for all in common and separately." Indeed, barring great hardships, life itself has "a certain joy and natural sweetness" and a "portion of the noble" (*Pol.* 1278b23–4). The political community achieves the common advantage, it seems, both in preserving mere life and in making possible noble action.

Using the common advantage as a standard, Aristotle returns to the division of regimes in order to distinguish the correct from the deviant ones. As in Book I, he begins by describing the form of rule that constitutes the master–slave relation as well as relations within the household. Recalling that mastery seeks the advantage both of the "slave by nature" and the "master by nature," he now acknowledges that such rule seeks primarily the advantage of the master and only incidentally that of the slave (*Pol.* 1278b32–5). By contrast, "household management" – rule over one's children and wife – is "in itself" for the sake of the ruled, but incidentally it may benefit the ruler. Household management is like the arts, such as medicine, gymnastic, and piloting, which aim at the advantage of the ruled but benefit also practitioners who are ruled by their own art (*Pol.* 1278b37–1279a4). Aristotle uses the arts as an analogy for a political regime of those who, being equal and similar, merit ruling in turn. Yet he indicates the source of corruption in the case of the regime. In the "natural" arrangement of equals, "the one worthy of serving in public offices in turn, also then [when not ruling] looks to his own good, just as before, when ruling, he looked to the advantage of another" (*Pol.* 1279a10–13). But this natural order contrasts with the more typical case – the case "now" – in which those who rule seek the benefits of office for their own profit and wish to rule continuously. By this standard, correct regimes are those in which the art of rule, pursuing its natural end, aims at the common advantage and thus accords with "the just simply," whereas deviant regimes seek the advantage of the rulers and accord with "mastery" (*Pol.* 1279a13–21).

Having insisted on the common advantage as a standard, however, Aristotle maintains also that "the city is a community of the free" (*Pol.* 1279a21), a claim he proceeds to underscore in arguing that the fundamental distinction between oligarchy and democracy does not rest on the number of those who rule – the few or the many – but on poverty and wealth. Consequently, the "cause of the dispute" between the few wealthy and many poor is that "the few are well off, but all share in freedom" (*Pol.* 1280a4–5). Every claim to rule is grounded in a specific principle of merit, and while the democratic claim in particular is typically framed in terms of freedom, all who dispute also share in the freedom the *demos* claims for itself. Moreover, as the effort to define the citizen has shown, each of the various regimes defines differently the "freedom" – achieved through birth, wealth, or virtue – on which it grounds its specific right to rule. The city is a community that seeks the common advantage, then, but also is a community of those who identify themselves as free with respect to one another. Although the democratic claim is the most extensive in this regard, it must compete with other, more exclusive, claims.

Aristotle's famous schema of correct and deviant regimes is determined first by regimes' orientations toward the common advantage and second by the number of those who rule in each case: the one, the few, or the many. Hence, in answer to the question of how many regimes there are, Aristotle concludes that there are six: kingship, aristocracy, and polity as correct regimes, and tyranny, oligarchy, and democracy as deviant (*Pol.* 1279a32–b10). As commentators have noted, Aristotle's schema is puzzling not least for the fact that, with regard to the fundamental criterion – the common advantage – the distinction between deviant and correct regimes would seem to collapse: If a citizen is one who shares in rule, and the city a multitude of citizens, then by definition the common advantage is the advantage of the rulers.[16] This puzzle may seem to be resolved by the suggestion that the common advantage refers to the advantage of both ruler and ruled. Yet, this suggestion overlooks the fact that with regard to the overarching question – who rules? – *every* regime is oligarchic. Just as the essential difference between oligarchy and democracy consists not in the number of those who rule, but in the specific claim the governing body makes regarding rule, so also each of the correct regimes, which are said to seek the common advantage, presents an exclusive claim to the ruling offices. Although Aristotle begins to sort through these claims by focusing on the debate between the oligarchs and the democrats, his effort at a resolution eventually takes account of all parties in the dispute. He indicates that the investigation now looks "not only to action," but to "making clear the truth" (*Pol.* 1279b13–15).

Aristotle turns to the dispute between oligarchs and democrats in the recognition that the "defining principles" (*horos*) and so the justice of oligarchy and democracy differ. For both groups agree that justice is "the equal" but diverge in defining equality. Recalling the discussion of distributive justice in the *Ethics*, Aristotle observes that "people agree on the equality of the object, but they disagree regarding

---

[16] See, for example, Newman, *The "Politics of Aristotle,"* I.216, n. 2; Simpson, *Philosophical Commentary*, p. 151; Morrison, "Aristotle's Definition of Citizenship," pp. 144–6.

for whom" (*Pol.* 1280a17–19).[17] The source of this disagreement is that they "judge badly about the things that concern themselves" and assume that, in speaking of justice in a partial sense, they are speaking of "the whole of justice in the authoritative sense" (*Pol.* 1280a19–22, 9–11). People assume, in other words, that because they are equal in one respect – for example, freedom – they are equal in all respects.

To resolve the dispute among these partial claims, Aristotle insists, we must be guided by the "most authoritative" consideration, which is the end for the sake of which the city exists. In light of this consideration, he proceeds to establish the insufficiency of the oligarchic and democratic principles of equality. For both wealth and freedom (or, more simply, security from harm) are necessary but not sufficient conditions of the city's highest and final end, which is not living but living well. Living well, he reiterates, involves "noble actions," and therefore those who "contribute most to this sort of community share more in the city than those who are equal or greater with respect to freedom and family but unequal in political virtue, or those who exceed in wealth but are exceeded in virtue" (*Pol.* 1281a4–8).

In coming to this conclusion, Aristotle places great emphasis on the necessity of virtue by underlining the inability of the law understood merely as a compact (*sunthēkē*) for protection or exchange to ensure the "good order" (*eunomia*) of the city. Rather, he insists, "whoever takes thought for good order considers thoroughly political virtue and vice" (*Pol.* 1280b5–6; see also 1280a36–40 and b7–11). Accordingly, virtue is a concern of every city worthy of the name, and while the law certainly must guarantee "the just things," it must also make citizens "good and just" (*Pol.* 1280b6–8, 10–12). By this account, virtue constitutes the superior claim to rule both because it contributes to the good order of the political community and because, as the essential

---

[17] As Bartlett notes, "Aristotle makes something of a new beginning at chapter 12 (cf. the beginnings of *Politics* 1 and 4 and the beginning of the *Nicomachean Ethics*). The political partisans are now said to agree not merely with one another but with 'the arguments in accord with philosophy' that justice is certain equality (cf. 1282b18–20 and 1280a9–22). Justice will now be considered from the highest point of view, that of 'political philosophy' (1282b23)" ("Aristotle's Science of the Best Regime," *American Political Science Review* 88 [March 1994], p. 147; see pp. 147–8 for a discussion of Aristotle's treatment of the good life that is the end of the regime).

ingredient of the complete and self-sufficient life, it constitutes the highest end for the sake of which the city exists. Since the best life is the most authoritative consideration in resolving the dispute over rule, and the contribution of any particular claimant to the city's highest end is the most authoritative ground of merit, virtue emerges as the correct principle of distribution for ruling offices (*Pol.* 1280a25, 1280b39–1281a4).[18]

Yet, even as he recognizes virtue's superior claim, Aristotle proceeds to deny it the full ground in the dispute: Virtue is the most authoritative claim, which is also to say that it is not the only one. The first reason Aristotle circumscribes virtue's claim, or refuses to identify it as the sole criterion of rule, is that all who dispute over rule – the free, wealthy, well-born, and virtuous – have a just claim, if a partial one. The partial justice of each claim is connected with the fact that the city is a composite whole in more than one way. For it is a compound not only of associations, but also of the elements that contribute to its very existence, including free persons, the wealthy, and the military. Insofar as each contributes to the existence of the city, each has a reasonable claim to honor, including the honors associated with ruling offices. As the "common advantage" in the full sense, therefore, justice must take account of the composite nature of the city and of the just claims that arise as a result (*Pol.* 1282b14–24, 1283a14–22). It is true, Aristotle observes, that each regime settles the question of rule in accord with its own authoritative principle, yet in considering the question from the point of view of justice, one has to acknowledge that when it comes

---

[18] Aristotle emphasizes how essential such a contribution is to citizenship. The effort by many modern students to make Aristotle's notion of citizenship more "democratic" would dilute the requirement of virtue or redefine virtue in democratic terms. See again Morrison, "Aristotle's Definition of Citizenship," pp. 145–55; Miller, *Nature, Justice, and Rights in Aristotle's "Politics"* (Oxford: Clarendon Press, 1995); Nichols, *Citizens and Statesmen*, chs. 2, 3; Frank, *A Democracy of Distinction: Aristotle and the Work of Politics* (Chicago: University of Chicago Press, 2005); as well as scholars such as Macedo, Galston, Gutmann, Nussbaum, and Berkowitz, discussed in Chapter 1, who define the virtues essential to liberal or democratic citizenship. Compare Simpson, who insists that the end of the city, "noble living," is the crucial criterion in assessing correct and deviant regimes (*Philosophical Commentary*, pp. 151–3). For highly qualified defenses of Aristotle in this regard, see Julia Annas, "Aristotle on Human Nature and Political Virtue," *Review of Metaphysics* 49 (June 1996): 731–53; Thomas Lindsay, "Aristotle's Qualified Defense of Democracy through 'Political Mixing,'" *The Journal of Politics* 54 (February 1992): 101–19; and Richard Mulgan, "Aristotle and the Value of Political Participation," *Political Theory* 18 (May 1990): 195–215.

to ruling offices, each regime, including the one grounded in virtue, is inherently oligarchic and so not wholly just (*Pol.* 1281a31–4).

The insistence by any one party that it is the "authoritative element" that "has resolved in a just manner" to distribute among its own members the goods common to all, in fact, would have the paradoxical effect that justice would be "destructive of the city" (*Pol.* 1281a14–21). In connection with this difficulty, Aristotle observes, one might point to the rule of law as the solution to the kind of tyrannical distribution of offices that each party undertakes in accordance with its partial claim. The inadequacy of this solution, however, is evident in the fact that the law itself is derivative of the regime – it is "oligarchic or democratic" (*Pol.* 1281a37).[19]

Aristotle's arbitration of the dispute over rule thus points to a second reason that he does not cede the full ground to virtue in this dispute. For he shows that even if we were to accept the authority of any one claim, this claim would be limited by its own principle of equality. Each criterion of merit, that is, establishes a ground upon which the preeminent with regard to that criterion may launch an exclusive claim to rule. Yet the law seeks equality, and citizenship in any particular regime involves the sharing of offices or "ruling and being ruled in turn" among those who share in this equality (*Pol.* 1283b42–1284a3). It is for this reason that Aristotle recommends ostracism as involving a "certain political justice" (*Pol.* 1284b15–16).[20] Ostracism is advantageous

---

[19] This difficulty will return in the discussion of kingship; as Mansfield observes, "It might seem that law is a refuge from relativism and a guarantor of impartiality, but law, as we shall see, is relative to the regime and thus reflects the relativism of regimes" (*Taming the Prince: The Ambivalence of Modern Executive Power* [New York: Free Press, 1989], p. 33).

[20] Miller acknowledges that Aristotle's approval of ostracism "presents a fundamental challenge to my interpretation, because it implies that justice is the overall advantage, rather than mutual advantage. This is especially the case if Aristotle means that it is unqualifiedly just to ostracize fully virtuous citizens in case they possess so much wealth or so many friends that the opportunity of others to exercise their virtue is thereby diminished" (*Nature, Justice, and Rights*, p. 247). He argues, however, that Aristotle's approval is qualified – ostracism is "a certain" or "sort of" political justice – and that ostracism is not required in the best regime: "The best constitution is *best* because it avoids genuine conflicts of interest among the citizens" (p. 247; emphasis in text). But this argument is unsupported by the text: In the case of kingship, in Book III, the principle of merit requires a revolution from aristocracy to a permanent kingship if there is one so preeminent as to outstrip the others in virtue, and in the best regime of Books VII and VIII, there is conventional slavery – in both cases, that is, there are genuine "conflicts of interest."

not only to tyrants and deviant regimes, but to "all regimes generally, including the correct ones" (*Pol.* 1284b3–4). In the absence of such a device, the preeminent are done an injustice by the city if they are considered worthy of equal things despite their being so unequal in virtue and political capacity. Aristotle reiterates that legislation necessarily applies to those who are equal; the preeminent are "like gods among human beings," and "they themselves are law" (*Pol.* 1284a3–15).

The dispute concerning distributive justice and rule thus leads Aristotle to consider the limits of every regime or of the regime as such. Citizenship, defined in terms of participation in political office, necessarily involves "ruling and being ruled in turn," and this arrangement "is already law" (*Pol.* 1283b42–1284a1, 1287a16–18). Given its inherent equality, the law is always vulnerable to an attack or argument on the part of those who are superior with respect to the principle of merit that underlies the law. In accord with a "certain political justice" – the common advantage defined by this principle of merit – the regime may rightly seek to preserve its inherent equality and so ostracize those who would threaten this equality.

Yet, in considering this solution, Aristotle raises the case of the best regime, concerning which "there is much perplexity as to what ought to be done if there happens to be someone who is superior not with respect to a preeminence in the other goods, such as strength, wealth, or many friends, but in point of virtue" (*Pol.* 1284b25–9). The problem is that the best regime, in aiming at the true good, should surely welcome as a kind of divine gift to the city the one who is preeminent in virtue, and to claim the right to rule over such a person would almost be like sharing political offices with Zeus. Accordingly, it would seem that the "natural" course is "for all to obey such a person gladly, so that these sorts will be perpetual kings in their cities" (*Pol.* 1284b32–4).[21] In such a circumstance, Aristotle rejects ostracism in favor of perpetual (*aidios*) kingship; he is therefore willing to allow a revolution from a regime in which those equal in virtue rule and are ruled in turn to a "kind of regime" in which one person "has authority over all matters"

---

[21] As Vander Waerdt argues, "To ostracize a man for his incomparable virtue therefore is incompatible with the best regime's end, the education of its citizens in accordance with the natural hierarchy of human goods" ("Kingship and Philosophy in Aristotle's Best Regime," *Phronesis: A Journal for Ancient Philosophy* 30[3] [1985], p. 255).

(*Pol.* 1286a1–6) and "acts in all things according to his own wish" (*Pol.* 1287a1–2).

But in making a concession he never retracts, and allowing for a revolution to absolute kingship (*pambasileia*) on the basis of virtue, Aristotle introduces another difficulty. For the investigation of absolute kingship ultimately raises a most fundamental question: "whether it is more advantageous to be ruled by the best man or by the best laws" (*Pol.* 1286a7–9). One of the deep problems raised by this question is that, regardless of the goodness of either the best laws or the best man, there exists an inherent tension between the two: If the one rules, the other does not. If the law does not rule, moreover, then it ceases to be the authoritative voice and highest object of reverence in the political community. Especially within the context of the regime that cares for virtue, then, it would seem that the law, and the arrangement of ruling offices that the law reflects and protects, could never securely possess the preeminence it claims for itself.[22]

Now, as he indicates more than once, Aristotle's probing investigation of the regime seeks to make clear the truth (see again *Pol.* 1279b13–15), yet in such a delicate matter as the authority of law, he also provides several practical reasons for respecting the rule of law. Immediately after he has drawn attention to the partial justice of democratic law, for example, he undertakes a lengthy examination of the claim that "the multitude ought to be authoritative, rather than those who are virtuous but few" – a claim that "involves some perplexity but perhaps also some truth" (*Pol.* 1281a40–1). Its major premise is that collectively the multitude is superior to the one or the few with regard to the most authoritative consideration, virtue. While Aristotle allows that this premise may be true in the case of "a certain kind of multitude," he gives voice to the objection of an unnamed oligarch or

---

[22] We can look to a modern thinker, Locke, for a similar articulation of the difficulty. In his chapter on Prerogative, after noting the natural tendency toward expansion of prerogative in the rule of the "wisest and best Princes," who rule with a view to the common good, Locke observes: "Such God-like Princes indeed had some Title to Arbitrary Power, by that Argument, that would prove Absolute Monarchy the best Government, as that which God himself governs the Universe by: because such Kings partake of his Wisdom and Goodness. Upon this is founded that saying, That the Reigns of good Princes have been always most dangerous to the Liberties of their People" (John Locke, *Two Treatises of Government*, ed. Peter Laslett [Cambridge: Cambridge University Press, 2003], pp. 377–8).

aristocrat that in some cases, there is no difference between a multitude and beasts (*Pol.* 1281b15–20). Moreover, insofar as a *demos* stakes its claim on the argument that it collectively exceeds others in virtue, it concedes the authoritative status of virtue and therefore the superior right to rule of any few or one who might exceed it in virtue. This defense of the multitude's authority, then, would not seem to establish its right to rule as any more authoritative than that of others.

Nevertheless, this defense does shed light on why, in practice, we might well cede authority over certain matters to the multitude and, more importantly, to the law: While it is not "safe" to allow those who are not just and prudent to share in "the greatest offices," neither is it safe simply to bar them from participation in rule, for then the city is "filled with enemies" (*Pol.* 1281b25–30). But over which offices or matters ought the multitude to have authority? Ought we to follow the example of Solon and others who allow them both to choose and audit officials even though this prerogative would seem to confer upon them the greatest authority (*Pol.* 1281b32–4)? Regarding this question, Aristotle proposes an avenue of compromise. It would seem that just as in the arts, the expert – the one with knowledge of the art – can best judge whether another has produced a good work or performed his art well, so also in the case of ruling. Nevertheless, perhaps those who use, rather than produce, the works of art may judge them better. Insofar as this metaphor and latter suggestion are true, the multitude ought to have authority over the choice and auditing of officials who occupy the greatest offices. As a collective body, at least, the multitude perhaps "justly has authority over greater things" (*Pol.* 1282a1–23). This argument proves also to underscore the importance of respecting law in practice, for it "makes nothing more evident than that it is laws, correctly enacted, that should be authoritative" (1282b1–3). Regarding the matters about which the law is able to speak, one ought not to rely on the judgment of any individual assembly member or even any particular assembly, but on the law itself. Aristotle makes this claim while also recalling that "it is necessary that the laws are poor or good [*spoudaios*], as well as just and unjust, in like manner with the regimes" (*Pol.* 1282b8–10). Even as he illuminates the limits of each regime's distributive principle, and of the laws that derive from that principle, then, Aristotle underlines the practical importance of the rule of law.

Furthermore, just as "'regime' and 'governing body' signify the same thing" (*Pol.* 1279a25–6), so also it is clear that "legislation necessarily concerns the equal both in kin [*genos*] and power, and that for other sorts, there is no law" (*Pol.* 1284a11–13). From this point of view, ostracism is both advantageous and just in preserving the common advantage of those among whom there is law. But in elucidating the partial justice of each governing body's claim to rule, including the most authoritative claim of virtue, Aristotle reveals also that no regime can accommodate the common advantage in the full sense: the advantage of the whole city – of every member who contributes to its existence and end – and the advantage of those who, as citizens, merit ruling and being ruled in turn (*Pol.* 1283b40–1284a1). The failure of any one regime to achieve the common advantage in this full sense may affect the many or the few, but every regime, limited as it is by its own distributive equality, will necessarily exclude "the one preeminent in virtue": the one who "acts in all things according to his own wish" and is thereby a law unto himself (*Pol.* 1284a13–14, 1287a1–2, 8–10). On this note, Aristotle turns to the examination of kingship and, in particular, the kind of kingship in which a single ruler possesses absolute authority.

In taking up absolute kingship, Aristotle distinguishes it from kingship "under law," indicating the existence of some disagreement as to which form deserves the name of kingship and of regime, properly speaking (*Pol.* 1287a1–12, 1286a2–5). Whereas kingship under law, exemplified by Sparta, grants "kingly" power in specified areas, such as war, foreign affairs, and some sacrifices, it by no means cedes all powers to a single ruler or king. As some argue, however, absolute kingship, in which one person has complete authority to act in accord with his own wish, is against nature among those who are equal and similar (*Pol.* 1287a10–12). The problem is that the regime and law reflect the equality that constitutes the governing body of a political community, whereas absolute rule arises from the inequality of a single one. For this reason also, the discussion of kingship necessarily begins from the question of "whether it is more advantageous to be ruled by the best man or by the best laws" (*Pol.* 1286a7–9; see also 1287b19–22). The practical reasons for respecting the rule of law do not address this deeper issue.[23]

---

[23] Several authors have revisited Aristotle's treatment of absolute kingship and the "kingly" man. See W. R. Newell, "Superlative Virtue: The Problem of Monarchy in Aristotle's *Politics*," *Western Political Quarterly* 40 (March 1987): 159–78; Thomas Lindsay,

Aristotle precedes the exploration of the arguments for and against absolute kingship with a summary of key points, focusing on the difficulty he addresses also in his discussion of equity in the *Ethics*: Law speaks "in general" (*kathalou*) and does not command with a view to particular circumstances. On these grounds, some suggest that it is foolish to rule in any art in accord with "writings" (*grammata*) and that the best regime itself is not based on written rules or laws. The potential inadequacy of law in particular cases is the reason that Egyptian doctors, for example, are permitted at some point to depart from the written rules. On the other hand, the "general reason" that is embodied in law and free of the "passionate element" in human beings ought to be available to a ruler (*Pol.* 1286a9–20). The arguments on each side of the issue point to a certain conclusion: It is necessary for a ruler to be a legislator and for laws to be laid down, but the law is not to be authoritative when it deviates in particular cases. The question that would seem to remain is whether, in these particular cases, a single human being or many ought to be the judge (*Pol.* 1286a21–8).

Aristotle offers a series of considerations that bear on this question without definitively resolving it. Central to these considerations are two claims: First, a multitude is superior as a collective to judge particular matters and less corruptible than a single human being, and second, the equality that constitutes the regime as such naturally opposes the rule of the one (*Pol.* 1286a28–35, 1286b8–22). With regard to the question of the best form of rule, the pivotal consideration is the first, the capacity for deliberation and judgment and, in general, superiority in virtue. Hence, for all the obstacles against absolute rule – not least, the natural resistance against it by others who wish to rule (*Pol.* 1286b27–33) – virtue remains the most fundamental standard in deciding who ought to rule.

Having thus indicated the tension between the equality inherent in the regime and this standard, Aristotle examines more closely the arguments in favor of the rule of law. For even as those who insist on the priority of law recognize the problem presented by its generality,

"The 'God-Like Man' versus the 'Best Laws': Politics and Religion in Aristotle's *Politics*," *Review of Politics* 53 (Summer 1991): 488–509; Barlett "Aristotle's Science of the Best Regime"; Vander Waerdt, "Kingship and Philosophy in Aristotle's Best Regime," pp. 249–73. Compare Newman, *The "Politics" of Aristotle*, I.268–83 and Ross, *Aristotle*, 6th ed. (London: Routledge Press, 1995), pp. 263–5.

they point to the importance of preserving the regime by respecting its inherent equality. Hence, they suggest, "whatever, on the basis of experience, is held to be better than the established law" ought to be handed over precisely to those whom the law has educated and who "by the most just decision" pronounce judgment in a particular case. These rulers act, accordingly, not as superior to the law but as its "guardians" and "servants" (*Pol.* 1287a25–8, 18–22).

The case for the priority of the law is supported also by the claim that "the one who bids that the law rule is held to be bidding the god and mind [*nous*] alone to rule, whereas the one who bids a man to rule adds the beast" (*Pol.* 1287a28–30).[24] Those who argue against kingship point to both desire and spirit (*thumos*) as inevitable sources by which rulers and the best men are corrupted and claim that the law, by contrast, is "mind without longing" (*Pol.* 1287a32). Contrary to the earlier argument from the arts – the good doctors of Egypt – those in political offices frequently act out of spite or to curry favor, and no one, not even the best doctor, tends to judge particularly well in his own case. For this reason, "it is clear that those who seek the just are seeking the mean [*meson*, or "the middle way," "impartiality"], and the law is a mean" (*Pol* 1287a32–b5).[25]

In addition, Aristotle mentions several other considerations, including the greater "steadiness" and authority of the "laws in accord with customs [*ethē*]," as well as the inability of one person to survey all and therefore the need for subordinate rulers, and he returns to an earlier suggestion, which he now buttresses with the authority of Homer, that two good men are better than one (*Pol.* 1287b5–15). But these considerations represent a fallback position on the part of those who reject absolute kingship, and the problem remains that the law itself must be

---

[24] On the "deification" of law entailed by this view, see Lindsay, "The 'God-Like Man' versus the 'Best Laws'," pp. 490–1. Also see Bartlett, "Aristotle's Science of the Best Regime," pp. 149–50, for a discussion of law and the "necessary recourse to providence." Moreover, as Bartlett observes, "a consideration of the context of the remarks...makes it clear that this is the view [of law] advanced by a republican partisan" (p. 145).

[25] See Mansfield's observation: "Thus, despite being intelligence without desire, law is not the best but the middle. Law abstracts from the desire of the best man in order to protect men from the distortion caused by his *thumos*, let alone that of others. But in this very abstraction it reflects the distortion it combats: to prevent the partiality of one, the law adopts the general, ostracizing envy of the many, and creates impartiality out of inferior vanities" (*Taming the Prince*, p. 42).

formulated and interpreted and that it is necessarily general.[26] For all
the difficulties with and obstacles to the absolute rule of the best one,
the dispute over the rule of law is thrown back on the fact that some
matters cannot be encompassed by law, and the law requires human
deliberation, and this fact is what "causes" the question to be raised
and investigated whether it is more choiceworthy for the best laws or
the best man to rule (*Pol.* 1287b19–22).

By insisting that "every ruler who has been educated by the law
judges nobly" (*Pol.* 1287b25–6), the defenders of law simply underline the problem at hand. In certain cases, Aristotle concludes, we
must allow that there is "a whole family or even one of the rest [who]
happens to arise who is distinguished in virtue so much as to exceed
that of all the rest" (*Pol.* 1288a15–17). When this occurs, then it is
just for either this family or single human being to be king and to
have authority over all (*Pol.* 1288a17–19). This argument is consistent
with the standard of justice asserted by those who are parties to the
dispute over rule – equal things for equal people – and with the view
that the one who contributes to the highest end of the city has the
most authoritative claim to rule. As Aristotle suggests, this "one" *is*
the city in this respect (*Pol.* 1288a19–28). Accordingly, as thorough
as the defense of law is, it does not resolve the difficulty presented by
the fact that ruling requires virtue, yet every regime is grounded in an
equality that must be preserved.[27]

Indeed, the laws that derive from the regime set out the education
of a citizen, and Aristotle's investigation points to the insufficiency of
this education in relation to the best simply, a subject to which he
returns at the end of Book III. From the point of view of the city,

---

[26] "The moral," Newman observes, "is that law is only a make-shift, that the best thing
is the unceasing guidance and supervision of a true King, and that if law exists, it is
essential that the King should be free to depart from it, wherever he can do so with
advantage" (*The "Politics" of Aristotle*, I.217).

[27] Moreover, as Lindsay notes, "the theoretically best political arrangement, bereft of
law and equality, is in truth not political: The distance between the human city and
the 'natural course' [see *Pol.* 1284b32–4] appears such as to deprive the natural city
of its political identity and, correlatively, to deprive existing cities of simply natural
foundations" ("The 'God-Like Man' versus the 'Best Laws',", p. 494). Or see Newell,
"Superlative Virtue," p. 162: "The claim of superlative virtue to exercise this kind of
authority [the kind that a master exercises over a household] leads to the destruction
of the city understood as a community of diverse contributions and interests."

the education supplied by the law constitutes the virtue of both man and citizen, and "the education and habits that make a man morally serious are nearly the same as those that make him a political or kingly ruler" (*Pol.* 1288a41–b2).[28] In light of the limits of the regime and of law, however, the question of the good human being and the best education remains. Aristotle's "kingly" man, who is a law unto himself, is something of a mystery, but about him we can say at least this much: He is not captured or captured fully within the framework of citizen virtue.[29]

Aristotle's exploration of law and the regime in Book III of the *Politics* sheds light on the treatment of the choiceworthy life and education in Books VII and VIII. For in negotiating the debate between those who prefer the active political life and those who argue that a certain theoretical life is best, Aristotle presents the life of leisure – an "active" life of thought – as the aim of the education of the best regime. He characterizes this life and its goodness by reinterpreting action and the active way of life as study and thinking that are "complete in themselves" and "for their own sake" (*Pol.* 1325b16–23). As he has emphasized in Book III, the best work or activity is free in being for

---

[28] Aristotle's qualification of this equation – "the education and habits that make a man morally serious are *nearly the same* as those that make him a political or kingly ruler" – is another indication that the virtues of a good citizen are not *exactly* the same (as Yack and others suggest) as those of a good human being (cf. Yack, *The Problems of a Political Animal*, p. 262).

[29] The mysteriousness of this extreme in Aristotle's account of the regimes is brought out by the different accounts offered by Mansfield and Vander Waerdt. Mansfield observes, "Aristotle is led to say, that if one or more so exceed the rest in virtue, he or they cannot be counted a part of the city. Such a one would be like a god among human beings; and a law could not apply to such, for they themselves are a law (1284a3–14; cf. 1253a25–30). This virtuous 'one' is usually not specified as a man or a human being. He or it would be literally 'monarchy,' a single ruler or ruling principle which so exceeds the rest that it becomes a law. Such a monarchy is above the other regimes, or in a way above all regimes, because it carries the human claims to rule to non-human extremes" (*Taming the Prince*, p. 39) Compare Vander Waerdt: The king's "natural title to rule consists not in *philosophia*, like Plato's philosopher-kings, but in a kind of heroic or even divine virtue which differs in *eidos* from both moral and philosophical virtue. The king's heroic virtue, being incomparable to that of his subjects, thus undermines the basis for *politikē archē*: their virtue, even if taken altogether, cannot exceed his, because it differs in *eidos*; consequently, since they cannot justly ostracize a man of outstanding virtue, the only course open to them is to accept his permanent rule" ("Philosophy and Kingship in Aristotle's Best Regime," p. 264).

one's own sake and use, and those who undertake such work also must be free from the "necessary things." In this regard, Aristotle finally sides in Book VII with those who reject the political life not only because it may involve injustice but also because it is an "impediment to one's own well-being" (*Pol.* 1324a35–7). According to a suggestion earlier in the *Politics*, the "action" of the theoretical life also involves a pleasure unaccompanied by pain and enjoyment through oneself alone (*Pol.* 1267a2–15), and, in this way, philosophy can supply a remedy for the greatest injustices, which arise from the desire for more than the necessary things and for a pleasure without pain. As Aristotle will say later in Book VII, in addition to moderation and justice, philosophy is needed in particular by those who are at leisure amid an abundance of good things (*Pol.* 1334a31–4).

But while Aristotle's characterization of theoretical activity is thus connected with considerations of the human good simply, the education that he presents in Books VII and VIII of the *Politics* is informed by the demands of citizenship, the claims involved in the dispute over rule, and the singular importance of law in human affairs. He shows that the political community naturally involves constraints that every citizen, even the one of preeminent virtue, must acknowledge: In this regard, the just things are "necessary," if not noble (see *Pol.* 1332a10–15). As a middle ground between the political and theoretical lives, the life of leisure in Books VII and VIII reflects the necessity of law and the law's limits with respect to education and the good. As I seek to show in the following chapter, Aristotle's presentation of an apparently minor virtue in the *Ethics*, wittiness, elucidates the perspective of the human being who occupies this middle ground – the human being who respects and obeys law yet is not simply in awe of it.

6

Political Wit and Enlightenment

Leading up to his account of justice in the *Nicomachean Ethics*, Aristotle discusses three virtues that pertain to "our associations" and "the speeches and deeds of our common relations": friendliness (*philia*, lit. "friendship"), truthfulness, and wittiness (*NE* 1126b11–12). His account of these virtues is prepared by his treatment of the nameless characteristic pertaining to anger, which he chooses to call "gentleness" (*praotēs*).[1] Generally speaking, the person who possesses this virtue becomes angry "in the circumstances and at whom he ought, and further in the manner, when, and for as much time as he ought" (*NE* 1125b31–2).[2] In choosing to name the virtue "gentleness," Aristotle

---

[1] Given that the object of gentleness is anger, a passion, it is at first puzzling that Aristotle does not discuss it along with courage and moderation, the two virtues that pertain to the "irrational parts" strictly speaking (*NE* 1117b23–34) – in fact, gentleness does take the third place in Aristotle's *Eudemian Ethics* (See Stewart, *Notes on the "Nicomachean Ethics," of Aristotle*, 2 vols. [Oxford: Clarendon Press, 1892], I:321–2). Grant observes, "Had the *Ethics* been composed on a psychological plan, what is said here might have been arranged under the head of *thumos*, and would have been connected with the relation of *thumos* to courage which is discussed above" (Grant, *The "Ethics" of Aristotle*, 2 vols. [New York: Arno Press, 1973], II.81).

[2] In an effort to capture this sense of *praotēs*, some translators and commentators suggest alternatives to "gentleness" in the English. Burnet suggests "patience" and "good temper" (*The "Ethics" of Aristotle* [London: Methuen & Co., 1900], p. 188); Thomson, "patience" (*The "Ethics" of Aristotle*, trans. J. A. K. Thomson [New York: Viking Penguin, 1976], p. 160); Welldon (*Aristotle, Nicomachean Ethics*, trans J. E. C. Welldon [Buffalo, NY: Prometheus Books, 1987], p. 129); Apostle (*Aristotle's "Nicomachean Ethics"* [Grinnell, IA: The Peripatetic Press, 1984], p. 70); and Ross (*Aristotle*, 6th ed. [London: Routledge Press, 1995], p. 96), "good temper"; but Ostwald (*Nicomachean Ethics*, p. 100) and Rackham (*Nicomachean Ethics*, p. 231) prefer "gentleness."

associates it with its also nameless deficiency, and the gentle person in fact tends toward a deficiency of anger. The gentle person, who "wishes to be calm and led not by passion but as reason would command," is more disposed to forgive than, as is more common, to seek revenge and punishment (*NE* 1125b33–1126a4, 1126a30). Indeed, this disposition toward forgiveness sometimes makes the gentle human being an object of blame rather than praise: He is thought to be a fool and slavish, for he appears to endure foul abuse and to overlook his own affairs (*NE* 1126a4–8). Moreover, in certain circumstances, not gentleness but harshness, the excess of anger identified as most opposed to the mean, is praised: Harsh human beings "are sometimes praised as manly on the grounds that they are able to rule" (*NE* 1126a36–b2). This contrast between harshness and gentleness manifests the tension between the necessities of ruling, especially punishment or punitive justice, and the forgiveness toward which reason by itself tends. The account of gentleness thus suggests that moral virtue points to divergent ends: on the one hand, toward rule, and on the other hand, away from rule toward something other than political activity. This latter possibility is indicated by Aristotle's observation that gentleness contributes to good relations among friends and associates (*NE* 1126a25–6, 1126a31), and it is explored in the subsequent account of the three virtues that pertain to our associations and the speeches and deeds of our common relations. In contrast to justice and the activity of ruling, these virtues are merely ancillary to the serious occupation of life, political action; yet in pointing away from political life, they help to illuminate both the grounds and the limits of our freedom from it.

NOBILITY AND IRONY

In his original list of the virtues in Book II, Aristotle had unqualifiedly identified the first virtue he discusses as friendship, implying that he meant nothing less than the full scope of associations treated in Books VIII and IX (*NE* 1108a26–30). But he now observes that the virtue he is describing is nameless and that although it resembles friendship, the person who is friendly without being a friend does not act out of passion or love for those with whom he is associating (*NE* 1126b22–5). Rather, "friendliness" as a virtue constitutes the proper disposition toward pleasures and pains in our associations. The friendly person is pleasant and approving of others insofar as he does not bring discredit or harm upon himself or his associates; when necessary, he will express his disapproval, even though to do so may cause pain (*NE* 1126b27–33). His company is clearly preferable to that of his fellows at the extremes: the obsequious man, who praises everything in order to please and opposes nothing, wishing never to pain anyone, and the quarrelsome one, who peevishly opposes everything, caring not about the pain he may cause (*NE* 1126b11–17). As a virtue, then, friendliness makes our "living together" pleasant.

In the course of his discussion of this virtue and its associated vices, however, Aristotle explicitly distinguishes among the ends of actions that would otherwise appear the same. Although both seek to please others, the obsequious person differs from the flatterer because the former seeks to please for no particular reason – as a matter of character – whereas the latter does so with a view to monetary gain. That virtuous or vicious actions can be judged also in relation to specific ends, rather than in relation to a mean, proves to be particularly significant in the account of the next virtue, truthfulness, in which Aristotle raises the question of whether the virtues are means.

Aristotle begins the discussion of the next virtue, which he calls "truthfulness," by acknowledging that it too is nameless (*NE* 1127a14–15). Both in this discussion and in his list of the virtues in Book II, he offers an apology for taking up nameless characteristics, arguing that we must discuss them not only to understand character better but to confirm that the virtues are means by seeing that in each case the mean is praiseworthy and the extremes are blameworthy (*NE* 1108a14–16, 1127a14–17). Given Aristotle's general definition of virtue as a mean, it is surprising that this principle suddenly requires confirmation (*NE* 1106b14–1107a7, 1109a20–6). Nonetheless, truthfulness proves to be complicated in this respect.[3]

Aristotle suggests that friendliness and truthfulness concern nearly the same thing, living together, but the former pertains to pleasure and

---

[3] Both Stewart and Grant remark on Aristotle's "inductive method," but do not consider the significance of his apology in light of the fact that truthfulness proves complicated as a mean (cf. Stewart, *Notes on the "Nicomachean Ethics" of Aristotle*, I.213 and Grant, *The "Ethics" of Aristotle*, I.507).

pain in our speeches and deeds, and the latter to truth and falsehood regarding what one is – one's attributes and abilities (*NE* 1127a17–20). As a straightforward "plain dealer" (*authekastos*),[4] the truthful person claims to be nothing more or less than he is. He is flanked on the one side by the boaster, who pretends to be greater than he is, and, on the other, by the person who pretends to be less than he is, whom Aristotle chooses to call "ironic" (*eirōnikos*) (*NE* 1127a19–26). Both extremes involve lying or dissembling and so appear blameworthy in contrast to the dedication to the truth that is of a piece with the virtuous person's love of the noble: "In itself, falsehood is base [*phaulon*] and blameworthy, but truth is noble and praiseworthy," and "in this way, furthermore, the truthful person, holding the mean, is praiseworthy, and the deceivers both are blameworthy" (*NE* 1127a28–32).

The praiseworthiness of truthfulness and blameworthiness of dissembling, however, become less obvious as Aristotle proceeds to analyze the virtue and its extremes, especially irony. The virtuous person is truthful in speech and deed not for the sake of some particular end but "because his characteristic is of this sort"; although "this kind of person would seem to be equitable," he can be distinguished from the one "who is truthful in agreements or in whatever is relevant to injustice and justice, for these things would belong to another virtue" (*NE* 1127a 34–b2; cf. 1126b20–1). According to Aristotle, since the one who is characteristically a lover of truth is truthful when it does not matter, such a person is unlikely to act out of character when the need for truthfulness is all the more pressing (*NE* 1127b2–5). Yet sometimes circumstances may warrant a departure from the truth: Justice may generally demand but is not identical with truthfulness, and there may be cases in which the truth, however noble, must bow to a greater imperative.[5] The mean represented by truthfulness in its own right, accordingly, may not always constitute right action.

The question of whether truthfulness is always a virtue or, more generally, whether the virtues are means is further complicated by the occasional praiseworthiness of one of the extremes, irony. The ironic person, who pretends to be less than he is, is most opposed to the

---

4 Welldon's suggestion for *authekastos*; see Welldon, *The Nicomachean Ethics* p. 135.
5 Compare Plato's *Republic* 331c1–9; also Gauthier and Jolif, *"L'Éthique à Nicomaque,"* 2nd ed., 2 vols. (Louvain, FR: Publications Universitaires de Louvain, 1970), p. 310.

boaster, who pretends to be greater than he is "for the sake of nothing" and who even seems to "take joy in falsehood" (*NE* 1127b9–11). Aristotle distinguishes this kind of boaster from the one who acts with a view to reputation or honor, though he absolves both from serious condemnation: The former appears silly rather than evil, and the latter is "not extremely blameworthy" since honor is a laudable end (*NE* 1127b11–13, 1115a12–14, 1116a27–9, 1125b11–12). The worst kind of boaster, rather, is one who dissembles with a view to gain or money – who pretends, for example, to be a prophet, a wise man, or a doctor for the sake of profit (*NE* 1127b13). By contrast, the virtuous person occasionally prefers irony as the more graceful manner of speech, for "ironical people, by disparaging themselves, appear more refined in character, since they are thought to speak not for the sake of gain but in order to avoid bombast" (*NE* 1127b6–9, 22–4, 29–31).

Indeed, those who are ironical deny possessing "especially the things of high repute" (*NE* 1127b25). Those who disclaim the small or obvious things "are called humbugs and are more despicable," and we see that we have come quite a distance from the virtue of courage when Aristotle takes aim at the martial Lacedaemonians, whose dress, as an exaggerated deficiency, is a form of boasting (*NE* 1127b27).[6] The measure of this distance becomes clearer in considering the fact that truthfulness and irony are first presented in Aristotle's account of the virtues as aspects of magnanimity or greatness of soul. The magnanimous man is open in hate and love, since "to be evasive and to care less for truth than for opinion is a sign of fearfulness," and he speaks and acts openly "on account of his disdain" (*NE* 1124b26–31). He is thus disposed toward truthfulness, "except whenever he is ironical, and he is ironical toward the many"; although it is proper to vaunt one's greatness among the eminent, "to do so among the humble is coarse, like exerting one's strength against the feeble" (*NE* 1124b30–1, 18–23). There is some connection, it appears, between the sense

---

[6] Since the manuscripts vary, there is an argument regarding whether the word is "pretend" (to the small or obvious things) or must be supplied as "disclaim." Given the context, the correct reading would seem to call for supplying the word "disclaim." Cf. Burnet, *The "Ethics" of Aristotle*, p. 196 and Stewart, *Notes on the "Nicomachean Ethics" of Aristotle*, I.364. Aristotle ridicules Lacedaemonian dress, but such external things are not conventionally considered unimportant, as evidenced by Aristotle's own description in the *Politics* of the ridicule heaped upon Hippodamus (*Pol.* 1267b22–30).

of greatness that distinguishes magnanimity and the nobility that the truthful person attributes to truth. Nevertheless, it belongs to Aristotle's pedagogy to define truthfulness and irony as characteristics in their own right rather than as extensions of magnanimity. He thus highlights the nobility involved in speaking and acting truthfully as an end in itself and suggests that this same dedication to the noble guides those who ironically deny that they possess the things of high repute. But when, regarding such ironical speech, Aristotle offers a rare example of one who possesses a characteristic, he points not to the magnanimous man, as his earlier discussion might lead us to expect, but to Socrates (*NE* 1127b25–6).[7]

Socrates, of course, was famous – or infamous – for his irony, and his notoriety in this department arose from what was seen to be his ironical disclaimer that he possessed wisdom. In the defense of his activity memorialized in Plato's *Apology of Socrates*, he observes that in contrast to those who claim to know things they do not know, he does not suppose himself to know the things he does not know (*Apology* 21d). But far from lending him an air of noble refinement, Socrates' disclaimer provoked great suspicion (cf. *Republic* 337a). This suspicion grew in part out of the investigation he claimed to have undertaken out of piety: his conversations with fellow Athenians – his relentless questioning of interlocutors who claimed to know something and were inevitably shown to be boasters. As Socrates observes in his defense speech, it was this activity in particular that caused hatred and slander to arise against him (*Apology* 22e–23a).

In the face of this hatred and slander, Aristotle rescues Socratic irony from the charge that it is mere dissembling by associating it with the graceful irony of the "noble and good" human being (or gentleman, *kalokagathos*).[8] Yet the two differ in important ways. The

---

[7] Stewart observes that "the notion of *eirōneia* was...enobled by the character of Socrates, and by the representation which Plato gave of him ... Aristotle is the first to make Socrates the type of true refined *Irony* (*Notes on the "Nicomachean Ethics" of Aristotle*, I.359). But compare Aristotle's *Posterior Analytics* 97b16–24, where Socrates is an example, alongside Alcibiades, of *megalopsychia* (see also Tessitore, *Reading Aristotle's "Ethics": Virtue, Rhetoric, and Political Philosophy* [Albany: State University of New York Press, 1996], pp. 31–5).

[8] As Gauthier and Jolif note (*"L'Éthique à Nicomaque,"* II.313), the first use of the term irony occurs in Aristophanes' *Clouds* (l. 449), whose author is identified by Socrates as one of his "silent" accusers. In Plato, see *Apology* 37e–38a, *Republic* 337a, *Sophist* 268a–d, *Symposium* 216e, 218d.

gentleman, who dissembles out of a sense of nobility, denies possessing something he believes himself to possess, and he is praised. By contrast, Socrates' disclaimer, while not entirely true, is not entirely false, and he is blamed. By his own account at least, the refuting activity for which he received the reputation of being "wise" is based not on the wisdom people suspected him of possessing – wisdom about the "greatest things" or the noble and good things – but on what he explicitly claims to know. As he observes after recounting a discussion with a politician reputed to be wise, "possibly neither of us knows anything noble and good . . . but at least I am probably a little bit wiser than he in this very thing: whatever I do not know, I do not even suppose I know" (*Apology* 21d).[9] Whereas the truthfulness and irony of a virtuous human being issue from a devotion to the noble, and so from correct opinion, Socrates' irony is bound up with his challenge to correct opinion and, in this connection, with his professed ignorance about the noble and good things.

In making his apology for discussing nameless virtues and vices, Aristotle insists that by undertaking this task, we will know better the things of character and will confirm that the virtues are means (*NE* 1127a15–17). That he chooses to reiterate his apology in the discussion of truthfulness suggests that this virtue is especially revealing of character and problematic as a mean (cf. again 1108a14–16 with 1127a14–15). Generally, the mean with respect to truth and falsehood in our associations is defined in relation to the extremes of

---

9 The question of Socrates' irony is made more complicated by the fact that Socrates' one use of the term refers to his claim about the god. He represents his activity in Athens as having been prompted by the pronouncement solicited by Chaerephon from the oracle at Delphi that no one was wiser than Socrates (20e–21b) – a pronouncement about which Socrates claims to be perplexed since he did not believe himself to be wise. He thus sought to investigate what he characterizes as the "riddle" of the oracle, and it is this investigation that underlies his conversations with those who are reputed to be wise. He represents these conversations as his way of "coming to the aid of the god" (23b). After having been found guilty, and speaking to the question of the penalty he ought to pay, Socrates rejects the possibility of keeping silent or of exile, saying, "Of this, it is hardest of all to persuade some of you. For if I say that this is to disobey the god and that on account of this it is impossible to keep quiet, you will still not be persuaded by me on the grounds that I am being ironic" (37e–38a). Those to whom he speaks will not be persuaded by Socrates' claim because the suspicion about his irony is closely linked with suspicion about his atheism (23d). From this point of view, Socrates' refuting activity clearly constitutes a challenge to conventional wisdom and to the source of that wisdom.

boasting and irony. But the mean changes when we see that the latter form of dissembling is sometimes practiced even by the gentleman and that the irony of Socrates was, for him, the best or necessary course of action (cf. 1126b28–31). When Aristotle concludes with a final condemnation of boastfulness, he has managed to match this particular extreme with the vice of supposing that one knows what one does not. In doing so, and in linking gentlemanly and Socratic irony, he prepares the way for his discussion of wittiness and the law.

POLITICS AND WIT

As the last of the virtues connected with our associations, Aristotle turns to wittiness, the virtue he originally classifies with friendliness because both have to do with pleasure: wittiness with pleasure in play (*paidia*) and friendliness with "the rest of pleasure, that in life" (*NE* 1108a26–7). He now recasts wittiness as pertaining to rest (*anapausis*), one part of life, and specifically to "passing the time [*diagogē*] in play," a part of rest (*NE* 1127b33–1128a1).[10] Rest and play are "necessary in life" (*NE* 1128b3–4); as he will later observe, citing the authority of Anacharsis, "we do not play for its own sake but in order to be serious. For play is like rest, and, being unable to labor continuously, people need rest" (*NE* 1176b33–1177a1). We play and rest, according to this argument, for the sake of further activity, and, for the morally virtuous human being, the serious activity of life to which play is ancillary is political action: As a relief from the cares and exertions of political life, the virtuous person turns to witty amusements.

This suggestion is echoed in the *Politics*: "Play is for the sake of rest, and it is necessary that play be pleasant, since it is a certain healing of the pain that comes from labors" (*Pol.* 1339b15–17). In the *Politics*, however, Aristotle discusses "music" as the virtue or activity pertaining to rest; sleep, drinking, and dancing are the only other activities he associates with play in this context (*Pol.* 1339a14–24). He never

---

[10] This is the first mention of *diagogē* in the *Ethics*. It is an important and difficult-to-translate term. "Passing the time" or "pastime" suits the context here, but *diagogē* also has more weighty meanings: a way or course of life, a course of instruction. Where appropriate, I will simply transliterate the Greek.

mentions wittiness and treats comedy only to comment on its delete-
rious effect upon the young: "The young should also be forbidden to
be spectators of lampoons and comedies until they reach the age at
which they are able to participate in reclining at table and drinking,
and education will make them entirely unaffected by the harm that
proceeds from such things" (*Pol.* 1336b20–3). Hence, we have warrant for asking why, in the *Ethics*, Aristotle singles out wittiness as the
virtue pertaining to play and rest.

As the virtue connected with play, wittiness is a mean between the
coarse jesting of buffoons, who always strive after a laugh and spare no
one, not even themselves, from pain or embarrassment, and the dour
humorlessness of boors, who will not abide any kind of fun, either
of their own or others' making. Regarding those who play "grace-
fully" ("harmoniously," *emmelōs*), Aristotle offers first an etymological observation: They are called witty (*eutrapelos*), "as in 'versatile'
[*eutropos*] since these kinds of things are thought to be movements
of character, and just as bodies are judged from their movements, so
also are characters" (*NE* 1128a9–12). The graceful or refined wit, by
this account, is the quick one.

But the mean and its extremes are properly understood also in the
context of two general considerations: First, "something laughable is
always within easy reach," and second, "most people enjoy play and
joking more than they ought" (*NE* 1128a13–14). These considerations
give the edge to buffoons, who, in always seeking a laugh, seem to stop
at nothing to win it. Nevertheless, although buffoons have a quick wit
and can be confused with genuinely witty human beings, the two differ
and "not a little." They differ in particular because the former lack what
Aristotle next identifies as "tact" (*epideksiotēs*), another quality, in addition to quickness, that distinguishes a good wit (*NE* 1128a15–16).[11] It is
not inappropriate for Aristotle to introduce a second quality or virtue
since he also identifies two other vices in relation to the extremes: Buffoons are called coarse and boors dour (cf. *NE* 1108a23–6 with 1128a4–
10). The person who possesses tact says and listens to the things
"appropriate to an equitable and liberal person" (*NE* 1128a16–19).

[11] "Tact" is the usual translation, but the full flavor of the word is captured by noting
that it also means cleverness, and in adjectival form (*epideksios*), dexterous, capable,
able, or clever.

Thus, it is the humor of a liberal and equitable human being that sets the standard for good wit and play (*NE* 1128a19–20).

Such liberal refinement is the basis upon which Aristotle both asserts the superiority of the amusements of free and educated human beings over those of the slavish and uneducated, and insists upon the superiority of the New Comedy to the Old. From the point of view of virtue, at least, the latter is characterized by crude language and jokes, whereas the former, in depending on graceful innuendo (*huponoia*, lit. "understatement"), reflects the virtue of a free and educated human being and makes "no small difference with a view to what is becoming" (*NE* 1128a19–25).[12] In this regard, New Comedy would appear to represent the "play" of a particular political class. As Aristotle maintains in the *Politics*, "liberal education" – the education to virtue – requires that a citizen not be subjected to the deforming effects of menial labor and other occupations (*Pol.* 1337b4–11), and this prerequisite necessitates a differentiation among the classes in the best regime. In the city that is "most happy" – "most nobly governed" and possessing just men – the citizens cannot live a "vulgar" or "mercantile" life. Rather, "with a view both to the growth of virtue and to political actions," they require leisure (*Pol.* 1328b23–1329a2). The citizens of the best regime are the class whose education has virtue as its aim and whose virtue justifies their leisure, political freedom, and rule.

Having established the quickness and tact of the liberal person as the standard of graceful play, Aristotle poses a question that this standard ought to settle: how to define the one with a good wit (*NE* 1128a25).

---

[12] Aristotle offers no examples, though the comedy of Aristophanes is the obvious representative of Old Comedy, and so his remark can rightly be taken as a criticism of Aristophanean comedy. Since Aristotle also does not offer an example of New Comedy, it is safe to suppose that he refers to the comedy of his time, the premier examples of which are the plays of Menander (for a discussion of the influence of Aristotelian thought on Menander, see Carnes Lord, "Aristotle, Menander and the *Adelphoe* of Terence," *Transactions of the American Philological Association* 107 [1977]: 183–202). But it is also helpful to recall the discussion among Socrates, Agathon, and Aristophanes at the end of Plato's *Symposium* in which Socrates argues that a poet must be able to write both comedy and tragedy. There is some evidence that the Platonic dialogues are in part a response to the comic poet whom Plato's Socrates identifies in his defense speech as his most dangerous accuser: We might compare, for example, the "female drama" of Book V of the *Republic* (451c1–3) to Aristophanes' *Ecclesiazusae* or Plato's *Theages* to the *Clouds*. In this regard, Plato's own dialogues may offer an illustration of the New Comedy to which Aristotle refers.

He considers three possibilities: one who speaks as befits a liberal man, one who does not pain his listener, or one who even delights his listener (*NE* 1128a26–7). As the latter two possibilities indicate, the question of humor also requires a consideration of the audience, for "different things are hateful and pleasant to different people" (*NE* 1128a27–8). A successful comic must take his bearings by the likes and dislikes of his audience. Indeed, because rest is found in the pleasures of play and everyone requires rest, a certain provision regarding music in the *Politics* is relevant also for comedy: The "twofold" nature of the audience – the one, liberal and educated, and the other, slavish and uneducated – necessitates a different music for each. Accordingly, a good comic, who provides pleasure in play for the sake of rest, conforms his wit to the character of his audience, and on this point, Aristotle plays with separate notions of "nature": For those whose "souls have been perverted from the characteristic that accords with nature," there needs to be a comedy that, by giving pleasure, suits each "by nature" (*Pol.* 1342a18–28). Aristotle's earlier observations that people tend to enjoy play and joking more than they ought and that something humorous is never far from the surface suggest that buffoonery, as opposed to graceful wit, will usually hold court (cf. *Pol.* 1341b10–18).

That the audience is not just determinative of the quality of comedy but also shaped by it, however, is the premise behind the prohibition against the exposure of the young to lampoons and comedies before education has made them immune to the harm that proceeds from these. Aristotle notes that the jokes a person endures hearing he will also be disposed to make (*NE* 1128a28–9). Nonetheless, the law establishes certain restrictions, "for a joke is a kind of slander, and lawgivers forbid slandering some things" (*NE* 1128a29–31).[13] Such is the rationale for the prohibition pertaining to comedy in the best regime, and Aristotle further elucidates the problem with the young's exposure to comedy and other bad influences by citing the remark of the tragic actor Theodorus "that never did he allow anyone to go out before he did, not even a poor actor, on the grounds that the spectators make most their own the first things they hear" (*Pol.* 1336b27–31). In general, human beings "always love more the first things," and "on

---

[13] For the comprehensiveness of the law, see again *NE* 1129b14–15, 1138a5–7, and especially 1145a10–11.

account of this, one ought to make everything that is wretched foreign to the young, especially those things that involve either wickedness or enmity" (*Pol.* 1336b31–5). These first experiences are crucial for the regime, since through them citizens come to embrace the conventions and habits established by the lawgiver. Having noted the lawgiver's prohibition against slander in his discussion of wittiness, therefore, Aristotle adds that "perhaps they needed also to forbid joking about some things" (*NE* 1128a31). The law must protect its authority against the power of comedy to mock it. The difficulty involved in such a task is underscored by the fact that our love of play typically disposes us to forgive the slander that lurks under the cover of humor and that a particularly well-wrought joke may easily pass the lawgiver's scrutiny unnoticed – a possibility especially true of New Comedy, since its understatedness, while graceful, is also more concealing.

In light of his call for the lawgiver to prohibit certain kinds of jokes and in the context of this apparently minor virtue, it is both impressive and curious that Aristotle should proceed to praise the witty human being as like "a law unto himself" (*NE* 1128a32), a characteristic that in the *Politics* he attributes to those preeminent in virtue and political capacity (*Pol.* 1284a3–15). The basis of his praise is illuminated by recalling the power of comedy. For humor can liberate a person from the conventions laid down by the lawgiver: To laugh at a convention is to free oneself from it, and to make others laugh at it is to liberate them. The one whose wit is moderated by the tact that buffoons and the Old Comedy lack is like a law unto himself because he combines law-abidingness with this liberation or potential for liberation from the conventions of the regime.[14] He acknowledges by his tactfulness the prohibitions of the lawmaker even as he shows by his humor that he is not simply in awe of them. As Aristotle observes in his *Rhetoric*, wittiness is "*hubris* that has been educated."[15]

[14] See Carnes Lord, *Education and Culture in the Political Thought of Aristotle:* (Ithaca, NY: Cornell University Press, 1983), pp. 165–77: "It is usually assumed without argument that Aristotle regarded tragedy as the highest form of poetry. One is compelled to wonder whether this assumption is really sound. . . . The obvious candidate as an alternative to tragedy is comedy" (p. 174).

[15] See Grant's remark: "We perhaps ought hardly to quit the present subject without alluding to the remarks which Aristotle has elsewhere thrown out on the nature of wit and of the ludicrous. The most striking are *Rhet.* II. xii. 16, where he defines wit as 'chastened insolence,' *hē gar eutrapelia pepaideumenē hubris estin*" (lit. "hubris that has

In this connection, we might note the absence of piety from Aristotle's discussion of the virtues. One of the few explicit statements regarding the morally virtuous person's attitude toward the gods occurs in the account of magnificence, the virtue pertaining to great wealth and specifically to fitting expenditures on a great scale (*NE* 1122a22–3). The person who is magnificent seeks to undertake the "greatest and most honored" expenditures, including foremost "those that have to do with the gods (such as votive offerings, buildings, and sacrifices) and that concern the entire divine realm" (*NE* 1122b19–23). In undertaking a magnificent work of this kind, the virtuous person aims at what is fitting to the work, the circumstances, and himself. He seeks especially to reflect his own noble and great virtue. Just as honor acts as a crown (or "ornament," *kosmos*) of the virtues in the case of magnanimity, so too does a great work in the case of magnificence (cf. *NE* 1123a7 with 1124a1–2). Of course, as Aristotle also adds, "the same thing is not fit for the gods and for human beings, nor for a shrine and a tomb" (*NE* 1123a9–10). Thus, a magnificent work that pertains to the divine must take account of the distance between gods and men, and not least, of the fact of human mortality. Yet the one who spends in a magnificent way seeks to produce a work that will "endure" – that not only reflects his great virtue but also endows him with a kind of immortality (*NE* 1123a7–9). Likewise, in longing for honor, the magnanimous man thinks himself worthy of the honor that is reserved in Book I for the gods (*NE* 1101b10–1102a4). The longing for the noble that belongs to virtue presents in this way a challenge to conventionally pious views, a challenge that is shared but also potentially moderated by the virtues of irony and wittiness.[16]

---

been educated"; see *The "Ethics" of Aristotle*, II.92). See also Leo Strauss's observation on Aristophanean comedy, "Both obscenities and blasphemies consist in publicly saying things which cannot be said publicly with propriety. They are ridiculous and hence pleasing to the extent to which propriety is sensed as a burden, as something imposed, as something owing its dignity to imposition, to convention, to *nomos*. In the background of the Aristophanean comedy we discern the distinction between *nomos* and *physis*." See Strauss, "The Problem of Socrates: First Lecture," in *The Rebirth of Classical Political Rationalism* (Chicago: University of Chicago Press, 1989), p. 115.

[16] Compare Aquinas, *Commentary on the "Nicomachean Ethics,"* 2 vols., trans. C. I. Litzinger (Chicago: Henry Regnery Company, 1964), I:719: "The gentiles...worshipped not only gods, i.e., certain separated substances, but also demons whom they held to be intermediaries between gods and men. Therefore, he [Aristotle] adds that everything expended on the worship of any demon whatsoever belongs to this same

EDUCATION, LIBERTY, AND LEISURE

That Aristotle should associate play and rest with wittiness and not music in the *Ethics* is striking precisely because the former tends away from the full devotion to moral virtue and political life that is the mark of the serious human being. The playfulness and quickness of a witty human being contrast with the seriousness and deliberateness of the magnanimous man, who is dedicated to moral virtue as an end and good in itself. Moreover, wittiness involves a liberation from law, albeit of an understated kind, which is in tension with the devotion to law characteristic of the just ruler (*NE* 1134b1–6). Thus, the virtue that provides relief from the cares and exertions of political activity also points beyond that activity.[17]

Where it points is further illuminated when Aristotle redraws the distinctions between rest and activity in book X of the *Ethics*. He newly divides life into leisure (*scholē*) and occupation, observing that occupation is for the sake of leisure since happiness depends on leisure (*NE* 1177b4–6). He then argues as before that *diagogē* in play is for the sake of further activity, namely, political action, yet he now adds that because political action is unleisurely, it must be for the sake of something beyond itself, namely, the activity appropriate to leisure (*NE* 1177b6–15). This transformation of the end is echoed in the *Politics*.[18] Whereas early in his discussion Aristotle largely posits political virtue as the aim of the best regime, he later establishes *diagogē* in leisure as its proper end (*Pol.* 1333a30–b5). Both the *Ethics* and the *Politics* make clear that play is for the sake of rest; the two works diverge, however, regarding the activity that constitutes our leisure and highest end.

---

classification. The Philosopher speaks here of a heathen custom that has been abrogated by the plain truth. Hence if someone now spent any money on the worship of a demon he would not be munificent but sacrilegious."

[17] Compare Stewart: "We must not overlook the way in which all 'the qualities of the Gentleman' (even the most superficial of them) are made to subserve earnest aims...the *eutrapelos* performs an important function, by lightening the incubus of ennui which tends to oppress life. He contributes to that *anapausis* which is sought not for its own sake, but because it makes us more capable of the performance of the earnest duties of life" (*Notes on the "Nicomachean Ethics" of Aristotle*, I.366).

[18] For a full discussion of this transformation, see Robert C. Bartlett, "The 'Realism' of Classical Political Science," *American Journal of Political Science* 38 (May 1994): 382–95. See also Lord, *Education and Culture*, pp. 36–41, 54–7.

In his account of the education of the young in the *Politics*, Aristotle insists that "there must be education with a view to the leisure that is in *diagogē*, and these objects of education and these studies must be treated as for their own sake whereas those which are unleisurely must be treated as necessary and for the sake of other things" (*Pol.* 1338a9–13). He establishes the content of this education by invoking the practice of the ancients, who instituted music as a part of education, "not as a necessary thing (since it possesses nothing of this kind), nor as a useful thing" but "with a view to the *diagogē* that is in leisure" (*Pol.* 1338a13–15, 21–2).

In focusing on music as "the *diagogē* of liberal human beings," however, Aristotle is silent about philosophy, which he had mentioned once in passing as "needed with a view to *diagogē* and leisure" (*Pol.* 1338a22–4, 1334a22–3).[19] His silence in this regard may be connected to the fact that the eighth book of the *Politics* has come down to us apparently incomplete, but it may also be the result of the limitation that Aristotle places on his account of the education of the young:

Since there is one end for the entire city, it is evident that there is also one education and that it is necessary that this one be the same for everyone and that the care of it be a common matter and not private, which is how each person now cares for his own children, in private and teaching whatever private studies he thinks best. But the training for things that are common ought to be made a common matter. At the same time, one ought not think that a certain individual citizen belongs to himself, but rather that all belong to the city, for each is a part of the city, and the care of each part naturally looks to the care of the whole. (*Pol.* 1337a21–30)

In his account of the music that constitutes the common education of the citizens, Aristotle raises three questions: whether music is for the

---

[19] See Lord, *Education and Culture*, p. 199: "The citizens of the best regime will also require, with a view to leisure alone, what Aristotle appears to call the 'virtue' of 'philosophy' (1334a16–28).... 'Philosophy' can mean one of two things. Either Aristotle is speaking of philosophy – theoretical speculation – in the precise sense, or he is speaking in a looser sense of what would today be called 'culture.' That philosophy in the precise sense can have been intended is, to judge from the argument of the opening chapter of Book VII, extremely unlikely; and Aristotle indicates in Chapter 14 itself that a capacity for speculative thought is not part of the equipment required of the citizens of the best regime (1333a25–30)." Compare again Simpson, *A Philosophical Commentary on the "Politics" of Aristotle* [Chapel Hill: University of North Carolina Press, 1998), pp. 206–10, 237–43.

sake of play and rest, or contributes to virtue, or contributes in some way to *diagogē* and prudence (*Pol.* 1339a10–26). After establishing that music is for the sake of play and rest, and dismissing the possibility that play is the end of human life simply, he takes up the question of whether music contributes to virtue or, as he puts it, to the character and the soul (*Pol.* 1339b31–1340a6). The extended discussion that follows concerning the influence of music on the soul, and specifically on the passions of pity, fear, and enthusiasm, proves to be concerned not with philosophy or theoretical virtue but with the virtue of one who "belongs to the city" or political virtue (*Pol.* 1340b40–1341a1).[20]

By contrast, the possibility with respect to leisure that is neglected in the *Politics* is the explicit focus of Aristotle's concluding discussion of happiness in the *Ethics*:

> If happiness is an activity in accord with virtue, it is reasonable that it be in accord with the best [*kratistē*], and this would be the one which is of the best [part]. Whether this is mind [*nous*] or something else that is thought to rule in accord with nature and to guide and to instill thought about noble and divine things, and whether it is itself divine or the most divine thing in us, the activity of this in accord with the virtue proper to it would be complete happiness. That it is theoretical activity has already been stated. (*NE* 1177a12–18)

In light of the conclusion that philosophic or theoretical activity is the most complete end of human life and so the proper activity of leisure, we can better understand why Aristotle chooses in the *Ethics* to single out wittiness as the virtue pertaining to play and rest: The liberation it makes possible – liberation from convention and our primary attachment to a regime – is preparatory to philosophy. Despite his statement that theoretical activity had earlier been identified as the most complete end of human life, the explicit disclosure of philosophy as our most complete end occurs only in Book X – only after, that is, the investigation of the virtue that distinguishes the political life and the citizen in the full sense.

---

[20] Lord argues persuasively that Aristotle here discusses the effects of music on both the young and adults (*Education and Culture*, pp. 92–104): "That the music education of the best regime does not end with youth or with the formation of moral character properly speaking – that the education in musical skills is only part of a larger music education 'with a view to political virtue' (1340b42–41a1) which extends through the years of maturity – is a suggestion for which Aristotle's audience cannot be wholly unprepared" (p. 102). But compare Simpson, *Philosophical Commentary*, pp. 273–83.

   This investigation acknowledges the political community's authoritative claim regarding the highest good for human beings and does
justice to the life of moral virtue as the law's highest and noblest pedagogic aim. But as we have seen, it shows also that the political community and the life it champions ultimately point to the need for wisdom as a guide in human action and thus to the activity and life that
have wisdom as their end. Acknowledging the weight of the political
community and its claim regarding the highest human good, then,
Aristotle proceeds with due regard for the law's authority and the concerns of moral virtue. Nevertheless, his clarity about the full character
of citizenship in this regard and, in particular, his investigation of the
complex relation between the virtues of justice and wisdom help us to
comprehend the political community's authority, as well as its limits,
in guiding human action.

   As a part of moral virtue that points beyond the political life, wittiness occupies the middle ground between a dogmatic commitment to
the law and skeptical alienation from it. For, in recognizing the seriousness and necessity of the law, the virtuous person does not permit
his "playfulness" to overrun the boundaries set by the lawgiver. Still,
even though the one who possesses a good wit does not mock the law,
neither is he a captive of it. In truth, the virtue of wittiness places its
possessor at a remove from the high seriousness that political matters,
in all their nobility and greatness, demand for themselves. Aristotle's
investigation of citizenship makes clear that the political community
is the arena of some of our deepest concerns – especially regarding
the "noble and just things" – and therefore is also the sphere in which
we enjoy great goods and may suffer great evils. Nevertheless, political
action is not the best simply. As a virtue, accordingly, wittiness shares in
the irony that Aristotle recalls with the example of Socrates: an irony
that acknowledges the power of our opinions regarding what is noble
and good even as it calls these opinions into question.

   When he concludes his discussion of wittiness, Aristotle offers a
summary of the three virtues that pertain to "certain speeches and
actions in our common relations" (*NE* 1128b4–6). Reminding us of his
original classification of the virtues – truthfulness concerns truth and
falsehood in our associations, and wittiness and "friendship" concern
pleasures in play and the rest of life – he recalls also the original
order of the virtues in his list in Book II: truthfulness, wittiness, and

friendship. In the original ordering of the virtues, friendship appeared to complete the full sphere of our associations. Yet while Aristotle unqualifiedly named this virtue friendship in Book II, he delays the full-blooded account of friendship until Books VIII and IX of the *Ethics*. This latter account occurs outside of the discussion of the moral virtues and illustrates that the complete human good involves actions and activities other than those constituted by the moral virtues proper.[21]

Notwithstanding the fact that Aristotle's discussion of wittiness likewise points to an end higher than political activity, the virtue that concludes his account of the particular virtues is justice. Before turning to justice, Aristotle discusses shame. Shame (or a sense of shame, *aidos*) is not a virtue: "it resembles a passion more than a characteristic" (*NE* 1128b10–11). This passion is appropriate only to the young because the force of their other passions makes them prone to many errors if shame is not present to restrain them (*NE* 1128b15–16). We thus approve of and praise modesty in the young but not in a mature person because "we suppose that he ought not do anything for which he is ashamed" (*NE* 1128b18–21). A mature human being, whose passions are under control, supposedly no longer requires the restraint that shame provides for the young. Thus, "shame is not the mark of one who is equitable because it arises as the result of wretched acts" and, Aristotle adds, whether these acts are shameful in truth or only by opinion does not matter (*NE* 1128b21–4). In comparison with his praise of the self-rule of a witty human being, Aristotle's suggestion that an equitable person ought to have regard for that which is shameful by opinion alone may seem to represent a descent in the account of the virtues. But such regard would have its basis in a just concern for the preservation of the political order. To put this suggestion in its best light: While the virtuous person is like a law unto himself, he is never lawless, which is appropriate to his virtue and especially his justice.

Justice is the distinctive virtue of the citizen, to which irony and wit pay homage. Nevertheless, in showing how the virtues and actions that

---

[21] See Grant, who thinks the new order of Book IV is an "improvement" on the grounds that "the quality which concerns the deportment and whole spirit of a man in society is rightly treated as most generic, and placed first"; Grant remarks on the substitution of friendship without noting its significance for the discussion (see *The "Ethics" of Aristotle*, II.84).

form the core of the political life point beyond themselves, Aristotle proposes that friendship and wisdom constitute goods that, by moral virtue's own standard, are more complete than the goods authorized and elevated by the political community. His investigation of the citizen thus offers a perspective on our existence as "political animals" that can appreciate and defend the benefits of a decent political community while remaining clear-eyed about its failings and limitations. Moreover, since such a perspective does not hold the community and its ends in complete awe, it does not despair in the face of the many tensions, conflicts, and evils that beset political life.[22] By this measure, it is appropriate that Aristotle should introduce wittiness into his list of moral virtues, for it reflects a "comic" vision in the highest sense: a vision that comprehends both the nobility and the limits of human striving and that sustains the quest for wisdom about human affairs.

[22] This "tragic" character of political, and human, life is brought out explicitly by Peter Euben in *The Tragedy of Political Theory: The Road Not Taken* (Princeton, NJ: Princeton University Press, 1990); see also his *Corrupting Youth: Political Education, Democratic Culture, and Political Theory* (Princeton, NJ: Princeton University Press, 1997). Such a view also informs Nussbaum's *The Fragility of Goodness: Luck and Ethics in Greek Tragedy and Philosophy*, rev. ed. (Cambridge: Cambridge University Press, 2001) and is implicit in much liberal thought, which takes the view that the political world is distinguished by the conflict of incommensurate views of the good (see Galston's *Liberal Pluralism: The Implications of Value Pluralism for Political Theory and Practice* [Cambridge: Cambridge University Press, 2002] for a recent presentation of this view). Compare Carnes Lord's presentation of Aristotle's view of tragedy in *Education and Culture*, pp. 34–5 and 165–79.

Conclusion

Aristotle and the Rediscovery of Citizenship

For Hobbes, there is nothing "more repugnant to government" or "more ignorantly" said than much of Aristotle's *Politics* and *Ethics*.[1] But it does not take such sharp wit to discern the tension between Aristotle's thought and a liberal tradition that prizes the freedom of each to pursue happiness as he or she sees fit. Indeed, one of the aims of this tradition has been to liberate the individual from the kind of religious authority and sectarian strife for which Hobbes blamed the "ghostly" Aristotelianism of his time. As Rawls notes, liberalism emerges as the solution to the problem of creedal and salvationist religions, and it is with a view to solving this problem for the sake of future peace that, in response to the attacks of September 11th, we are now attempting to remake the world in our image. Given the political goods of liberalism, then, perhaps we should simply abandon Aristotle's political philosophy, as Hobbes advises, or reformulate it to make it consistent with the democratic pluralism of our age, as some scholars today urge. I have argued, to the contrary, that it is precisely because Aristotle does not share liberal presuppositions that his thought becomes useful to us. In particular, by exploring dimensions of the moral and political world that we neglect or obscure, he illuminates the question central to his political philosophy and before us once again: What is a citizen?

[1] Thomas Hobbes, *Leviathan*, ed. Edwin Curley (Indianapolis, IN: Hackett Publishing Company, 1994), IV.11.

To draw out this suggestion, I recall some of the arguments of the contemporary theorists taken up in Chapter 1.

The question of citizenship is alive in part because the evolution of liberal thought has resulted in the radical claim that the rational principles espoused by early modern thinkers – the "self-evident truths" of the Declaration of Independence, for example – are contingent historical facts that may be superseded by different, equally contingent, facts in the future. Even as we celebrate the goods of liberal democracy and seek to bring them to others, it seems, we are not convinced of the truth of some of its fundamental tenets. More particularly, criticisms of liberalism and its prerequisites have convinced many scholars, even those committed to its ends, that liberal thought fundamentally misconstrues the relation between the individual and the political community. Against the orthodoxy that the individual is prior to the community, these doubts have weighed in favor of the older Aristotelian view that human beings are political animals.

Our own doubts have thus made it inadvisable to abandon Aristotle's thought. But the return to the older view is not a small step and, as the current debate indicates, raises difficult questions in our rediscovery of citizenship. As political animals and so parts of a larger community, are human beings ruled by an authority other than their own desire or will or "creative self"? Contrary to its self-understanding, does liberalism entail unconditional submission to authoritative principles, such as the primacy of the individual, the separation between private and public, the priority of the right over the good, or "the idea of public reason"? Are there educative prerequisites and ends of the liberal polity that shape the individual pursuit of the good? What are the grounds of liberalism's claim that the good is an open question? If the good is not truly an open question, then what is the effect of liberalism's claim to the contrary? The difficulty with the current debate is that our own commitments or hopes resist the investigation that these questions admit of and require. Aristotle's political philosophy may be in tension with these commitments and hopes, but it also provides a clarity about them and about citizenship that we need and cannot ourselves supply.

Although the contemporary discussion has moved beyond the narrow view that the central concern of citizenship has to do with individual rights and political equality, this discussion nonetheless continues to assert the separation between the public world of the citizen and the private world of the individual. To understand Aristotle's view and its significance for us, however, it is necessary to underline his beginning point. For Aristotle opens his investigation of the good by assuming no separation between public and private or, to use his terms, between the highest end of politics, moral virtue, and the human good. By his account, we can comprehend the nature and significance of our existence as citizens only if we first acknowledge and investigate the claim of the political community to establish the good for human beings and to be our moral educator.

Now, many scholars today concede the role of virtue in support of a liberal order and even allow, as Aristotle would insist, that the virtues demanded of citizens must also be good for their possessor. Nevertheless, these scholars maintain, a liberal order draws a bright line between public and private; as Rawls and Galston argue, liberalism does not legislate a way of life for its citizens – it does not constitute a regime. The liberal separation between the public requirements or obligations of a citizen and the private pursuit of the good thus assumes that this separation is at some level viable. Even if the liberal virtues should require a defense of their goodness, that is, they also serve an end other than themselves, the freedom of each to live as he or she sees fit. The good in the "comprehensive" sense – the pursuits and practices that constitute individual happiness – is said to reside in this private sphere.

But does this argument truly confront the central concern of citizenship raised by the current debate and fully elucidated in Aristotle's treatment of the political community: the relation between virtue, especially justice, and the good? In the first place, the claim that liberalism is not a regime merely deflects the question of the goodness of the liberal virtues. Indeed, scholars offer lengthy and conflicting lists of these virtues, from marital fidelity and piety to autonomy and critical thinking. These lists cannot be adjudicated by determining the utility of a virtue to the free pursuit of the good in the private sphere, for the very differences among them reflect deep disagreements about the nature of freedom and about the goods that freedom consists in or supports. More importantly, as many scholars today acknowledge, the relation between liberal virtues or "norms" and the private sphere is more direct and complex than the effort to separate public and private acknowledges. On the one hand, as Macedo observes, liberal politics shapes and transforms private pursuits: "Liberal political norms have a private life: they help shape and structure the private lives of liberal citizens."[2] According to Gutmann and Thompson, on the other hand, the converse is also true: Ideas of the good are not confined to the private sphere but inevitably make their way into political disputes. One way or the other, the public and the private spheres merge, or, as Macedo remarks, "To a greater extent than liberals usually allow, freedom is a way of life."[3]

To be sure, even as scholars underscore the relation between the political sphere and the individual good, they also grapple with the claim that liberalism is not a regime or way of life properly speaking. For this reason, Macedo, and Gutmann and Thompson ultimately fall back on a Rawlsian version of public reason as a way of adjudicating disputes at the public level without dictating private beliefs or privileging particular ideas of the good. Yet, in light of the acknowledged connection between the norms or principles of the political sphere and these beliefs and ideas, what justifies the claim that the management of these disputes does not favor one view of the good over another or that private beliefs are not shaped by the political order? In short, does the idea of public reason or "the fact of reasonable pluralism" that is said to reflect the plural nature of the good obscure a deeper homogeneity – a fundamentally liberal view of the good?

According to Galston, liberal pluralism is defensible because it accords with the true structure of the normative world, in which conflicting but reasonable, comprehensive views of the good reflect the basic human desire for liberty – the desire to go one's own way. In contrast to the ancient regime, then, the great accomplishment of liberal politics has been to create an institutional order within which diverse ways of life can coexist. The freedom of individuals in this sense undergirds liberalism's presumption in favor of human liberty, in the face of which coercion or, more simply, authority requires justification, and this presumption makes possible a core human value: "expressive liberty" or "the ability to live one's life in a manner that freely expresses

---

[2] Macedo, *Liberal Virtues* (Oxford: Oxford University Press, 1996), p. 265.
[3] Ibid.

one's deepest convictions about the sources of value and meaning."[4] This account of the goods of liberalism is central to its defense. Even Rorty, for whom democracy represents an historical and thus potentially temporary victory of one worldview over another, celebrates the greatest benefit of liberalism as "the freedom of individuals to work out their own salvation."[5]

But the principle of individual or expressive liberty itself proves to be the first and most radically formative liberal principle. Galston's own argument in defense of pluralism – that it is reasonable because it accords with the basic human desire for liberty and the structure of the moral universe – calls into doubt any way of life that fails this argument's test. A way of life that rejects the presumption in favor of individual liberty is not reasonable, and an authority that denies this presumption is in error as to the true structure of the moral universe. Simple consistency on this point requires Galston finally to invoke "the right of exit" with regard to every community: "In short, while liberal pluralism rejects state promotion of individual autonomy as an intrinsic good, there is a form of liberty that is a higher-order liberal pluralist political good: namely, individuals' right of exit from groups and associations that make up civil society." This right requires "affirmative state protections" to secure individuals against "oppression carried out by groups against their members."[6] In this way, every community must be made to be liberal, and Galston's claim that liberal pluralism "rejects state promotion of individual autonomy as an intrinsic good" proves to be a distinction without a difference. In short, by asserting the primacy of the individual, the principle of liberty transforms any community that, locating authority elsewhere, rejects the claim that individual desire or choice or will is authoritative concerning the good.[7]

But if we leave aside Galston's comprehensive defense of pluralism, and in the tradition of Rawls we seek a "free-standing" theory of

---

[4] Galston, *Liberal Pluralism; The Implication of Value Pluralism for Political Theory and Practice* (Cambridge: Cambridge University Press, 2002), p. 28.

[5] Rorty, "The Priority of Democracy to Philosophy," in *The Virginia Statute for Religious Freedom: Its Evolution and Consequences in American History*, eds. Merrill D. Peterson and Robert C. Vaughan (Cambridge: Cambridge University Press, 1988), p. 272.

[6] Galston, *Liberal Pluralism*, pp. 122–3.

[7] See Galston's effort to address this difficulty in *Liberal Pluralism*, pp. 52–3, an effort that still insists that a "traditional" – nonliberal – way of life rests on an "illusion."

liberal justice, we must still consider the influence of a liberal order on the deepest convictions of its citizens. When one looks at liberalism through the lens provided by Aristotle, it is not self-evident that individuals are independently working out their own salvation or that a liberal society is as pluralistic or heterogeneous as Rawls and Galston insist. First, even or especially for a liberal order, the consummate virtue is justice. Liberal justice is the first virtue of social institutions, according to Rawls, but, as the current debate acknowledges, it is also required as a virtue in citizens who must tolerate a diversity of pursuits. In this important respect, individuals must bow to an authority other than their own will or way of life. Liberal thought contends that this submission is grounded in a rational calculation: For the sake of peace, one tolerates pursuits and practices one might otherwise condemn and seek to extirpate. But this calculation relies on a revaluation or demotion of core beliefs: To take only the most important example, there are no heretics or blasphemers in the liberal world.

Moreover, Aristotle's analysis illustrates how the public elevation of particular virtues infuses them with the weight of community opinion and actively informs the individual's understanding of a good human being and good action. As the complex logic of his account of the virtues shows, the community praises particular virtues – courage on the battlefield and moderation of the appetites, for example – with a view to its own preservation and perpetuation, but the honor it bestows upon noble and just acts elevates them as choiceworthy in their own right. Even though the education to virtue is intimately tied to the good of the community, it is never a wholly mercenary affair – no virtue is ever simply political.

Even as a liberal order allows individuals to go about their business, such logic suggests, it quietly remaps the road to happiness and salvation in accord with the virtues of the good liberal citizen. Tolerance, reciprocity, and open-mindedness, for example, are prized in liberal societies not simply as public virtues necessary to good order but as the qualities of a good human being. The education to "self-aware pluralism" or tolerant liberalism produces a character that remains fixed across the public–private divide; public virtues do not suddenly become private vices, and in contrast to the self-aware pluralist or tolerant liberal, the pious believer and other such "absolutists" appear at the very least naive, if not dogmatic, irrational, intolerant, and even

fanatical.[8] It is certainly possible for communities within a liberal order
to resist, if only for a time, its education; yet, as Macedo confesses,
"What we want are healthy forms of diversity, and from a political
standpoint that means forms of diversity supportive of basic principles
of justice and a liberal democratic civic life."[9]

While Aristotle has no difficulty accepting the fact of political education, he nonetheless asks the question that we avoid: Is health "from
a political standpoint" the true health of a human being? By insisting that the good is an open question, liberalism denies not only its
educative influence but, more importantly, the possibility of the investigation that Aristotle indicates is central to understanding our good
as human beings. This investigation, he shows, begins from the serious
and careful consideration of the full meaning of citizenship for living
well. In undertaking this consideration, moreover, Aristotle does more
than challenge the liberal claim that the good is an open question. He
also compels us to explore a crucial dimension of citizenship that liberal individualism naturally obscures: the complex relation between
the noble *(to kalon)* and the good.

The morally serious citizen and human being, Aristotle contends,
seeks to undertake a noble deed and identifies this deed as the highest
human good. Contrary to the current understanding of virtue as either
a quality instrumental to the welfare of the community or a quality of
individual flourishing, Aristotle establishes that at one and the same
time, virtue seeks to be good for the community and for the person
who possesses and exercises it. This aspect of virtue – that its goodness
consists in its nobility – reveals itself not in a discursive analysis of
the good but in the action of the particular virtues. Hence, it is no
accident that Aristotle should identify the end of virtue as the noble
only when he turns to his account of courage and that he reiterates
this connection between virtue and nobility through the discussion
of the particular virtues. From the risks taken by courageous soldiers
in behalf of their country and comrades to acts of justice directed at
the common good, we see that a virtuous human being seeks his or

---

[8] See again, for example, Galston's remark in *Liberal Pluralism* that in contrast to the
life of a "self-aware value pluralist," a traditional way of life "allows or even requires
illusion" (p. 53).

[9] Macedo, *Diversity and Distrust: Civic Education in a Multicultural Democracy* (Cambridge,
MA: Harvard University Press, 2000), p. 134.

her good in an act that is not simply self-serving – in an act of noble self-forgetting. For the good citizen and morally serious human being, the life of noble action is the best life simply.

By emphasizing the role of self-interest and calculation in human action and denying the existence of a highest good, liberal thought bars us from exploring, if not experiencing, the possibility that the best life consists in noble and just action in behalf of fellow citizens and friends. For us, the ends and actions involved in the pursuit of happiness are as many and varied as the desires and interests of each. Or, as scholars today maintain, the good is "plural." By this measure, noble action is a preference in the same category as all other preferences: If action is understood simply in terms of self-interest, that is, throwing oneself on a grenade to save a comrade in combat is not finally different from closing a big real estate deal; giving is no better than receiving; endowing a university or children's hospital is no finer a deed than adding to one's vintage car collection; and the just act is, at bottom, a cost–benefit analysis. By contrast, in beginning from a consideration of the noble and just life as best, Aristotle is able to explore a question and an answer that our own premises deny.

For us, the question at the heart of Aristotle's political philosophy – the question of the best life – necessarily disappears, as does the answer that the morally serious life is the end of the political community and the highest human good. It is not surprising, consequently, that modern students of Aristotle are typically interested more in the form than in the substance of his accounts of the virtues, citizen, and best regime. Insofar as neo-Aristotelians, for instance, take guidance from Aristotle, they either emphasize the participatory and deliberative character of Aristotelian politics or articulate a notion of the good that is thicker than that of Rawlsian liberalism but still vague enough to preserve liberal individualism.[10] Yet the full meaning of citizenship for living well

---

[10] The emphasis on an Aristotelian notion of participation and deliberation is most readily associated with the work of Hannah Arendt, but as noted in Chapter 1, several scholars today employ some strand of this idea, as does, most recently, Jill Frank in *A Democracy of Distinction: Aristotle and the Work of Politics* (Chicago: University of Chicago Press, 2005). Liberal scholars who find inspiration in Aristotelianism also seek to find a way to balance a richer or thicker notion of the good with individual liberty. This effort distinguishes the early Aristotelianism of Martha Nussbaum, but also the efforts of several other scholars, including Galston, Macedo, and Sandel.

emerges from the rich substance of Aristotle's thought: his accounts of the virtues from courage through wittiness; his analyses of magnanimity and justice; his investigation of the nature and end of the political community; his arbitration of the dispute over distributive justice and rule; and his careful and sustained exploration of education and the best regime.

In helping us to rediscover the full scope of citizenship, moreover, Aristotle provides much needed clarity about law as the vehicle by which human beings first come to know and seek the good. For the morally serious life requires an education to virtue that finds its articulation in law. Aristotle concedes that most political communities neglect the education to virtue, such that it falls to the individual "to lay down what is right for his wife and children" (*NE* 1180a26–9). Nevertheless, he argues, this education necessarily involves law and law-giving. Broadly speaking, it is the law, "written and unwritten," that defines the virtues, such as courage, moderation, and liberality, whose exercise constitutes good action (*NE* 1180a26–b2). For all of the defects of actual regimes, not to say of politics simply, every political order needs and encourages specific virtues and thus, however dimly or distantly, establishes an association between the lawful and the good.

More importantly, the education to virtue falls under law because justice, which is required by every political community, pertains to relations among individuals and to goods that are common, and justice exists "among those for whom there is law" (*NE* 1134a30–1). According to Aristotle's formulation, we achieve our completion as parts – as citizens – of the city, and from the city's perspective, this completion consists in justice: Human beings are "the best of the animals" when perfected, but when separated from law and justice (*dikē*), we are the "worst of all" (*Pol.* 1253a31–9). Alone among the virtues, justice is held to be "another's good," but like the other virtues, it also constitutes a perfection of the one who possesses and exercises it. As the sum of the virtues directed toward the good of the community, justice is the highest end of the law and most complete virtue of a human being – "neither the evening nor the morning star is so wondrous" (*NE* 1129b27–9).

For all its emphasis on the priority of justice, however, liberal thought has traditionally sought to strip it of its completeness as a virtue by insisting with Hobbes, for example, that justice is simply the keeping of the contract for the sake of peace and self-preservation or, with Smith, that, compared to the "free gift" of beneficence, the sentiment of justice issues from resentment and from fear of disapprobation and punishment.[11] As his tough-minded discussions of reciprocity and of distributive and corrective justice illustrate, Aristotle is hardly unaware of such brute facts. Yet, even as he insists that we are the "worst of all" when separated from law, he does not present these facts as the whole of human experience, and he is able to explore fully the claim so central to citizenship that justice is the perfection and highest good of a human being.

In contending from the outset that there is no such perfection or completion – no highest good – but only the pursuit of individual goods, liberalism correspondingly narrows the scope of law. The contemporary opposition to Aristotle's contention that "what the law does not command, it forbids" is summed up by his great antagonist, Hobbes, who maintains that what the law does not forbid, it allows.[12] Liberalism's denial of a highest good is thus connected with its rejection of the view that law constitutes the authoritative education to virtue. But if, as Aristotle's thought suggests, the law is intimately connected with the question of the human good, then our view places a nearly insurmountable roadblock on the path to self-understanding. For all of its great benefits, especially the liberty that follows from its narrow view of law, liberalism comes at a price.

Given its insistence on the priority of justice and on universal or human rights, it is true, liberal thought would appear to have a deeply moral or moralistic character; as Sandel notes about Rawlsian liberalism in particular, "it affirms justice, not nihilism."[13] But in reckoning with Aristotle, we see that our principles, and the liberty that follows from them, obscure the most serious question that citizenship poses for the individual: whether justice is what it wishes to be, the highest perfection and good of a human being. This question can come fully to sight only with the comprehensive examination of the law as the

---

[11] Hobbes, *Leviathan*, II.21; Adam Smith, *The Theory of Moral Sentiments*, ed. D. D. Raphael and A. L. Macphie (Indianapolis, IN: Liberty Fund, 1982), pp. 79–81.

[12] Compare *NE* 1138a7 with Hobbes, *Leviathan*, II.21.

[13] Sandel, *Liberalism and the Limits of Justice*, 2nd ed. (Cambridge: Cambridge University Press, 1998), p. 176.

source of our completion as human beings – an examination that we preempt by denying this possibility. In giving full due to the law as educator, Aristotle is able both to articulate its aims and to establish its limits. In doing so, moreover, he illuminates the grounds upon which the investigation of the good must acknowledge political authority and upon which it may move beyond it.

As we have seen, Aristotle's treatment of citizenship in his *Nicomachean Ethics* and *Politics* does not complete his account of the good – although the political community establishes the "authoritative" good for human beings, it also points beyond itself. One of the first indications of this fact is moral virtue's own claim to be an independent end. The morally virtuous life strives to transcend its origin in the city, and it is on this basis that one might propose a distinction between civic or political virtue in the strictest sense – what is instrumental to the common good – and moral virtue. Yet Aristotle's accounts of justice and citizen virtue establish that this distinction actually reflects a tension *within* moral virtue. As a completion, moral virtue seeks at one and the same time to achieve the common good and to constitute a good in its own right, but even in the best case, it cannot fully attain this completion.

This tension between the dedication to the common good and moral virtue as an independent end – between civic virtue and the virtue of a good human being – is inherent in political life. Indeed, it is built into every regime, since, as the dispute over distributive justice reveals, every regime is constituted on the basis of a partial claim to justice. Aristotle's analysis of this dispute thus establishes the limits of the political community also by way of the different requirements of justice: Justice as the common good preserves the city, but as the distributive principle "to each in accord with his merit," it looks to the advantage or good of the individual. In light of these different requirements, the question of the good, originally settled by the political authority, reemerges – not least for the person who loves virtue and sees the city as the locus of morally serious action. For, as Aristotle's treatment of this problem indicates, if there are limits to the perfection that the political community and the law can offer, we must consider also the meaning of these limits for our good simply.

In acknowledging the educative authority of the political community, Aristotle examines it on its own terms, and if he is thus more open-minded regarding the scope and influence of politics, he is also more penetrating in his analysis of it. Moreover, we may begin to understand better the grounds upon which wisdom emerges in Aristotle's investigation as potentially the highest human good. Even though his treatment of the political life establishes that the law is not authoritative simply, he does not then rush to embrace relativism. Contrary to liberal thought, Aristotle does not make the good relative to the individual's desire or wish, or even, simply speaking, to each circumstance. Rather, he indicates first the necessity of wisdom. Choices must be made, actions taken, and when the law falls short, it requires guidance from a source other than itself. In the first place, that is, wisdom comes to sight as a corrective of, if a potential competitor to, law, which cannot judge its own deficiencies or the departures from its command that may be necessary and good. More importantly, Aristotle ultimately looks beyond the law to settle the question over which the political community claims purview: Wisdom provides guidance, he argues in the latter half of the *Nicomachean Ethics*, because it constitutes the highest good of a human being.

Aristotle's investigation of citizenship thus speaks to the individual, suggesting that for those who seek the good and are "ambitious with a view to virtue," there are two possibilities: the political life and the theoretical life. The question of the good does not remain open in this regard – a political life of noble and just action is not the same life as one devoted to contemplation or theoretical activity. According to Aristotle, the choice between the two depends most fundamentally on a judgment about which kind of action is better, and he lays out the grounds on which he ranks theoretical activity as best in the latter half of the *Ethics*. This is a ranking that his investigation of citizenship and the political community prepares for but does not establish. As we have seen, in preparing the way, Aristotle gives full due to the nobility and greatness of the political life, but he also illuminates the tensions within it, the necessities underpinning the law, the dispute over distributive justice that informs every regime, the limits that this dispute places on the political community's highest end, and the significance of these limits for both the community and the individual. Aristotle's care in presenting the full scope of politics – its heights as well as its necessities – reflects the seriousness and greatness of political life while moderating the good citizen's highest hopes regarding its possibilities.

His care on both counts is worthy of emulation, since our own rediscovery of citizenship continues to obscure the link between citizenship
and the good while insisting on new programs of civic education. More
importantly, in helping us to recall the view of justice and law that liberal thought rejected in the name of the individual good, Aristotle's
investigation of the citizen proves to be necessary for understanding
our good, especially in its connection with justice and nobility. For
Aristotle speaks to those "deepest convictions about the sources of
value and meaning" that we claim are reserved for the private sphere
of freedom. He thus compels us not only to confront fully our own
doubts about this claim, but also to recollect problems and concerns
that our thought obscures or resists. For us especially, Aristotle redraws
the terrain within which we must explore the question of the good,
and in showing the connection of this question with citizenship and
the life of moral virtue, he makes it possible for us to consider fully the
"source of their value and meaning" and the hopes, for happiness in
particular, that attend them.

By recovering a central part of Aristotle's philosophy of human
affairs – a philosophy that, in speaking to enduring human concerns,
has traveled across traditions and eras – this study has sought to show
how the "old Morall Philosopher" continues to enlighten us today
regarding the life of the citizen. Aristotle's thought cannot solve our
every problem, nor does it always flatter us. But one need not deny the
great political achievements of liberalism to recognize also its defects
or deficiencies, and in times such as these, when we confront both
doubts from within and challenges from without, Aristotle's investigation of citizenship – his rich account of its relation to moral virtue
and the good, connection with the law and justice, and significance for
education and happiness – serves to correct these defects and deficiencies. His wisdom thus offers guidance for us, as it did for generations
past, and it will persevere as long as there are political communities
that require citizens, and citizens who love justice and seek the wisdom
to which his philosophy of human affairs finally gives pride of place.

Bibliography

Allen, Anita L. and Regan, Milton C., Jr., eds. 1998. *Debating Democracy's Discontent: Essays on American Politics, Law, and Public Philosophy*. Oxford: Oxford University Press.

Ambler, Wayne H. 1985. "Aristotle's Understanding of the Naturalness of the City," *Review of Politics* 47 (Winter): 163–85.

Annas, Julia. 1996. "Aristotle on Human Nature and Political Virtue," *Review of Metaphysics* 49 (June): 731–53.

Anscombe, G. E. M. 1958. "Modern Moral Philosophy," *Philosophy* 33 (January): 1–19.

Apostle, G. 1984. *Aristotle's Nicomachean Ethics*. Grinnell, IA: The Peripatetic Press.

Aquinas, Thomas. 1964. *Commentary on the "Nicomachean Ethics,"* 2 vols, trans. C. I. Litzinger. Chicago: Henry Regnery Company.

Arendt, Hannah. 1998. *The Human Condition*. Chicago: University of Chicago Press.

Aristotle. 1959. *Ars Rhetorica*, ed. W. D. Ross. Oxford: Oxford University Press.

Aristotle. 1964. *Analytica Priora et Posteriora*, ed. W. D. Ross. Oxford: Oxford University Press.

Aristotle. 1986. *Politica*, ed. W. D. Ross. Oxford: Oxford University Press.

Aristotle. 1988. *Ethica Nicomachea*, ed. I. Bywater. Oxford: Oxford University Press.

Aristotle. 1991. *Ethica Eudemia*, ed. R. R. Walzer and J. M. Mingay. Oxford: Oxford University Press.

Arnhart, Larry. 1983. "Statesmanship as Magnanimity: Classical, Christian, and Modern," *Polity* 16 (Winter): 263–83.

Aspasius. 1889. *Commentaria in Aristotelem graeca*: Vol. 19, *Aspasii in Ethica Nicomachea*, ed. Gustavus Heylbut. Berlin: G. Reimeri.

Aubenque, Pierre. 1995. "The Twofold Natural Foundation of Justice According to Aristotle," in *Aristotle and Moral Realism*, ed. Robert Heinamen. Boulder, CO: Westview Press.

Bartlett, Robert C. 1994. "The 'Realism' of Classical Political Science," *American Journal of Political Science* 38 (May): 381–402.

Bartlett, Robert C. 1994. "Aristotle's Science of the Best Regime," *American Political Science Review* 88 (March): 143–54.

Bartlett, Robert C. and Collins, Susan D., eds. 1999. *Action and Contemplation: Studies in the Moral and Political Thought of Aristotle*. Albany: State University of New York Press.

Beiner, Ronald. 1998. "Introduction" to *Debating Democracy's Discontent: Essays on American Politics, Law, and Public Philosophy*, eds. Anita L. Allen and Milton C. Regan, Jr. Oxford: Oxford University Press.

Berkowitz, Peter. 1999. *Virtue and the Making of Modern Liberalism*. Princeton, NJ: Princeton University Press.

Berns, Walter. 2001. *Making Patriots*. Chicago: University of Chicago Press.

Bodéüs, Richard. 1993. *The Political Dimensions of Aristotle's "Ethics,"* trans. Jan Edward Garrett. Albany: State University of New York Press.

Bodéüs, Richard. 1999. "The Natural Foundations of Right" in *Action and Contemplation: Studies in the Moral and Political Thought of Aristotle*. Albany: State University of New York Press.

Bohman, James and Rehg, William, eds. 1997. *Deliberative Democracy: Essays on Reason and Politics*. Cambridge, MA: MIT Press.

Broadie, Sarah. 1991. *Ethics with Aristotle*. Oxford: Oxford University Press.

Burnet, John, ed. 1900. *The "Ethics" of Aristotle*. London: Methuen & Co. (reprint ed. Ayer Company Publishers, 1988).

Collins, Susan D. 2002. "Justice and the Dilemma of Virtue" in *Aristotle and Modern Politics: The Persistence of Political Philosophy*, ed. Aristide Tessitore. Notre Dame, IN: University of Notre Dame Press.

Cooper, John M. 1975. *Reason and Human Good in Aristotle*. Cambridge, MA: Harvard University Press.

Cooper, John M. 1996. "Justice and Rights in Aristotle's *Politics*," *Review of Metaphysics* 49 (June): 859–72.

Copleston, Frederick. 1950. *A History of Philosophy*, Vol II: *Mediaeval Philosophy: Augustine to Scotus*. Westminster, MD: Newman Press.

Crisp, Roger and Slote, Michael, eds. 1997. *Virtue Ethics*. Oxford: Oxford University Press.

Cropsey, Joseph. 1977. *Political Philosophy and the Issues of Politics*. Chicago: University of Chicago Press.

Delaney, C. F. 1994. *The Liberalism–Communitarianism Debate*. Lanham, MD: Rowman & Littlefield.

Dobbs, Darrell. 1994. "Natural Right and the Problem of Aristotle's Defense of Slavery," *Journal of Politics* 56 (February): 69–94.

Dobbs, Darrell. 1996. "Family Matters: Aristotle's Appreciation of Women and the Plural Structure of Society," *American Political Science Review* 90 (March): 74–89.

Downing, Lyle A. and Thigpen, Robert B. 1993. "Virtue and the Common Good in Liberal Theory," *The Journal of Politics* 55 (November): 1046–59.

Dworkin, Ronald. 1985. *A Matter of Principle*. Cambridge, MA: Harvard University Press.

Elshtain, Jean Bethke. 1981. *Public Man, Private Woman*. Princeton, NJ: Princeton University Press.

Etzioni, Amitai, ed. 1995. *Rights and the Common Good: The Communitarian Perspective*. New York: St. Martin's Press.

Euben, Peter. 1990. *The Tragedy of Political Theory: The Road Not Taken*. Princeton, NJ: Princeton University Press.

Euben, Peter. 1997. *Corrupting Youth: Political Education, Democratic Culture, and Political Theory*. Princeton, NJ: Princeton University Press.

Fish, Stanley. 1999. "Mutual Respect as a Device of Exclusion" in *Deliberative Politics: Essays on "Democracy and Disagreement."* Oxford: Oxford University Press.

Foot, Philippa. 2001. *Natural Goodness*. Oxford: Clarendon Press.

Frank, Jill. 2005. *A Democracy of Distinction: Aristotle and the Work of Politics*. Chicago: University of Chicago Press.

Galston, William. 1980. *Justice and the Human Good*. Chicago: University of Chicago Press.

Galston, William. 1991. *Liberal Purposes: Goods, Virtues, and Diversity in the Liberal State*. Cambridge: Cambridge University Press.

Galston, William. 1995. "Two Concepts of Liberalism," *Ethics* 105 (April): 516–34.

Galston, William. 1998. "Review of Gutmann and Thompson's *Democracy and Disagreement*," *Ethics* 108 (April): 607–10.

Galston, William. 2002. *Liberal Pluralism: The Implications of Value Pluralism for Political Theory and Practice*. Cambridge: Cambridge University Press.

Galston, William. 2002. "Review of Stephen Macedo's *Diversity and Distrust: Civic Education in a Multicultural Democracy*," *Ethics* 112 (January): 386–91.

Gauthier, R. A. 1951. *Magnanimité: L'ideal de la grandeur dans la Philosophie Païenne et dans la Théologie Chrétienne*. Paris: Librairie Philosophique J. Vrin.

Gauthier, R. A. and Jolif, J. Y. 1970. *"L'Éthique à Nicomaque,"* 2nd ed., 2 vols. Louvain, FR: Publications Universitaires de Louvain.

Grant, Sir Alexander. 1877. *Aristotle*. London: William Blackwood & Sons.

Grant, Sir Alexander. 1973. *The "Ethics" of Aristotle*, 2 vols. New York: Arno Press.

Griswold, Charles L., Jr. 1999. *Adam Smith and the Virtues of Enlightenment*. Cambridge: Cambridge University Press.

Gutmann, Amy. 1999. *Democratic Education, With a New Preface and Epilogue*. Princeton, NJ: Princeton University Press.

Gutmann, Amy. 2003. *Identity in Democracy*. Cambridge: Cambridge University Press.

Gutmann, Amy and Thompson, Dennis. 1996. *Democracy and Disagreement*. Cambridge, MA: Harvard University Press.

Gutmann, Amy and Thompson, Dennis. 2000. "Why Deliberative Democracy Is Different," *Social Philosophy and Policy* 17 (Winter): 161–80.

Habermas, Jürgen. 1995. "Reconciliation Through the Public Use of Reason: Remarks on John Rawls' *Political Liberalism,*" *Journal of Philosophy* 92 (March): 109–31.

Habermas, Jürgen. 1998. *Between Facts and Norms: Contribution to a Discourse Theory of Law and Democracy,* trans. William Rehg. Cambridge, MA: MIT Press.

Halberstam, David. 2002. "Interview on Newsnight with Aaron Brown," CNN, September 9.

Hanley, Ryan Patrick. 2002. "Aristotle on the Greatness of the Greatness of Soul," *History of Political Thought* 23 (Spring): 1–20.

Hardie, W. F. R. 1968. *Aristotle's Ethical Theory.* London: Oxford University Press.

Hardie, W. F. R. 1978. "Magnanimity in Aristotle's *Ethics,*" *Phronesis: A Journal for Ancient Philosophy* 23(1): 63–79.

Hobbes, Thomas. 1994. *Leviathan,* ed. Edwin Curley. Indianapolis, IN: Hackett Publishing Co.

Howland, Jacob. 2002. "Aristotle's Great-Souled Man," *Review of Politics* 64 (Winter): 27–56.

Hursthouse, Rosalind. 1999. *On Virtue Ethics.* Oxford: Oxford University Press.

Irwin, Terence, trans. 1985. *Aristotle: Nicomachean Ethics.* Indianapolis, IN: Hackett Publishing Co.

Jaffa, Harry V. 1952. *Thomism and Aristotelianism: A Study of the Commentary by Thomas Aquinas on the "Nicomachean Ethics."* Chicago: University of Chicago Press.

Janoski, Thomas. 1998. *Citizenship and Civil Society.* Cambridge: Cambridge University Press.

Joachim, H. H. 1951. *Aristotle: The "Nicomachean Ethics."* Oxford: Clarendon Press.

Johnson, Curtis. 1984. "Who Is Aristotle's Citizen?" *Phronesis: A Journal for Ancient Philosophy* 29(1): 73–90.

Kant, Immanuel. 1964. *Groundwork of the Metaphysics of Morals,* trans. H. J. Paton. New York: Harper & Row.

Keys, Mary. 2001. "Aquinas's Two Pedagogies: A Reconsideration of the Relation between Law and Moral Virtue," *American Journal of Political Science* 45 (July): 519–31.

Keyt, David. 1995. "Supplementary Essay" in *Aristotle: "Politics" Books III and IV,* trans. with Introduction and Comments by Richard Robinson, Oxford: Clarendon Press.

Keyt, David and Miller, Fred D., Jr., eds. 1991. *A Companion to Aristotle's "Politics."* Oxford: Blackwell.

Konstan, David. 1997. *Friendship in the Classical World.* Cambridge: Cambridge University Press.

Krause, Sharon. 2002. *Liberalism with Honor.* Cambridge, MA: Harvard University Press.

Kraut, Richard. 1989. *Aristotle and the Human Good*. Princeton, NJ: Princeton University Press.

Kraut, Richard. 2002. *Aristotle: Political Philosophy*. Oxford: Oxford University Press.

Kukathas, Chandran and Pettit, Philip. 1990. *Rawls: "A Theory of Justice" and Its Critics*. Stanford, CA: Stanford University Press.

Kymlicka, Will. 2001. *Politics in the Vernacular: Nationalism, Multiculturalism, and Citizenship*. Oxford: Oxford University Press.

Larmore, Charles. 1987. *Patterns of Moral Complexity*. Cambridge: Cambridge University Press.

Levy, Harold. 1990. "Does Aristotle Exclude Women from Politics?" *Review of Politics* 52 (Summer): 397–416.

Lindsay, Thomas K. 1991. "The 'God-Like Man' versus the 'Best Laws': Politics and Religion in Aristotle's *Politics*," *Review of Politics* 53 (Summer): 488–509.

Lindsay, Thomas, K. 1992. "Aristotle's Qualified Defense of Democracy through 'Political Mixing,'" *The Journal of Politics* 54 (February): 101–19.

Lindsay, Thomas K. 1994. "Was Aristotle Racist, Sexist, and Anti-Democratic?: A Review Essay," *Review of Politics* 56 (Winter): 127–51.

Lister, Ruth. 2003. *Citizenship: Feminist Perspectives*. New York: New York University Press.

Locke, John. 2003. *Two Treatises of Government*, ed. Peter Laslett. Cambridge: Cambridge University Press.

Lord, Carnes. 1977. "Aristotle, Menander and the *Adelphoe* of Terence," *Transactions of the American Philological Association* 107: 183–202.

Lord, Carnes. 1983. *Education and Culture in the Political Thought of Aristotle*. Ithaca, NY: Cornell University Press.

Lord, Carnes, trans. 1984. *Aristotle: The "Politics."* Chicago: University of Chicago Press.

MacIntyre, Alasdair. 1981. *After Virtue: A Study in Moral Theory*. Notre Dame, IN: University of Notre Dame Press.

MacIntyre, Alasdair. 1990. "The Privatization of the Good: An Inaugural Lecture," *Review of Politics* 52 (Summer): 344–61.

MacIntyre, Alasdair. 1995. "The Spectre of Communitarianism," *Radical Philosophy* 70 (March–April): 34–5.

MacIntyre, Alasdair. 1999. *Dependent Rational Animals: Why Human Beings Need the Virtues*. Chicago: Open Court Press.

Macedo, Stephen. 1996. *Liberal Virtues*. Oxford: Oxford University Press.

Macedo, Stephen, ed. 1999. *Deliberative Politics: Essays on Democracy and Disagreement*. Oxford: Oxford University Press.

Macedo, Stephen. 2000. *Diversity and Distrust: Civic Education in a Multicultural Democracy*. Cambridge, MA: Harvard University Press.

Mansfield, Harvey C. 1989. *Taming the Prince: The Ambivalence of Modern Executive Power*. New York: Free Press.

Mansfield, Harvey C. 1994. *Responsible Citizenship Ancient and Modern*. Eugene: University of Oregon Books.

Miller, Fred D. 1995. *Nature, Justice, and Rights in Aristotle's "Politics."* Oxford: Clarendon Press.

Miller, Fred D. 1999. "Aristotle on Natural Law and Justice" in *A Companion to Aristotle's "Politics,"* eds. David Keyt and Fred D. Miller. Oxford: Blackwell Publishers.

Miller, David. 2000. *Citizenship and National Identity.* Oxford: Blackwell Publishers.

Morrison, Donald. 1999. "Aristotle's Definition of Citizenship: A Problem and Some Solutions," *History of Philosophy Quarterly* 16 (April): 143–65.

Morrison, Donald. 2001. "Politics as a Vocation, According to Aristotle," *History of Political Thought* 22 (Summer): 221–41.

Mulgan, Richard. 1990. "Aristotle and the Value of Political Participation," *Political Theory* 18 (May): 195–215.

Newell, W. R. 1987. "Superlative Virtue: The Problem of Monarchy in Aristotle's *Politics,*" *Western Political Quarterly* 40 (March): 159–78.

Newman, W. L. 1902. *The "Politics" of Aristotle,* 4 vols. Oxford: Oxford University Press.

Nichols, Mary P. 1992. *Citizens and Statesmen: A Study of Aristotle's "Politics."* Savage, MD: Rowman & Littlefield Publishers.

Nussbaum, Martha C. 1987. "Shame, Separateness, and Political Unity: Aristotle's Criticism of Plato," *in Essays on Aristotle's "Ethics,"* ed. Amélie Oksenberg Rorty. Berkeley: University of California Press.

Nussbaum, Martha C. 1988. "Non-Relative Virtues: An Aristotelian Approach," in *Midwest Studies in Philosophy. Vol. XIII: Ethical Theory, Character, and Virtue,* ed. Peter A. French, Theodore E. Uehling, Jr., and Howard K. Wettstein. Notre Dame, IN: University of Notre Dame Press.

Nussbaum, Martha C. 1992. "Human Functioning and Social Justice: In Defense of Aristotelian Essentialism," *Political Theory* 20 (May): 202–46.

Nussbaum, Martha C. 1996. *For Love of Country: Debating the Limits of Patriotism.* Boston: Beacon Press.

Nussbaum, Martha C. 1999. "Virtue Ethics: A Misleading Category? *The Journal of Ethics* 3(3): 163–201.

Nussbaum, Martha C. 2001. *The Fragility of Goodness: Luck and Ethics in Greek Tragedy and Philosophy,* rev. ed. Cambridge: Cambridge University Press.

Nussbaum, Martha C. 2002. "Aristotelian Social Democracy," in *Aristotle and Modern Politics: The Persistence of Political Philosophy,* ed. Aristide Tessitore (Notre Dame, IN: University of Notre Dame Press.

O'Connor, David. 1991. "The Aetiology of Justice,." In *Essays on the Foundations of Aristotelian Political Thought,* eds. Carnes Lord and David O'Connor. Berkeley: University of California Press.

Okin, Susan Mollar. 1989. *Justice, Gender, and the Family.* New York: Basic Books.

Ostwald, Martin, trans. 1999. *Nicomachean Ethics.* Upper Saddle River, NJ: Prentice Hall (Library of Liberal Arts).

Pakaluk, Michael. 1998. *Nicomachean Ethics. Books VIII and IX.* Oxford: Oxford University Press.

Pangle, Lorraine Smith. 2003. *Aristotle and the Philosophy of Friendship.* Cambridge: Cambridge University Press.

Pangle, Thomas. 1998. "The Retrieval of Civic Virtue: A Critical Appreciation of Sandel's *Democracy's Discontent*" in *Debating Democracy's Discontent: Essays on American Politics, Law, and Public Philosophy.* Oxford: Oxford University Press.

Pickus, Noah M. J., ed. 1998. *Immigration and Citizenship in the Twenty-First Century.* Lanham, MD: Rowman & Littlefield.

Price, A. W. 1989. *Love and Friendship in Plato and Aristotle.* Oxford: Oxford University Press.

Plato. 1946. *Euthyphro, Apologia, Crito, Phaedo, Cratylus, Theaetetus, Sophista, Politicus,* ed. John Burnet. Oxford: Oxford Classical Texts.

Rackham, H. trans. 1982. *Aristotle: "Nicomachean Ethics."* Cambridge, MA: Harvard University Press (Loeb Classical Library).

Rahe, Paul. A. 1994. *Republics Ancient and Modern: The Ancien Régime in Classical Greece.* Chapel Hill: University of North Carolina Press.

Ramsauer, G., ed. 1987. *Aristotle, Nicomachean Ethics,* vol. 2 of *Greek and Roman Philosophy.* New York: Garland Publishing.

Ravitch, Diane and Viteritti, Joseph P., eds. 2001. *Making Good Citizens: Education and Civil Society.* New Haven, CT: Yale University Press.

Rawls, John. 1971. *A Theory of Justice.* Cambridge, MA: Harvard University Press.

Rawls, John. 1980. "Kantian Constructivism in Moral Theory," *Journal of Philosophy* 77 (August): 515–72.

Rawls, John. 1993. *Political Liberalism.* New York: Columbia University Press.

Rawls, John. 1995. "Political Liberalism: Reply to Habermas," *Journal of Philosophy* 92 (March): 132–80.

Rawls, John. 1999. *The Law of Peoples, with "The Idea of Public Reason Revisited."* Cambridge, MA: Harvard University Press.

Rawls, John. 2001. *Justice as Fairness: A Restatement.* Cambridge, MA: Harvard University Press.

Reeve, C. D. C. 1992. *Practices of Reason: Aristotle's "Nicomachean Ethics."* Oxford: Oxford University Press.

Ritchie, D. G. 1894. "Aristotle's Subdivisions of Particular Justice," *The Classical Review* 8 (May): 185–93.

Rorty, Amélie Oksenberg, ed. 1980. *Essays on Aristotle's "Ethics."* Berkeley: University of California Press.

Rorty, Richard. 1988. "The Priority of Democracy to Philosophy," in *The Virginia Statute for Religious Freedom: Its Evolution and Consequences in American History,* eds. Merrill D. Peterson and Robert C. Vaughan. Cambridge: Cambridge University Press.

Rorty, Richard. 1998. *Achieving Our Country: Leftist Thought in Twentieth-Century America.* Cambridge MA: Harvard University Press.

Rorty, Richard. 1999. *Philosophy and Social Hope.* London: Penguin Books.

Ross, David. 1995. *Aristotle,* 6th ed. London: Routledge Press.

Ruderman, Richard. 1997. "Aristotle and the Recovery of Political Judgment," *American Political Science Review* 91 (June): 409–20.

Salkever, Stephen G. 1990. *Finding the Mean: Theory and Practice in Aristotelian Political Philosophy.* Princeton, NJ: Princeton University Press.

Salkever, Stephen G. 1990. "'Lopp'd and Bound': How Liberal Theory Obscures the Goods of Liberal Practices," in *Liberalism and the Good*, eds. R. Bruce Douglass, Gerald R. Mara, and Henry S. Richardson. New York: Routledge.

Salkever, Stephen G. 2002. "The Deliberative Model of Democracy and Aristotle's Ethics of Natural Questions" in *Aristotle and Modern Politics: The Persistence of Political Philosophy*, ed. Aristotle Tessitore. Notre Dame, IN: University of Notre Dame Press.

Sandel, Michael, ed. 1984. *Liberalism and Its Critics.* New York: New York University Press.

Sandel, Michael. 1994. "Political Liberalism," *Harvard Law Review* 107(7) (May): 1765–94.

Sandel, Michael. 1996. *Democracy's Discontent: America in Search of a Public Philosophy.* Cambridge, MA: Harvard University Press.

Sandel, Michael. 1998. *Liberalism and the Limits of Justice*, 2nd ed. Cambridge: Cambridge University Press.

Saxonhouse, Arlene. 1985. *Women in the History of Political* Thought. New York: Praeger.

Saxonhouse, Arlene. 1992. *Fear of Diversity: The Birth of Political Science in Ancient Greek Thought.* Chicago: University of Chicago Press.

Schofield, Malcolm. 1999. *Saving the City: Philosopher-Kings and Other Classical Paradigms.* New York: Routledge.

Schollmeier, Paul. 1994. *Other Selves: Aristotle on Personal and Political Friendship.* Albany: State University of New York Press.

Shklar, Judith. 1991. *American Citizenship: The Quest for Inclusion.* Cambridge, MA: Harvard University Press.

Simpson, Peter L. Phillips. 1992. "Contemporary Virtue Ethics and Aristotle," *Review of Metaphysics* 45 (March): 503–24.

Simpson, Peter L. Phillips, trans. 1997. *The "Politics" of Aristotle.* Chapel Hill: University of North Carolina Press.

Simpson, Peter L. Phillips. 1998. *A Philosophical Commentary on the "Politics" of Aristotle."* Chapel Hill: University of North Carolina Press.

Smith, Adam. 1982. *The Theory of Moral Sentiments*, ed. D. D. Raphael and A. L. Macphie. Indianapolis, IN: Liberty Fund.

Smith, Rogers M. 1997. *Civic Ideals: Conflicting Visions of Citizenship in U.S. History.* New Haven, CT. Yale University Press.

Smith, Thomas W. 2001. *Revaluing Ethics: Aristotle's Dialectical Pedagogy.* Albany: State University of New York Press.

Stern-Gillet, Suzanne. 1995. *Aristotle's Philosophy of Friendship.* Albany: State University of New York Press.

Stewart, J. A. 1892. *Notes on the "Nicomachean Ethics" of Aristotle*, 2 vols. Oxford: Clarendon Press.

Strauss, Leo. 1953. *Natural Right and History.* Chicago: University of Chicago Press.

Strauss, Leo. 1989. *The Rebirth of Classical Political Rationalism.* Chicago: University of Chicago Press.

Swanson, Judith. 1992. *The Public and the Private in Aristotle's Political Philosophy.* Ithaca, NY: Cornell University Press.

Swanson, Judith. 1999. "Aristotle on Nature, Human Nature, and Justice: A Consideration of the Natural Functions of Men and Women in the City," *in Action and Contemplation: Studies in the Moral and Political Thought of Aristotle,* ed. Robert C. Bartlett and Susan D. Collins. Albany: State University of New York Press.

Taylor, Charles. 1998. "Living with Difference," in *Debating Democracy's Discontent: Essays on American Politics, Law and Public Philosophy,* eds. Anita L. Allen and Milton C. Regan, Jr. Oxford: Oxford University Press.

Tessitore, Aristide. 1996. *Reading Aristotle's "Ethics": Virtue, Rhetoric, and Political Philosophy.* Albany: State University of New York Press.

Tessitore, Aristide, ed. 2002. *Aristotle and Modern Politics: The Persistence of Political Philosophy.* Notre Dame, IN: University of Notre Dame Press.

Thomson, J. A. K., trans. 1976. *The "Ethics" of Aristotle.* New York: Viking Penguin.

Trianosky, Gregory. 1990. "What Is Virtue Ethics All About?" *American Philosophical Quarterly* 27 (October): 335–44.

Vander Waerdt, P. A. 1985. "Kingship and Philosophy in Aristotle's Best Regime," *Phronesis: A Journal for Ancient Philosophy* 30(3): 249–73.

Vander Waerdt, P. A. 1985. "The Political Intention of Aristotle's Moral Philosophy," *Ancient Philosophy* 5 (Spring): 77–90.

Villa, Dana. 2001. *Socratic Citizenship.* Princeton, NJ: Princeton University Press.

Wallach, John C. 1992. "Contemporary Aristotelianism," *Political Theory* 20 (November): 613–41.

Walzer, Michael. 1990. "The Communitarian Critique of Liberalism," *Political Theory* 18 (February): 6–23.

Ward, Lee. 2001. "Nobility and Necessity: The Problem of Courage in Aristotle's *Nicomachean Ethics,*" *American Political Science Review* 95 (March): 71–83.

Welldon, J. E. C., trans. 1987. *The Nicomachean Ethics.* Buffalo, NY: Prometheus Books.

Williams, Bernard. 1980. "Justice as a Virtue," in *Essays on Aristotle's "Ethics,"* ed. Amélie Oksenberg Rorty. Berkeley: University of California Press.

Winthrop, Delba. 1978. "Aristotle and Theories of Justice," *American Political Science Review* 72 (December): 1201–16.

Yack, Bernard. 1993. *The Problems of a Political Animal: Community, Justice, and Conflict in Aristotelian Political Thought.* Berkeley: University of California Press.

Young, Iris Marion. 2000. *Inclusion and Democracy.* Oxford: Oxford University Press.

Zuckert, Catherine H. 1983. "Aristotle on the Satisfactions and Limits of Political Life," *Interpretation* 11 (May): 185–206.

Index

Allen, Anita L., 15
Ambler, Wayne H., 103, 105
Annas, Julia, 136
Anscombe, G. E. M., 13
Aquinas, Thomas, 46, 48, 57, 58, 70,
    75, 85, 102, 159
Arendt, Hannah, 23, 105, 173
Aristotelianism, 2, 7, 166
Aristotle
  Nicomachean Ethics
    courage, 45, 48, 50–8, 63–4, 69,
        77, 79, 151, 171–4
    education, 2–4, 5, 22, 40–6, 54,
        78–80, 94–101, 157, 171, 174,
        178
    friendliness, 49, 147, 148–50,
        154
    friendship, 93, 96, 98, 117, 147,
        148, 163, 164, 165
    gentleness, 49, 69, 147–8
    good life, 2, 4, 43, 82, 96–8, 173
    human good, 2, 3–4, 5, 40–6,
        63, 68, 74, 76–8, 82–4,
        89–90, 92–8, 100–2, 108, 163,
        164, 175–8
    intellectual virtue, 44, 89, 91,
        92, 95

irony, 150–4, 159, 163, 164
justice, 45, 50, 117, 147, 174
    equity, 80, 86–9, 117, 142
    general justice, 68–72, 76
    natural justice, 80, 84–6, 117
    particular justice, 68–9, 71–3,
        76–80
    political justice, 82–5, 137,
        138
    reciprocity, 69, 73–6, 82, 175
law, 2–4, 22, 42–6, 52, 54, 65,
    69–89, 91–4, 98–101, 117,
    142, 146, 154, 157–8, 160,
    162–3, 175–8
leisure, 160–2
liberality, 48, 58–9, 64, 65, 77,
    174
magnanimity, 45, 48, 52, 59–64,
    68, 70, 77, 115, 151–2, 159,
    174
magnificence, 48, 59–61, 159
moderation, 48, 50, 58, 69, 81,
    171, 174
moral virtue, 2, 3, 22, 40–6, 47,
    55, 56, 61, 64, 65, 73, 78–81,
    89, 92–8, 108, 125, 148, 160,
    163, 165, 176, 178

Aristotle *(cont.)*
  nameless virtues, 49, 148–9, 153
  noble *(to kalon)*, 4, 43, 45,
    52–61, 79, 89, 98–9, 150,
    151–3, 159, 163, 165, 171–3
  philosophy, 97, 101, 162, 178
  piety, 159
  prudence, 5, 90, 91, 92, 93–4,
    99
  regime *(politeia)*, 69, 72–3, 76,
    78, 86, 97–8, 100, 162
  right reason, 42, 44, 80–2, 89,
    91–2, 99, 117
  truthfulness, 49, 147, 149–54,
    163–4
  wisdom, 46, 86, 92–7, 117, 163,
    165, 177
  wittiness, 5, 49, 146, 147, 154–6,
    158, 159, 160, 162–4, 165, 174
Politics
  best regime, 64–6, 108–9, 111,
    112, 116–17, 124–30, 131, 138,
    142, 145, 156, 157, 160, 173,
    174
  citizen virtue, 107, 115, 129,
    145, 173, 176
  courage, 110, 111, 113
  education, 5, 108, 115–17, 126,
    130, 131, 144–6, 154–7,
    160–2, 174
  good citizen and good man, 66,
    117, 124–9, 130, 145
  good life, 107–14, 116, 136
  human good, 4, 5, 119, 146
  intellectual virtue, 128, 162
  justice, 5, 102, 105–11, 114,
    122–8, 134, 136, 146
  law, 3, 4, 46, 82, 90, 101–8,
    115–18, 120, 130–2, 135–46,
    174, 176
  leisure, 116–17, 145–6, 156,
    160–2

moderation, 110, 114, 125,
  127–8, 146
noble *(to kalon)*, 110–11, 114–15,
  132
philosophy, 112, 116–17, 146,
  161
prudence, 110–11, 117, 125,
  127–8, 162
regime *(politeia)*, 4, 5, 46, 73,
  82, 90, 102, 106, 109, 112–13,
  115, 126, 129–34, 136–45,
  158, 176, 177
wisdom, 106, 117
works other than *NE* and *Pol.*
  Eudemian Ethics, 64, 131,
    147
  Posterior Analytics, 65, 152
  Rhetoric, 158
Arnhart, Larry, 60, 62
Aspasius, 53, 63
Aubenque, Pierre, 67

Bartlett, Robert C., 51, 78, 116, 135,
  141, 143, 160
Beiner, Ronald, 26
Berkowitz, Peter, 2, 10, 16, 18, 23, 27,
  37, 40, 69, 136
Berns, Walter, 39
Bodéüs, Richard, 45, 85, 88, 92, 93,
  94, 98, 100, 109, 116
Bohman, James, 23, 28
Broadie, Sarah, 92
Burnet, John, 42, 59, 62, 73, 75, 78,
  80, 81, 125, 147, 151

Cooper, John M., 44, 94, 107
Copleston, Frederick, 48, 85
Crisp, Roger, 13, 67
Cropsey, Joseph, 60

Delaney, C. F., 10
Dobbs, Darrell, 51, 115

Downing, Lyle A., 16
Dworkin, Ronald, 34, 35

Elshtain, Jean Bethke, 51
Etzioni, Amitai, 10
Euben, Peter, 165

Fish, Stanley, 25
Foot, Philippa, 13
Frank, Jill, 40, 74, 97, 103, 136, 173

Galston, William, 2, 7, 10, 13, 14, 15,
    16, 18, 20, 21, 23, 25, 26, 29,
    32–40, 43, 69, 95, 136, 165,
    168, 169, 170, 171, 172, 173
Gauthier, R. A., 45, 48, 50, 63, 85,
    93, 150, 152
Grant, Sir Alexander, 45, 47, 48, 53,
    56, 57, 69, 81, 85, 147, 149,
    158, 164
Griswold, Charles, 10
Gutmann, Amy, 2, 18, 22–6, 28, 33,
    39, 136, 169

Habermas, Jürgen, 10, 11, 17, 19
Halberstam, David, 1, 5
Hanley, Ryan Patrick, 61, 62
Hardie, W. F. R., 46, 48, 62, 85, 92
Hegel, Georg Wilhelm Friedrich, 9,
    17
Hobbes, Thomas, 1, 2, 8, 28, 81, 107,
    166, 175
Howland, Jacob, 45, 53, 61, 62, 63,
    65
Hursthouse, Rosalind, 13, 67

Irwin, Terence, 81

Jaffa, Harry V., 46, 48, 60, 63, 65, 85
Janoski, Thomas, 39
Joachim, H. H., 45, 47, 49, 62, 85,
    125

Johnson, Curtis, 121, 122
Jolif, J. Y., 45, 48, 50, 85, 93, 150, 152

Kant, Immanuel, 1, 7, 8–13, 14, 16,
    19, 21, 36, 41, 42
Keyt, David, 74, 131
Konstan, David, 97
Krause, Sharon, 16
Kraut, Richard, 43, 51, 60, 68, 77, 85,
    88, 89
Kukathas, Chandran, 21
Kymlicka, Will, 39

Larmore, Charles, 29
Levy, Harold, 51
liberalism
    citizen virtue, 30, 171
    citizenship, 6, 11, 18, 28–30, 34
    education, 3, 18, 22, 23, 27–9, 31,
        35, 37, 40, 172, 178
    enlightenment, 3, 7, 8, 9, 17, 21
    good citizen and good human
        being, 37
    human good, 8, 20, 22, 26–7,
        35–7, 40, 168–70, 172, 173
Lindsay, Thomas K., 51, 136, 141,
    143, 144
Lister, Ruth, 40
Locke, John, 8, 28, 30, 107, 139
Lord, Carnes, 67, 109, 116, 156, 158,
    160, 161, 162, 165

Macedo, Stephen, 2, 10, 18, 23, 24,
    29–33, 34–5, 36, 40, 69, 136,
    169, 172, 173
MacIntyre, Alasdair, 2, 7, 9–10, 13,
    14, 17, 26, 43, 49, 63, 95
Mansfield, Harvey C., 122, 137, 143,
    145
Miller, David, 40
Miller, Fred D., 74, 85, 107, 136,
    137

Morrison, Donald, 129, 134, 136
Mulgan, Richard, 136

Newell, W. R., 141, 144
Newman, W. L., 109, 110, 120,
    123, 124, 125, 126, 134,
    142, 144
Nichols, Mary P., 52, 107, 127, 128,
    136
Nietzsche, Friedrich, 9
Nussbaum, Martha, 2, 10, 16, 17, 39,
    43, 51, 95, 136, 165, 173

O'Connor, David, 67, 70, 71, 78
Okin, Susan Mollar, 17

Pakaluk, Michael, 96
Pangle, Lorraine Smith, 96
Pangle, Thomas, 28
Plato, 98, 145, 152
    Apology of Socrates, 152, 153
    Republic, 70, 150, 152
    Symposium, 156
Price, A. W., 96

Rahe, Paul, 105, 106
Ramsauer, G., 42, 83
Ravitch, Diane, 39
Rawls, John, 17, 18, 36
    A Theory of Justice, 7, 11, 17, 19
    constitutional democracy, 23–4
    justice, 12, 19–20, 25
    liberalism, 2, 13, 19, 25–30, 32, 36,
        40, 166, 168, 170, 171
    pluralism, 22, 25, 171
    political liberalism, 3, 16, 19, 20,
        22–3
    Political Liberalism, 16, 25
    public reason, 19, 20, 32
Reeve, C. D. C., 92, 94
Regan Jr., Milton C., 15
Rehg, William, 11, 23, 28

Ritchie, D. G., 74, 75, 79
Rorty, Amélie Oksenberg, 51, 67
Rorty, Richard, 2, 10, 11, 17, 21, 25–6,
    39, 170
Ross, David, 46, 47, 48, 142, 147
Rousseau, Jean-Jacques, 1, 8, 12, 28

Salkever, Stephen G., 7, 16, 19, 43,
    45, 50, 51, 52, 69, 104, 186
Sandel, Michael, 2, 10, 11, 12–15, 17,
    18, 21, 22, 25–8, 36, 40, 173,
    175
Saxonhouse, Arlene, 51
Schofield, Malcolm, 10, 49, 103, 107,
    119
Shklar, Judith, 6
Simpson, Peter, 7, 13, 44, 102, 108,
    109, 116, 119, 124, 126, 127,
    134, 136, 161, 162
Slote, Michael, 13, 67
Smith, Adam, 175
Smith, Thomas W., 45, 53, 61, 63, 64,
    65, 67, 70, 71, 77, 80, 95, 96,
    97, 125, 131
Socrates, 38, 152–4, 156, 159, 163
Stern-Gillet, Suzanne, 97
Stewart, J. A., 45, 48, 53, 56, 57, 61,
    64, 70, 81, 83, 85, 88, 98, 147,
    149, 151, 152, 160
Strauss, Leo, 85, 159
Swanson, Judith, 51, 52

Taylor, Charles, 15
Tessitore, Aristide, 10, 45, 61, 63, 65,
    71, 77, 80, 88, 94, 96, 152
Thigpen, Robert B., 16
Thompson, Dennis, 2, 18, 22–6, 33,
    169

Vander Waerdt, P. A., 94, 102, 116,
    138, 142, 145
Villa, Dana, 40

Walzer, Michael, 9, 16
Ward, Lee, 53, 54, 65
Welldon, J. E. C., 147, 150
Williams, Bernard, 67
Winthrop, Delba, 75, 79

Yack, Bernard, 85, 125, 145
Young, Iris Marion, 29

Zuckert, Catherine H., 105

LaVergne, TN USA
07 July 2010
188548LV00003B/52/P